How to Read
the Bible
for All Its Worth

Also by Gordon D. Fee and Douglas Stuart

How to Read the Bible Book by Book

Also by Gordon D. Fee and Mark L. Strauss

How to Choose a Translation for All Its Worth

FOURTH EDITION

How to Read the Bible for All Its Worth

Gordon D. Fee
Douglas Stuart

ZONDERVAN®

ZONDERVAN

How to Read the Bible for All Its Worth
Copyright © 1981, 1993, 2003, 2014 by Douglas Stuart and Gordon D. Fee

This title is also available as a Zondervan ebook. Visit www.zondervan.com/ebooks.

This title is also available in a Zondervan audio edition. Visit www.zondervan.fm.

Requests for information should be addressed to:

Zondervan, 3900 Sparks Dr. SE, *Grand Rapids, Michigan 49546*

Library of Congress Cataloging-in-Publication Data

Fee, Gordon D.
    How to read the bible for all its worth/ Gordon D. Fee and Douglas Stuart. —
Fourth Edition
        pages cm.
    Includes index.
    ISBN 978-0-310-51782-5 (softcover)
    1. Bible—Study and teaching. I. Stuart, Douglas K. II. Title
BS600.3.F44 2014
220.6'1—dc23   2013041169

Cover design and illustration: JuiceBox Designs
Interior design: Matthew Van Zomeren

Printed in the United States of America

17 18 19 20 21 22 /DCI/ 20 19 18 17 16 15 14 13 12 11 10

For our parents
Donald and Grace Fee
and
Streeter and Merle Stuart,
from whom we learned
our love for the Word

Contents

Abbreviations   8

Abbreviations of Translations   9

Preface to the Fourth Edition   11

Preface to the Third Edition   13

Preface to the First Edition   16

1. Introduction: The Need to Interpret   21

2. The Basic Tool: A Good Translation   36

3. The Epistles: Learning to Think Contextually   57

4. The Epistles: The Hermeneutical Questions   74

5. The Old Testament Narratives: Their Proper Use   93

6. Acts: The Question of Historical Precedent   112

7. The Gospels: One Story, Many Dimensions   132

8. The Parables: Do You Get the Point?   154

9. The Law(s): Covenant Stipulations for Israel   168

10. The Prophets: Enforcing the Covenant in Israel   187

11. The Psalms: Israel's Prayers and Ours   212

12. Wisdom: Then and Now   233

13. Revelation: Images of Judgment and Hope   258

Appendix: The Evaluation and Use of Commentaries   275

Scripture Index   291

Names Index   301

Abbreviations

OLD TESTAMENT

Gen	Genesis	Song	Song of Songs
Exod	Exodus	Isa	Isaiah
Lev	Leviticus	Jer	Jeremiah
Num	Numbers	Lam	Lamentations
Deut	Deuteronomy	Ezek	Ezekiel
Josh	Joshua	Dan	Daniel
Judg	Judges	Hos	Hosea
Ruth	Ruth	Joel	Joel
1–2 Sam	1–2 Samuel	Amos	Amos
1–2 Kgs	1–2 Kings	Obad	Obadiah
1–2 Chr	1–2 Chronicles	Jonah	Jonah
Ezra	Ezra	Mic	Micah
Neh	Nehemiah	Nah	Nahum
Esth	Esther	Hab	Habakkuk
Job	Job	Zeph	Zephaniah
Ps/Pss	Psalms	Hag	Haggai
Prov	Proverbs	Zech	Zechariah
Eccl	Ecclesiastes	Mal	Malachi

NEW TESTAMENT

Matt	Matthew	1–2 Thess	1–2 Thessalonians
Mark	Mark	1–2 Tim	1–2 Timothy
Luke	Luke	Titus	Titus
John	John	Phlm	Philemon
Acts	Acts	Heb	Hebrews
Rom	Romans	Jas	James
1–2 Cor	1–2 Corinthians	1–2 Pet	1–2 Peter
Gal	Galatians	1–2–3 John	1–2–3 John
Eph	Ephesians	Jude	Jude
Phil	Philippians	Rev	Revelation
Col	Colossians		

AD	anno Domini (in the year of [our] Lord)	et al.	*et alii*, and others
		etc.	*et cetera*, and the rest
BC	before Christ	i.e.	*id est*, that is
ca.	*circa*, about, approximately	*How to 1*	*How to Read the Bible for All Its Worth*
cf.	*confer*, compare	*How to 2*	*How to Read the Bible Book by Book*
ch(s).	chapter(s)		
ed.	edited by	NT	New Testament
p(p).	page(s)	OT	Old Testament
e.g.	*exempli gratia*, for example	vol(s).	volume(s)
		v(v).	verse(s)

Abbreviations of Translations

ESV	The English Standard Version, 2001
GNB	The Good News Bible, 1992
HCSB	The Holman Christian Standard Bible, 2003
JB	The Jerusalem Bible, 1966
KJV	The King James Version (also known as the Authorized Version), 1611
LB	The Living Bible, 1971
NAB	The New American Bible, 1970
NASB	The New American Standard Bible, 1995
NEB	The New English Bible, 1961
NIV	The New International Version, 2011
NJB	The New Jerusalem Bible, 1985
NKJV	The New King James Version, 1982
NLT	The New Living Translation, 1997
NRSV	The New Revised Standard Version, 1991
REB	The Revised English Bible, 1989
RSV	The Revised Standard Version, 1952

Abbreviations of Commentary Series

AB	Anchor Bible
BCOT	Baker Commentary on the Old Testament
BNTC	Black's New Testament Commentaries
BST	The Bible Speaks Today
CC	Concordia Commentary
EBC	Expositor's Bible Commentary
HNTC	Harper's New Testament Commentary
Int	*Interpretation*
NAC	New American Commentary
NCBC	New Century Bible Commentary
NIBC	New International Biblical Commentary
NICNT	New International Commentary on the New Testament
NICOT	New International Commentary on the Old Testament
NIGTC	New International Greek Testament Commentary
NIVAC	The NIV Application Commentary
OTL	Old Testament Library
REC	Reformed Expository Commentary
SP	Sacra pagina
TNTC	Tyndale New Testament Commentaries
UBCS	Understanding the Bible Commentary Series
TNTC	Tyndale New Testament Commentaries
TOTC	Tyndale Old Testament Commentaries
WBC	Word Biblical Commentary

Copyrights of Translations

Preface to
the Fourth Edition

This fourth edition of *How to Read the Bible for All Its Worth* was prompted by a phone call from Doug having to do with updating the bibliographies in the Appendix. It did not take much reading of the third edition to realize how much things had changed in the past decade. Not only did the bibliography need to be brought up to date, but so did several other matters. Thus as is my wont, I took down a copy from my shelf and marked up page after page with red ink, so much so that it became clear that a thoroughgoing rewrite was necessary. At the top of the list was my own longtime passion of "getting rid of the numbers," so that people will read the Bible the way they would read any book. In this edition the numbers, that is, the chapter and verse notations, are kept, of course, but now appear only in parentheses at the end of a sentence or paragraph. Understandably this involved restructuring various sentences; but it also gave us the opportunity to bring several other matters up to date as well. The result is a fourth edition of the same book that seems to have benefitted so many readers of the Bible.

It turned out that the most serious need for revision had to do with the biblical text itself. The need was clear, since the original NIV, also known as the 1984 NIV, is no longer published. As a longtime member of the Committee for Bible Translation, who are responsible for the NIV, it has been for me a privilege to bring the biblical text used throughout the book up to speed, in this case now based on the 2011 NIV. Thus as with any "revision" of a book, things have here been "updated" on almost every page.

But the basic content has remained the same. Our aim here has been to make our own book more readable, but far beyond that to encourage an ongoing *reading* of the Bible on the part of God's people. So we conclude this preface by repeating those words that St. Augustine heard that led to his conversion: *Tolle, lege*— "Take up and read!" meaning, of course, Scripture itself, hopefully with this little book helping you to read God's Word better, with worship and obedience as the ultimate goal!

Gordon D. Fee
July 2013

Preface to
the Third Edition

The appearance of *How to Read the Bible Book by Book* (2002) prompted the authors to revisit this first book and give it a thorough updating. In part this was occasioned by the fact that we regularly cross-referenced the present book (dubbed *How to 1* in that book, which in turn has been cross-referenced in the present edition as *How to 2*). In the process of this cross-referencing we came to realize how much we ourselves had learned since we wrote the first book in 1979 and 1980, and how out of date some of the material had become in the meantime. Not only did we need to change all "century" references from the "twentieth" to the "twenty-first"(!), but we became aware of other "dated" items as well (indeed, the mention of our secretaries' typing and retyping the first edition [p. 23] made us both feel a bit Neanderthal!). We also wanted to reflect several significant advances in scholarship (especially regarding biblical narrative). So that in brief explains the *why* of this present edition. But a few further explanations are needed as well.

The most obvious chapter that needed reworking was chapter 2. Although most of the explanation and examples of translational theory remain the same, every translation listed in the second edition except for the NRSV has undergone revision within the last two decades. That not only made much of the discussion of the translations themselves out of date, but also required some additional explanations of the reasons for the revisions of these well-established and well-loved expressions of the Bible in English. In the first edition we offered many of our comments in contrast to the King James

Version; and we have become aware of how few among the majority of people in the United States and Canada (namely, those under age thirty-five!) presently have any serious acquaintance with the KJV. So that, too, needed to be revised in this edition of *How to 1*.

The other obvious item that needed serious revision—and will need revision again as soon as this edition becomes available(!)—is the list of suggested commentaries in the appendix. New, good commentaries appear with some regularity. So, as before, we remind readers that they need to be aware of this and try to find help where they can. Even so, our present list will provide excellent help for years to come.

But we felt other chapters needed some overhaul as well. And this, too, reflects both our own growth and what we perceive to be a change in the climate and makeup of our readership over the past two decades. At the time of our first writing, we had both come from backgrounds where poor interpretation of Scripture was an unfortunately frequent phenomenon. That caused us in some chapters to lean heavily toward how *not* to read certain genres. Our sense is that many of today's readership know less about these poor ways of "doing Bible," in part because we are also going through a period where we find a frighteningly large number of people who, by and large, are biblically illiterate. So in some chapters our emphasis has changed decidedly toward how to read well, with less emphasis on the ways texts were abused in the past.

We also hope that those who have read thus far will go on to read the preface to the first edition, where we made only one slight change to a sentence to give it greater clarity. Though some things there are dated (especially the mention of other books of this kind), it still serves as a genuine preface to the book and should help orient you to what you can expect.

A word about the title—since we have received as many "corrective" comments here as about anything else in the book. No, neither we nor the publishers made a mistake. The "Its" is a deliberate wordplay that works *only* when it appears without the apostrophe; and in the end our own emphasis lies with this possessive. Scripture is God's Word, and we want people to read it because of its great value to them. And if they do it "for all it's worth," hopefully they will also find its worth.

Again, we are glad to thank several people to whom we are indebted for helping to make this a better book. Maudine Fee has read every word several times over, with a keen eye for things that only scholars would understand(!); special thanks also to V. Phillips Long, Bruce W. Waltke, and Bill Barker for input of various kinds.

We are both humbled and delighted with the measure of success this book has had over the past two decades. We pray that this new edition may prove to be equally helpful.

Gordon D. Fee
Douglas Stuart
Advent 2002

Preface to
the First Edition

In one of our lighter moments we toyed with the idea of calling this book *Not Just Another Book on How to Understand the Bible*. Wisdom prevailed, and the "title" lost out. But such a title would in fact describe the kind of urgency that caused this book to be written.

How-to-understand-the-Bible books abound. Some are good; others are not so good. Few are written by biblical scholars. Some of these books approach the subject from the variety of methods one can use in studying Scripture; others try to be basic primers in hermeneutics (the science of interpretation) for the layperson. The latter usually give a long section of general rules (rules that apply to all biblical texts) and another section of specific rules (rules that govern special types of problems: prophecy, typology, figures of speech, etc.).

Of the "basic primer" type books we recommend especially *Knowing Scripture* by R. C. Sproul (InterVarsity Press). For a heavier and less readable, but very helpful, dose of the same, one should see A. Berkeley Mickelson's *Interpreting the Bible* (Eerdmans). The closest comparison to the kind of book we have written is *Better Bible Study* by Berkeley and Alvera Mickelson (Regal).

But this is "not just another book"—we hope. The uniqueness of what we have tried to do has several facets:

1. As one may note from a glance at the table of contents, the basic concern of this book is with the understanding of the different types of literature (the *genres*) that make up the Bible. Although we do speak to other issues, this generic approach has

controlled all that has been done. We affirm that there is a real difference between a psalm, on the one hand, and an epistle on the other. Our concern is to help the reader to read and study the Psalms as poems, and the Epistles as letters. We hope to show that these differences are vital and should affect both the way one reads them and how one is to understand their message for today.

2. Even though throughout the book we have repeatedly given guidelines for *studying* each genre of Scripture, we are equally concerned with the intelligent *reading* of Scripture—since that is what most of us do the most. Anyone who has tried, for example, to read through Leviticus, Jeremiah, or Proverbs, as over against 1 Samuel or Acts, knows full well that there are many differences. One can get bogged down in Leviticus, and who has not felt the frustration of completing the reading of Isaiah or Jeremiah and then wondering what the "plot" was? In contrast, 1 Samuel and Acts are especially readable. We hope to help the reader appreciate these differences so that he or she can read intelligently and profitably the nonnarrative parts of the Bible.

3. This book was written by two seminary professors, those sometimes dry and stodgy people that other books are written to get around. It has often been said that one does not have to have a seminary education in order to understand the Bible. This is true, and we believe it with all our hearts. But we are also concerned about the (sometimes) hidden agenda that suggests that a seminary education or seminary professors are thereby a *hindrance* to understanding the Bible. We are so bold as to think that even the "experts" may have something to say.

Furthermore, these two seminary professors also happen to be believers, who think we should *obey* the biblical texts, not merely read or study them. It is precisely this concern that led us to become scholars in the first place. We had a great desire to understand as carefully and as fully as possible what it is that we are to know about God and his will in the twentieth (and now the twenty-first) century.

These two seminary professors also regularly preach and teach the Word in a variety of church settings. Thus we are regularly called upon not simply to be scholars but to wrestle with how the Bible applies, and this leads to our fourth item.

4. The great urgency that gave birth to this book is hermeneutics; we wrote especially to help believers wrestle with the ques-

tions of application. Many of the urgent problems in the church today are basically struggles with bridging the hermeneutical gap—with moving from the "then and there" of the original text to the "here and now" of our own life settings. But this also means bridging the gap between the scholar and layperson. The concern of the scholar is primarily with what the text *meant*; the concern of the layperson is usually with what it *means*. The believing scholar insists that we must have both. Reading the Bible with an eye *only* to its meaning for us can lead to a great deal of nonsense as well as to every imaginable kind of error—because it lacks controls. Fortunately, most believers are blessed with at least a measure of that most important of all hermeneutical skills—common sense.

On the other hand, nothing can be so dry and lifeless for the church as making biblical study purely an academic exercise in historical investigation. Even though the Word was originally given in a concrete historical context, its uniqueness centers in the fact that, though historically given and conditioned, this Word is ever a living Word.

Our concern, therefore, must be with both dimensions. The believing scholar insists that the biblical texts first of all *mean what they meant*. That is, we believe that God's Word for us today is first of all precisely what his Word was to them. Thus we have two tasks: First, our task is to find out what the text originally meant; this is called *exegesis*. Second, we must learn to hear that same meaning in the variety of new or different contexts of our own day; we call this second task *hermeneutics*. In its classical usage, the term "hermeneutics" covers both tasks, but in this book we consistently use it only in this narrower sense. To do both tasks well should be the goal of Bible study.

Thus in chapters 3 through 13, which deal in turn with ten different kinds of literary genres, we have given attention to both needs. Since exegesis is always the first task, we have spent much of our time emphasizing the uniqueness of each of the genres. What is a biblical psalm? What are their different kinds? What is the nature of Hebrew poetry? How does all this affect our understanding? But we are also concerned with how the various psalms function as the Word of God. What is God trying to say? What are we to learn, or how are we to obey? Here we have avoided giving rules. What we have offered are guidelines, suggestions, helps.

We recognize that the first task—exegesis—is often considered to be a matter for the expert. At times this is true. But one does not have to be an expert to learn to do the basic tasks of exegesis well. The secret lies in learning to ask the right questions of the text. We hope, therefore, to guide the reader in learning to ask the right questions of each biblical genre. There will be times when one will finally want to consult the experts as well. We shall also give some practical guidelines in this matter.

Each author is responsible for those chapters that fall within his area of specialty. Thus, Professor Fee wrote chapters 1 to 4, 6 to 8, and 13, and Professor Stuart wrote chapters 5 and 9 to 12. Although each author had considerable input into the other's chapters, and although we consider the book to be a truly joint effort, the careful reader will also observe that each author has his own style and manner of presentation. Special thanks go to some friends and family who have read several of the chapters and offered helpful advice: Frank DeRemer, Bill Jackson, Judy Peace, and Maudine, Cherith, Craig, and Brian Fee. Special thanks also to our secretaries, Carrie Powell and Holly Greening, for typing both the rough drafts and the final copy.

In the words of the child that moved Augustine to read a passage from Romans at his conversion experience, we say, "*Tolle, lege*"—"Take up and read." The Bible is God's eternal word. Read it, understand it, obey it.[1]

---

1. Permission has been granted by Baker Book House, Grand Rapids, Michigan, to use material in chapters 3, 4, and 6 that appeared earlier in different form as "Hermeneutics and Common Sense: An Exploratory Essay on the Hermeneutics of the Epistles," in *Inerrancy and Common Sense* (ed. J. R. Michaels and R. R. Nicole, 1980), pages 161–86; and "Hermeneutics and Historical Precedent—A Major Problem in Pentecostal Hermeneutics," in *Perspectives on the New Pentecostalism* (ed. R. P. Spittler, 1976), pages 118–32.

CHAPTER 1

Introduction:
The Need to Interpret

Every so often we meet someone who says with great feeling, "You don't have to interpret the Bible; just read it and do what it says." Usually, such a remark reflects the layperson's protest against the "professional" scholar, pastor, teacher, or Sunday school teacher, who by "interpreting" seems to be taking the Bible away from the common person. It is their way of saying that the Bible is not an obscure book. "After all," it is argued, "anyone with half a brain can read it and understand it. The problem with too many preachers and teachers is that they dig around so much they tend to muddy the waters. What was clear to us when we read it isn't so clear anymore."

There is a lot of truth in this protest. We agree that Christians should learn to read, believe, and obey the Bible. And we especially agree that the Bible need not be an obscure book if read and studied properly. In fact we are convinced that the single most serious problem people have with the Bible is not with a lack of understanding but with the fact that they understand many things too well! For example, with such a text as "Do everything without grumbling or arguing" (Phil 2:14), the problem is not understanding it but obeying it—putting it into practice.

We are also agreed that the preacher or teacher is all too often prone to dig first and look later, and thereby at times to cover up the plain meaning of the text, which often lies on the surface. Let it be said at the outset—and repeated throughout—that the aim of good interpretation is not uniqueness; one is not trying to discover what no one else has ever seen before.

Interpretation that aims at, or thrives on, uniqueness can usually be attributed to pride (an attempt to "outclever" the rest of the world), a false understanding of spirituality (wherein the Bible is full of deeply buried truths waiting to be mined by the spiritually sensitive person with special insight), or vested interests (the need to support a theological bias, especially in dealing with texts that seem to go against that bias). Unique interpretations are usually wrong. This is not to say that the correct understanding of a passage may not often seem unique to someone who hears it for the first time. But it is to say that uniqueness is *not* the aim of our task.

The aim of good interpretation is simple: to get at the "plain meaning of the text," the author's intended meaning. And the most important ingredient one brings to this task is an enlightened common sense. The test of good interpretation is that it makes good sense of what is written. Correct interpretation, therefore, brings relief to the mind as well as a prick or prod to the heart.

But if the plain meaning is what interpretation is all about, then why interpret? Why not just read? Does not the plain meaning come simply from reading? In a sense, yes. But in a truer sense, such an argument is both naive and unrealistic because of two factors: the nature of the reader and the nature of Scripture.

THE READER AS AN INTERPRETER

The first reason one needs to learn *how* to interpret is that, whether one likes it or not, every reader is at the same time an interpreter. That is, most of us assume as we read that we also understand what we read. We also tend to think that *our understanding* is the same as the Holy Spirit's or human author's *intent*. However, we invariably bring to the text all that we are, with all of our experiences, culture, and prior understandings of words and ideas. Sometimes what we bring to the text, unintentionally to be sure, leads us astray, or else causes us to read all kinds of foreign ideas into the text.

Thus, when a person in our culture hears the word "cross," centuries of Christian art and symbolism cause most people automatically to think of a Roman cross (✝), although there is little likelihood that that was the shape of Jesus' cross, which was probably shaped like a T. Most Protestants, and Catholics as well, when they read passages about the church at worship, automatically envision people sitting in a building with "pews" much like their own. When Paul says, "Make no provision for the flesh, to fulfill its lusts" (Rom 13:14 NKJV), people in most English-speaking cultures are apt to think that "flesh" means the "body" and therefore that Paul is speaking of "bodily appetites."

But the word "flesh," as Paul uses it, seldom refers to the body—and in this text it almost certainly did not—but to a spiritual malady sometimes called "the sinful nature," denoting totally self-centered existence. Therefore, without intending to do so, the reader is interpreting as he or she reads, and unfortunately all too often interprets incorrectly.

This leads us to note further, that in any case the reader of an English Bible is already involved in interpretation. For translation is in itself a (necessary) form of interpretation. Your Bible, whatever translation you use, which is your *beginning* point, is in fact the *end result* of much scholarly work. Translators are regularly called upon to make choices regarding meanings, and *their* choices are going to affect how *you* understand.

Good translators, therefore, take the problem of our language differences into consideration. But it is not an easy task. In Romans 13:14, for example, shall we translate "flesh" (as in KJV, NIV, NRSV, NASB, ESV, etc.) because this is the word Paul used, and then leave it to an interpreter to tell us that "flesh" here does not mean "body"? Or shall we "help" the reader and translate "sinful nature" (NIV 1984, GNB, NLT, etc.) or "disordered natural inclinations" (NJB) because these more closely approximate what Paul's word really *means*? We will take up this matter in greater detail in the next chapter. For now it is sufficient to point out how the *fact* of translation in itself has already involved one in the task of interpretation.

The need to interpret is also found by noting what goes on around us all the time. A simple look at the contemporary church, for example, makes it abundantly clear that not all "plain meanings" are equally plain to all. It is of more than passing interest that most of those in today's church who argue that, despite contrary evidence in 1 Corinthians 11:2–3, women should keep silent in church, on the basis of 1 Corinthians 14:34–35, at the same time deny the validity of speaking in tongues and prophecy, the very context in which the "silence" passage occurs. And those who affirm, on the basis of 1 Corinthians 11:2–16, that women as well as men should pray and prophesy, usually deny that women must do so with some form of head covering. For some, the Bible "plainly teaches" believers' baptism by immersion; others believe they can make a biblical case for infant baptism. Both "eternal security" and the possibility of "losing one's salvation" are preached in today's churches, though never by the same person! Yet both are affirmed as the plain meaning of biblical texts. Even the two authors of this book have some disagreements as to what certain texts "plainly" mean. Yet all of us are reading the same Bible, and we all are trying to be obedient to what the text "plainly" means.

Besides these recognizable differences among Bible-believing Christians, there are also all kinds of strange things afloat. One can usually recognize the cults, for example, because they have an authority in addition to the Bible. But not all of them do; and in every case they bend the truth by the way they select texts from the Bible itself. Every imaginable heresy or practice, from the Arianism (denying Christ's deity) of the Jehovah's Witnesses, to baptizing for the dead among Mormons, to snake handling among Appalachian sects, claims to be "supported" by a biblical text.

Even among more theologically orthodox individuals, many strange ideas manage to gain acceptance in various quarters. For example, one of the current rages among American Protestants, especially charismatics, is the so-called wealth and health gospel. The "good news" is that God's will for you is financial and material prosperity! One of the advocates of this "gospel" begins his book by arguing for the "plain sense" of Scripture and claiming that he puts the Word of God first and foremost throughout his study. He says that it is not what we *think* it says but what it *actually* says that counts. The "plain meaning" is what he is after. But one begins to wonder what the "plain meaning" really is when financial prosperity is argued as the will of God from such a passage as, "Beloved, I wish above all things that thou mayest prosper and be in health, even as thy soul prospereth" (3 John 2, KJV)—a text that in fact has nothing at all to do with financial prosperity. Another example takes the plain meaning of the story of the rich young man (Mark 10:17–22) as precisely the opposite of "what it actually says" and attributes the "interpretation" to the Holy Spirit. One may rightly question whether the plain meaning is being sought at all; perhaps, the plain meaning is simply what such a writer wants the text to mean in order to support some pet ideas.

Given all this diversity, both inside and outside the church, and all the differences even among scholars, who supposedly know "the rules," it is no wonder that some argue for no interpretation, just reading. But as we have noted, this is a false option. The antidote to *bad* interpretation is not *no* interpretation but *good* interpretation, based on commonsense guidelines.

The authors of this book labor under no illusions that by reading and following our guidelines everyone will finally agree on the "plain meaning," *our* meaning! What we do hope to achieve is to heighten the reader's sensitivity to specific problems inherent in each genre, to help the reader know *why* different options exist and how to make commonsense judgments, and especially, to enable the reader to discern between good and not-so-good interpretations—and to know what makes them one or the other.

THE NATURE OF SCRIPTURE

A more significant reason for the need to interpret lies in the nature of Scripture itself. Historically the church has understood the nature of Scripture much the same as it has understood the person of Christ—the Bible is at the same time both human and divine. "The Bible," it has been correctly said, "is the Word of God given in human words in history." It is this dual nature of the Bible that demands of us the task of interpretation.

Because the Bible is *God's* message, it has *eternal relevance*; it speaks to all humankind, in every age and in every culture. Because it is the word of God, we must listen—and obey. But because God chose to speak his word through *human words in history,* every book in the Bible also has *historical particularity;* each document is conditioned by the language, time, and culture in which it was originally written (and in some cases also by the oral history it had before it was written down). Interpretation of the Bible is demanded by the "tension" that exists between its *eternal relevance* and its *historical particularity.*

There are some, of course, who believe that the Bible is merely a human book, and that it contains only human words in history. For these people the task of interpreting is limited to historical inquiry. Their interest, as with reading Cicero or Milton, is with the religious ideas of the Jews, Jesus, or the early church. The task for them, therefore, is purely a historical one. What did these words mean to the people who wrote them? What did they think about God? How did they understand themselves?

On the other hand, there are those who think of the Bible only in terms of its eternal relevance. Because it is the word of God, they tend to think of it only as a collection of propositions to be believed and imperatives to be obeyed—although invariably there is a great deal of picking and choosing among the propositions and imperatives. There are, for example, Christians who, on the basis of Deuteronomy 22:5 ("A woman must not wear men's clothing"), argue that a woman should not wear slacks or shorts, because these are deemed to be "men's clothing." But the same people seldom take literally the other imperatives in this list, which include building a parapet around the roof of one's house (v. 8), not planting two kinds of seeds in a vineyard (v. 9), and making tassels on the four corners of one's cloak (v. 12).

The Bible, however, is *not* a series of propositions and imperatives; it is not simply a collection of "Sayings from Chairman God," as though he looked down on us from heaven and said: "Hey you down there, learn these truths. Number 1, There is no God but One, and I am that One. Number 2, I am the Creator of all things, including humankind"—and so on, all the way through proposition number 7,777 and imperative number 777.

These propositions of course are true, and they are found in the Bible (though not quite in that form). Indeed such a book might have made some things easier for us. But, fortunately, that is not how God chose to speak to us. Rather, he chose to speak his eternal truths within the particular circumstances and events of human history. This also is what gives us hope. Precisely because God chose to speak in the context of real human history, we may take courage that these same words will speak again and again in our own "real" history, as they have throughout the history of the church.

The fact that the Bible has a human side is our encouragement; it is also our challenge, and the reason that we need to interpret. Two items should be noted in this regard:

1. One of the most important aspects of the human side of the Bible is that, in order to communicate his word to all human conditions, God chose to use almost every available kind of communication: narrative history, genealogies, chronicles, laws of all kinds, poetry of all kinds, proverbs, prophetic oracles, riddles, drama, biographical sketches, parables, letters, sermons, and apocalypses.

To interpret properly the "then and there" of the biblical texts, one must not only know some general rules that apply to all the words of the Bible, but one also needs to learn the special rules that apply to each of these literary forms (genres). The way God communicates the divine word to us in the "here and now" will often differ from one form to another. For example, we need to know *how* a psalm, a form often addressed *to God*, functions as God's word *to us*, and how certain psalms differ from others, and how all of them differ from "the laws," which were often addressed to people in cultural situations no longer in existence. *How* do such "laws" speak to us, and how do they differ from the moral "laws," which are always valid in all circumstances? Such are the questions the dual nature of the Bible forces on us.

2. In speaking through real persons, in a variety of circumstances, over a 1,500-year period, God's Word was expressed in the vocabulary and thought patterns of those persons and conditioned by the culture of those times and circumstances. That is to say, God's word to us was first of all God's word to them. If they were going to hear it, it could only have come through events and in language *they* could have understood. Our problem is that we are so far removed from them in time, and sometimes in thought. This is the major reason one needs to learn to *interpret* the Bible. If God's word about women wearing men's clothing or people having parapets around houses is to speak to us, we first need to know what it said to its original hearers—and why.

Thus the task of interpreting involves the student/reader at two levels. First, one has to hear the word they heard; we must try to understand what was said to them back *then and there* (exegesis). Second, we must learn to hear that same word in the *here and now* (hermeneutics). A few preliminary words are needed about these two tasks.

THE FIRST TASK: EXEGESIS

The first task of the interpreter is called *exegesis*. This involves the careful, systematic study of the Scripture to discover the original, intended meaning. This is primarily a historical task. It is the attempt to hear the Word as the original recipients were to have heard it, to find out what was *the original intent of the words of the Bible*. This is the task that often calls for the help of the "expert," a person trained to know well the language and circumstances of a text in its original setting. But one does not have to be an expert to do good exegesis.

In fact, everyone is an exegete of sorts. The only real question is whether you will be a good one. How many times, for example, have you heard or said, "What Jesus *meant* by that was ..." or, "Back in those days, they used to ..."? These are exegetical expressions. Most often they are employed to explain the differences between "them" and "us"—why we do not build parapets around our houses, for example—or to give a reason for our using a text in a new or different way—why handshaking has often taken the place of the "holy kiss." Even when such ideas are not articulated, they are in fact practiced all the time in a kind of commonsense way.

The problem with much of this, however, is (1) that such exegesis is often too selective and (2) that often the sources consulted are not written by true "experts," that is, they are secondary sources that also often use other secondary sources rather than the primary sources. A few words about each of these must be given.

1. Although everyone employs exegesis at times, and although quite often such exegesis is well done, it nonetheless tends to be employed *only* when there is an obvious problem between the biblical texts and modern culture. Whereas it must indeed be employed for such texts, we insist that it is *the first step in reading EVERY text*. At first, this will not be easy to do, but learning to think exegetically will pay rich dividends in understanding and will make even the reading, not to mention the studying, of the Bible a much more exciting experience. But note well: Learning to think exegetically is not the *only* task; it is simply the *first* task.

The real problem with "selective" exegesis is that one will often read one's own, completely foreign, ideas into a text and thereby make God's word something other than what God really said. For example, one of the authors of this book once received a letter from a well-known evangelical, who argued that the author should not appear in a conference with another well-known person, whose orthodoxy on a point was thought to be suspect. The biblical reason given for avoiding the conference was the command to: "Abstain from all appearance of evil" (1 Thess 5:22 KJV). But had our brother learned to read the Bible exegetically, he would not have used the text in that way. For this is Paul's final word in a *paragraph* to the Thessalonians regarding Spirit manifestations in the community. What Paul really says, in current English, is: "Do not treat prophecies with contempt, but test them all; hold on to what is good, reject every kind of evil" (NIV). The "avoidance of evil" had to do with "prophecies," which, when tested, were found not to be of the Spirit. To make this text mean something God did not intend is to abuse the text, not use it. To avoid making such mistakes one needs to learn to think exegetically, that is, to begin back then and there, and to do so with *every* text.

2. As we will soon note, one does not begin by consulting the "experts." But when it is necessary to do so, one should try to use the better sources. For example, at the conclusion of the story of the rich young man in Mark 10:24 (Matt 19:23; Luke 18:24), Jesus says, "How hard it is to enter the kingdom of God!" He then adds: "It is easier for a camel to go through the eye of a needle than for someone who is rich to enter the kingdom of God." You will sometimes hear it said that there was a gate in Jerusalem known as the "Needle's Eye," which camels could go through only by kneeling, and with great difficulty. The point of this "interpretation" is that a camel could in fact go through the "Needle's Eye." The trouble with this "exegesis," however, is that it is simply not true. There never was such a gate in Jerusalem at any time in its history. The earliest known "evidence" for this idea is found in the eleventh century(!) in a commentary by a Greek churchman named Theophylact, who had the same difficulty with the text that many later readers do. After all, it is *impossible* for a camel to go through the eye of a needle, and that was precisely Jesus' point. It is impossible for someone who is rich to enter the kingdom. It takes a miracle for a rich person to get saved, which is quite the point of what follows: "All things are possible with God."

LEARNING TO DO EXEGESIS

How, then, do we learn to do good exegesis and at the same time avoid the pitfalls along the way? The first part of most of the chapters in this book will explain how one goes about this task for each of the genres in particular. Here we simply want to overview what is involved in the exegesis of any text.

At its highest level, of course, exegesis requires knowledge of many things we do not necessarily expect the readers of this book to know: the biblical languages; the Jewish, Semitic, and Greco-Roman backgrounds to much of what is written; how to determine the original text when early copies (produced by hand) have differing readings; the use of all kinds of primary sources and tools. But you can learn to do good exegesis even if you do not have access to all of these skills and tools. To do so, however, you must learn first what you can do with your own skills, and second how to use the work of others.

The key to good exegesis, and therefore to a more intelligent reading of the Bible, is to learn to read the text carefully and to ask the right questions of the text. One of the best steps one could do in this regard would be to read Mortimer J. Adler's still popular classic *How to Read a Book* (1940, revised edition, with Charles Van Doren [New York: Simon and Schuster, 1972]). Our experience over many years in college and seminary teaching is that many people simply do not know how to read well. To read or study the Bible intelligently demands careful reading, and this includes learning to ask the right questions of the text.

There are two basic kinds of questions one should ask of every biblical passage: those that relate to *context* and those that relate to *content*. The questions of context are also of two kinds: historical and literary. Let us briefly note each of these.

The Historical Context

The historical context, which will differ from book to book, has to do with several matters: the time and culture of the author and audience, that is, the geographical, topographical, and political factors that are relevant to the author's setting; and the historical occasion of the book, letter, psalm, prophetic oracle, or other genre. All such matters are especially important for understanding.

1. It makes a considerable difference in understanding to know the eighth-century BC background of Amos, Hosea, or Isaiah, or that Haggai prophesied after the exile, or to know the messianic expectations of Israel when John the Baptist and Jesus appeared on the scene, or to understand the differences between the cities of Corinth and Philippi and how these differences affected the churches in each, and thus Paul's letters in each case. One's reading of Jesus' parables is greatly enhanced by knowing something about the customs of Jesus' day. Surely it makes a difference in understanding to know that the *"denarius"* ("penny" KJV!) offered to the workers in Matthew 20:1–16 was the equivalent of a full day's wage. Even matters of topography are important. Those raised in

the American West — or East for that matter — must be careful not to think of "the mountains [that] surround Jerusalem" (Ps 125:2) in terms of their own experience of mountains, since they are actually low hills and plateaus.

To answer most of these kinds of questions, you will need some outside help. A good Bible dictionary, such as the four-volume *International Standard Bible Encyclopedia* (ed. G. W. Bromiley [Grand Rapids: Eerdmans, 1995]) or the one-volume *Zondervan Illustrated Bible Dictionary* (J. D. Douglas and Merrill C. Tenney; ed. Moises Silva [Grand Rapids: Zondervan, 2011]) or *Eerdmans Dictionary of the Bible* (ed. David Noel Freedman [Grand Rapids: Eerdmans, 2000]), will generally supply the need here. If you wish to pursue a matter further, the bibliographies at the end of each article in these dictionaries would be a good place to start.

2. The more important question of historical context, however, has to do with the *occasion* and *purpose* of each biblical book and/or its various parts. Here one wants to have an idea of what was going on in Israel or the church that called forth such a document, or what the situation of the author was that caused him to speak or write. Again, this will vary from book to book; it is after all somewhat less crucial for Proverbs, for example, than for 1 Corinthians.

The answer to this question is usually to be found — when it can be found — within the book itself. But one needs to learn to read with their eyes open for such matters. If you want to corroborate your own findings on these questions, you might consult your Bible dictionary again or the introduction to a good commentary on the book (see the appendix on p. 275). But make your own observations first!

The Literary Context

The literary context is what most people mean when they talk about reading something in its context. Indeed this is *the* crucial task in exegesis, and fortunately it is something one can learn to do well without necessarily having to consult the "experts." Essentially, *literary context* means first that words only have meaning in sentences, and second that biblical sentences for the most part have full and clear meaning only in relation to preceding and succeeding sentences.

The most important contextual question you will ever ask — and it must be asked over and over of every sentence and every paragraph—is: What's the point? We must try to trace the author's train of thought. What is the author saying, and why does he say it right here? Having made that point, what is he saying next, and why?

This question will vary from genre to genre, but it is *always* the crucial question. The goal of exegesis, you remember, is to find out what the original author intended. To do this task well, it is imperative that one use a translation that recognizes poetry and paragraphs. One of the major causes of inadequate exegesis by readers of the King James Version and, to a lesser degree, of the New American Standard Bible, is that every verse has been printed as a paragraph. Such an arrangement tends to obscure the author's own logic. Above all else, therefore, one must learn to recognize units of thought, whether paragraphs (for prose) or lines and sections (for poetry). And, with the aid of an adequate translation, this is something any good reader can do with practice.

The Questions of Content

The second major category of questions one needs to ask of any text relates to the author's actual content. "Content" has to do with the meanings of words, their grammatical relationships in sentences, and the choice of the original text where the manuscripts (handwritten copies) differ from one another (see next chapter). It also includes a number of the items mentioned above under "historical context," for example, the meaning of a denarius, or a Sabbath day's journey, or high places, etc.

For the most part, these are the questions of meaning that people ordinarily ask of the biblical text. When Paul writes to the believers in Corinth, "Even though we have known Christ according to the flesh, yet now we know Him in this way no longer" (2 Cor 5:16, NASB), you should want to know *who* is "according to the flesh"—Christ or the one knowing him? It makes a considerable difference in meaning to learn that "we" know Christ no longer "from a worldly point of view" (NIV) is what Paul intends, not that we know Christ no longer "in his earthly life."

To answer these kinds of questions a reader will ordinarily need to seek outside help. Again, the quality of one's answers to such questions will usually depend on the quality of the sources being used. This is the place where you will finally want to consult a good exegetical commentary. But note that from our view, consulting a commentary, as essential as this will be at times, is the last task you perform.

The Tools

For the most part, then, you can do good exegesis with a minimum amount of outside help, provided that the help is of the highest quality. We have mentioned three such tools: a good translation, a good Bible dictionary, and good commentaries. There are other kinds of tools, of course, especially for topical or thematic kinds of study. But for reading or studying the Bible book by book, these are the essential ones.

Because a good translation (or better, several good translations) is the absolutely basic tool for one who does not know the original languages, the next chapter is devoted to this matter. Learning to choose a good commentary is also important, but because this is the last task one does, an appendix on commentaries concludes the book.

THE SECOND TASK: HERMENEUTICS

Although the word "hermeneutics" ordinarily covers the whole field of interpretation, including exegesis, it is also used in the narrower sense of seeking the contemporary relevance of ancient texts. In this book we will use it exclusively in this way—to ask questions about the Bible's meaning in the "here and now"—even though we know this is not the most common meaning of the term.

This matter of the here and now, after all, is what brings us to the Bible in the first place. So why not start here? Why worry about exegesis? Surely the same Spirit who inspired the writing of the Bible can equally inspire one's reading of it. In a sense this is true, and we do not by this book intend to take from anyone the joy of devotional reading of the Bible and the sense of direct communication involved in such reading. But devotional reading is not the only kind one should do. One must also read for learning and understanding. In short, you must also learn to study the Bible, which in turn must inform your devotional reading. And this brings us back to our insistence that proper "hermeneutics" begins with solid "exegesis."

The reason you must *not begin* with the here and now is that the only proper control for hermeneutics is to be found *in the original intent of the biblical text.* As noted earlier in this chapter, this is the "plain meaning" one is after. Otherwise biblical texts can be made to mean whatever they might mean to any given reader. But such hermeneutics becomes total subjectivity, and who then is to say that one person's interpretation is right and another's is wrong? Anything goes.

In contrast to such subjectivity, we insist that the original meaning of the text — as much as it is in our power to discern it — is the objective point of control. We are convinced that the Mormons' baptizing for the dead on the basis of 1 Corinthians 15:29, or the Jehovah's Witnesses' rejection of the deity of Christ, or the snake handlers' use of Mark 16:18, or the prosperity evangelists' advocating of the American dream as a Christian right on the basis of 3 John 2 are all *improper* interpretations. In each case the error is in their hermeneutics, precisely because their hermeneutics is not controlled by good exegesis. They have started with the here and now and have read into the texts "meanings" that were not originally intended. And what is to keep one from killing one's daughter because of a foolish vow, as did Jephthah (Judg 11:29–40), or to argue, as one preacher is reported to have done, that women should never wear their hair up in a topknot ("bun") because the Bible says "topknot go down" ("Let him that is on the housetop not go down" [Mark 13:15 KJV])?

It will be argued, of course, that common sense will keep one from such foolishness. Unfortunately common sense is not always so common. We want to know what the Bible means *for us* — legitimately so. But we cannot make it mean anything that pleases us and then give the Holy Spirit "credit" for it. The Holy Spirit cannot be brought into the process to contradict what is said, since the Spirit is the one who inspired the original intent. Therefore, the Spirit's help for us will come in our discovering that original intent and in guiding us as we try faithfully to apply that meaning to our own situations.

The questions of hermeneutics are not at all easy, which is probably why so few books are written on this aspect of our subject. Nor will all agree on how one goes about this task. But this is the crucial area, and believers need to learn to talk to one another about these questions — and to listen. On this one statement, however, there must surely be agreement: *A text cannot mean what it could never have meant for its original readers/hearers.* Or to put it in a positive way, the true meaning of the biblical text for us is what God originally intended it to mean when it was first spoken or written. This is the starting point. How we work it out from that point is what this book is basically all about.

Someone will surely ask, "But is it not possible for a text to have an additional [or fuller or deeper] meaning beyond its original intent? After all, this happens in the New Testament itself in the way it sometimes uses the Old Testament." In the case of prophecy, we would not close the door to such a possibility, and we would argue that, with careful controls, a second, or ultimate, intended meaning is possible. But how does one justify it at other points? Our problem is a simple one: Who speaks for God? Roman Catholicism has less of a problem here; the magisterium, the authority vested in the official teaching of the church, determines for all the fuller sense of the text. Protestants, however, have no magisterium and we should be properly concerned whenever anyone says they have God's deeper meaning to a text—especially if the text never meant what it is now made to mean. Of such interpretations are all the cults born, and innumerable lesser heresies.

It is difficult to give rules for hermeneutics. What we offer throughout the following chapters, therefore, are guidelines. You may not agree with our guidelines. We do hope that your disagreements will be bathed in Christian charity, and perhaps our guidelines will serve to stimulate your own thinking on these matters.

CHAPTER 2

The Basic Tool:
A Good Translation

The sixty-six books of the Protestant Bible were originally written in three different languages: Hebrew (most of the Old Testament), Aramaic (a sister language to Hebrew used in half of Daniel and two passages in Ezra), and Greek (all of the New Testament). We assume that most of the readers of this book do not know these languages. This means, therefore, that one's basic tool for reading and studying the Bible is a contemporary English translation or, as will be argued in this chapter, *several* such translations.

As we noted in the last chapter, the very fact that you are reading God's Word in translation means that you are already involved in interpretation—and this is so whether one likes it or not. To read in translation is not a bad thing, of course; it is simply the only thing available and therefore the necessary thing. What this means further, however, is that, in a certain sense, the person who reads the Bible only in English is at the mercy of the translator(s), and translators have often had to make choices as to what in fact the original Hebrew or Greek author was really intending to express.

The trouble, then, with using only *one* translation, be it ever so good, is that you are thereby committed to the particular exegetical choices of that translation as the Word of God. The translation you are using will, of course, be correct most of the time; but at times it also may not be.

Let's take, for example, the following four translations of 1 Corinthians 7:36:

NKJV: "If any man thinks that he is behaving improperly
          toward his virgin …"
NASB: "If any man thinks that he is acting unbecomingly
          toward his virgin *daughter* …"
NIV: "If anyone is worried that he might not be acting
          honorably toward the virgin he is engaged to …"
NEB: "If a man has a partner in celibacy and feels that he is
          not behaving properly towards her …"

The NKJV is very literal but not very helpful, since it leaves the term "virgin" and the relationship between the "man" and "his virgin" quite ambiguous. Of one item, however, you may be absolutely certain: Paul did not *intend* to be ambiguous. He intended one of the other three options, and the Corinthians, who had raised the problem in their letter, knew which one; indeed they knew nothing of the other two.

It should be noted here that none of these other three is a *bad* translation, since any of them is a legitimate option as to Paul's intent. However, only one of them can be the *correct* translation. The problem is which one? For a number of reasons, the NIV reflects the best exegetical option here (in fact the NEB reading is now a marginal note in the newer REB). However, if you regularly read only the NASB (which also has a less likely option here), then you are committed to an *interpretation* of the text that is quite unlikely to be what Paul intended. And this kind of example can be illustrated hundreds of times over. So, what to do?

First, it is probably a good practice to regularly read one main translation, provided it really is a good one. This will aid in memorization as well as give you consistency. Also, if you are using one of the better translations, it will have notes in the margin at many of the places where there are difficulties. However, for the *study* of the Bible, you should use *several* well-chosen translations. The best option is to use translations that *one knows in advance will tend to differ*. This will highlight where many of the difficult problems of interpretation lie. To resolve these matters you will usually want to consult one or more commentaries.

But which translation should you use, and which of the several should you study from? No one can really speak for someone else on this matter. But your choice should not be simply because "I like it" or "This one is so readable." You should indeed like your translation, and if it is a really good one, it will be readable.

However, to make an intelligent choice, you need to know something about the science of translation itself as well as about some of the various English translations.

THE SCIENCE OF TRANSLATION

There are two kinds of choices that translators must make: textual and linguistic. The first kind has to do with the actual wording of the original text. The second has to do with the translators' theory of translation that underlies their rendering of the text into English.

The Question of Text

The first concern of translators is to be sure that the Hebrew or Greek text they are using is as close as possible to the original wording as it left the author's hands (or the hands of the scribe taking it down by dictation). Is this what the psalmist actually wrote? Are these the very words of Mark or Paul? Indeed, why should anyone think otherwise?

Although the details of the problem of text in the Old and New Testaments differ, the basic concerns are the same. (1) Unlike Thomas Jefferson's "Declaration of Independence," for example, whose handwritten original is preserved in America's national archives, no such handwritten "original" exists for any biblical book. (2) What does exist are thousands of copies produced by hand (thus called "manuscripts") and copied repeatedly over a period of about 1,400 years (for the NT; even longer for the OT). (3) Although the vast majority of manuscripts, which for both Testaments come from the later medieval period, are very much alike, for the New Testament these later manuscripts differ significantly from the earlier copies and translations. In fact, there are over five thousand Greek manuscripts of part or all of the New Testament, as well as thousands in Latin; and because these hand copies were made before the invention of the printing press (which helped guarantee uniformity), no two of them anywhere in existence are exactly alike.

The problem, therefore, is to sift through all the available material, compare the places where the manuscripts differ (these are called "variants"), and determine which of the variants represent errors and which one most likely represents the original text.

Although this may seem like an imposing task—and in some ways it is—translators do not despair, because they also know something about textual criticism, the science that attempts to discover the original texts of ancient documents.

It is not our purpose here to give the reader a primer in textual criticism. This you may find in convenient form in the articles by Bruce Waltke (Old Testament) and Gordon Fee (New Testament) in volume 1 of *The Expositor's Bible Commentary* (ed. Frank Gaebelein [Grand Rapids: Zondervan, 1979], pp. 211–22, 419–33). Our purpose here is to give some basic information about what is involved in textual criticism so that you will know why translators must do it and so that you can make better sense of the marginal notes in your translation that say, "Other ancient authorities add ..." or, "Some manuscripts do not have ..."

For the purposes of this chapter, you need to be aware of two items:

1. *Textual criticism is a science that works with careful controls.* There are two kinds of evidence that translators consider in making textual choices: external evidence (the character and quality of the manuscripts) and the internal evidence (the kinds of mistakes to which copyists were susceptible). Scholars sometimes differ as to how much weight they give either of these strands of evidence, but all are agreed that the combination of strong external and strong internal evidence together makes the vast majority of choices somewhat routine. But for the remainder, where these two lines of evidence seem to collide, the choices are more difficult.

The *external evidence* has to do with the quality and age of the manuscripts that support a given variant. For the Old Testament this often amounts to a choice among the Hebrew manuscripts preserved in the Masoretic Text (MT), primarily medieval copies (based on a very careful copying tradition), earlier Hebrew manuscripts that have been preserved, in part, in the Dead Sea Scrolls (DSS; dated before the first Christian century), and manuscripts of ancient translations such as the Greek Septuagint (LXX; produced in Egypt around 250–150 BC). A well-preserved copy of Isaiah found among the Dead Sea Scrolls has demonstrated that the Masoretic tradition has carefully preserved a very ancient text; nonetheless, it often needs emendation from the Septuagint. Sometimes neither the Hebrew nor Greek yields a tolerable sense, at which times conjectures are necessary.

For the New Testament, the better external evidence was preserved in Egypt, where again, a very reliable copying tradition existed. When this early evidence is also supported by equally early evidence from other sectors of the Roman Empire, such evidence is usually seen to be conclusive.

The *internal evidence* has to do with the copyists and authors. When translators are faced with a choice between two or more variants, they usually can detect which readings are the mistakes because scribal habits and tendencies have been carefully analyzed by scholars and are now well-known. Usually the variant that best explains how all the others came about is the one presumed to be the original text. It is also important for the translator to know a given biblical author's style and vocabulary, because these, too, play a role in making textual choices.

As already noted, for the vast majority of variants found among the manuscripts, the best (or good) external evidence combined with the best internal evidence yields us an extraordinarily high degree of certainty about the original text. This may be illustrated thousands of times over simply by comparing the NKJV (which is based on poor, late manuscripts) with almost all other contemporary translations, such as the NRSV or NIV. We will note three variants as illustrations of the work of textual criticism:

1 Samuel 8:16

NKJV/NASB: "he will take ... your finest young men and your
            donkeys"
NRSV/NIV: "he will take ... the best of your cattle and donkeys"

The text of the NRSV/NIV ("your cattle") comes from the Septuagint, the usually reliable Greek translation of the Old Testament. The NKJV/NASB follows the Masoretic Text, reading "young men," a rather unlikely term to be used in parallel to "donkeys." The origin of the miscopy in the Hebrew text, which the NKJV followed, is easy to understand. The expression for "your young men" in Hebrew is *bhwrykm*, while "your cattle" is *bqrykm* (they are as much alike as "television" and "telephone" — i.e., the error could not have been oral). The incorrect copying of a single character by a scribe resulted in a change of meaning. The Septuagint was translated some time before the miscopy was made, so it preserved the original "your cattle." The accidental change to "your young men" was made later, affecting medieval Hebrew manuscripts, but too late to affect the premedieval Septuagint.

Mark 1:2

NKJV: "As it is written in the Prophets ..."
NIV: "as it is written in Isaiah the prophet ..."

The text of the NIV is found in all the best early Greek manuscripts. It is also the only text found in all the earliest (second-century) translations (Latin, Coptic, and Syriac) and is the only text known among all but one of the church fathers before the ninth century. It is easy to see what happened in the later Greek manuscripts. Since the citation that follows is a combination of Malachi 3:1 and Isaiah 40:3, a later copyist "corrected" Mark's original text to make it more precise.

1 Corinthians 6:20

NKJV: "therefore glorify God in your body and in your spirit, which are God's."
NIV: "Therefore honor God with your bodies."

This example was chosen to illustrate that, on occasion, changes to the original text were made by copyists for theological reasons. The words "and in your spirit, which are God's," though found in most of the late-medieval Greek manuscripts, do not appear in any early Greek evidence or in the Latin-speaking church in the West. Had they been in Paul's original letter, it is nearly impossible to explain either how or why copyists would have left them out so early and so often. But their late appearance in Greek manuscripts can be easily explained. All such manuscripts were copied in monasteries at a time when Greek philosophy, with its low view of the body, had made inroads into Christian theology. So, some monks added "in your spirit" and then concluded that both body and spirit "are God's." While this is true, these additional words deflect Paul's obvious concern with the body in this passage and are thus no part of the Spirit's inspiration of the apostle.

It should be noted here that, for the most part, translators work from Greek and Hebrew texts edited by careful, rigorous scholarship. For the New Testament this means that the "best text" has been edited and published by scholars who are experts in this field. But it also means, for both Testaments, that the translators themselves have access to an "apparatus" (textual information in footnotes) that includes the significant variants along with their manuscript support.

2. *Although textual criticism is a science, it is not an exact science, because it deals with many human variables.* Occasionally, especially when the translation is the work of a committee, the translators will themselves be divided as to which variant represents the original text and which is (are) the scribal error(s). Usually at such times the majority choice will be found in the actual translation, while the minority choice will be in the margin.

The reason for the uncertainty may be either that the best manuscript evidence conflicts with the best explanation of how the error came about, or that the manuscript evidence is evenly divided and either variant can explain how the other came to be. We can illustrate this from 1 Corinthians 13:3, which in the 1984 NIV looks like this:

NIV text 1984: "surrender my body to the flames"
NIV note: "surrender my body that I may boast"

But in the 2011 NIV, the verse now looks like this (cf. NRSV, NLT):

NIV text 2011: "give over my body to hardship that I may boast
NIV note: "give over my body to the flames"

In Greek the difference is only one letter: *kauthēsōmai/ kauchēsōmai.* The word "boast" has the best and earliest Greek support; the word "flames" appeared first in Latin translation (at a time when Christians were being burned at the stake). In this case *both* readings have some inherent difficulties: "Flames" represents a form that is ungrammatical in Greek; moreover, Paul's letter was written well before Christians were martyred by burning—and no one ever voluntarily "gave over their bodies" to be burned at the stake! On the other hand, while supported by what is easily the best evidence, it has been difficult to find an adequate meaning for "that I may boast." Here is one of those places where a good commentary will probably be necessary in order for you to make up your own mind.

The preceding example is a good place for us also to refer you back to the last chapter. You will note that the choice of the correct text is one of the *content* questions. A good exegete must know, if it is possible to know, which of these words Paul actually wrote. On the other hand, it should also be noted that Paul's final *point* here is little affected by that choice. In either case, he means that if one gives the body over to some extreme sacrifice, or the like, but lacks love, it is all for nothing.

This, then, is what it means to say that translators must make textual choices, and it also explains one of the reasons why translations will sometimes differ—and also why translators are themselves interpreters. Before we go on to the second reason why translations differ, we need to make a note here about the King James Version and its most recent revision, the New King James Version.

The KJV for a long time was the most widely used translation in the world; it also served for several centuries as the classic expression of the English language. Indeed, its translators coined phrases that will be forever embedded in our language ("coals of fire," "the skin of my teeth," "tongues of fire"). However, for the New Testament, the only Greek text available to the translators of the 1611 edition was based on late manuscripts, which had accumulated the mistakes of over a thousand years of copying. Few of these mistakes—and we must note that there are many of them—make any difference to us doctrinally, but they often do make a difference in the meaning of certain specific texts. Recognizing that the English of the KJV was no longer a living language—and thoroughly dissatisfied with its modern revision (RSV/NRSV)—it was decided by some to "update" the KJV by ridding it of its "archaic" way of speaking. But in so doing, the NKJV revisers eliminated the best feature of the KJV (its marvelous expression of the English language) and kept the worst (its flawed Greek text).

This is why for study *you should use almost any modern translation other than the KJV or the NKJV.* But how to choose between modern translations takes us to the next kinds of choices translators have to make.

The Questions of Language

The next two kinds of choices—verbal and grammatical—bring us to the actual science of translation. The difficulty has to do with the transferring of words and ideas from one language to another. To understand what various theories underlie our modern translations, you will need to become acquainted with the following technical terms:

Original language: the language that one is translating *from;* in our case, Hebrew, Aramaic, or Greek. For convenience, we will usually say just "Hebrew or Greek."

Receptor language: the language that one is translating *into*; in our case, English.

Historical distance: has to do with the differences that exist between the original language and the receptor language, both in matters of words, grammar, and idioms as well as in matters of culture and history.

Formal equivalence: the attempt to keep as close to the "form" of the Hebrew or Greek, both words and grammar, as can be conveniently put into understandable English. The closer one stays to the Hebrew or Greek idiom, the closer one moves toward a theory of translation often described as "literal." Translations based on formal equivalence will keep historical distance intact at all points. The problem here, however, is that "understandable" English is not the goal of good translation; rather the goal is good "contemporary" English that is comparable in language and meaning to the original author's intent—as much as that can be determined from the context.

Functional equivalence: the attempt to keep the meaning of the Hebrew or Greek but to put their words and idioms into what would be the normal way of saying the same thing in English. The more one is willing to forego formal equivalence for functional equivalence, the closer one moves toward a theory of translation frequently described as "dynamic equivalent." Such translations sustain historical distance on all historical and factual matters but "update" matters of language, grammar, and style.

Free translation: the attempt to translate the *ideas* from one language to another, with less concern about using the exact words of the original. A free translation, sometimes also called a paraphrase, tries to eliminate as much of the historical distance as possible and still be faithful to the intent of the original text. The danger here is that a free translation can easily become *too* free-reflecting how the translator wishes the concepts would have been conveyed, rather than reflecting faithfully how they actually are conveyed in the original text.

Theory of translation has basically to do with whether one puts primary emphasis on formal or on functional equivalency, that is, the degree to which one is willing to go in order to bridge the gap between the two languages, either in use of words and grammar or in bridging the historical distance by offering a modern equivalent. For example, should "lamp" be translated "flashlight" or "torch" in cultures where these serve the purpose a lamp once did?

Or should one translate it "lamp," and let readers bridge the gap for themselves? Should "holy kiss" be translated "the handshake of Christian love" in cultures where public kissing is offensive? Should "coals of fire" become "burning embers/coals," since this is more normal English? Should "endurance inspired by hope" (1 Thess 1:3), a formal equivalent that is almost meaningless in English, be rendered "your endurance inspired by hope," which is what Paul's Greek actually means?

Translators are not always consistent, but one of these theories will govern all translators' basic approach to their task. At times the free or literal translations can be excessive, so much so that Clarence Jordan in his Cotton Patch Version "translated" Paul's letter to Rome as to Washington (!), while Robert Young, in a literal rendering published in 1862, transformed one Pauline sentence into this impossible English (?): "Whoredom is actually heard of among you, and such whoredom as is not even named among the nations—as that one hath the wife of the father" (1 Cor 5:1). This is not a valid translation at all.

The several translations of the whole Bible that are most easily accessible may be placed on a formal or functional equivalent and historical distance scale, as shown on the following graph (line 1 represents the original translations, line 2 their various revisions; note that in the case of the RSV, both the NRSV and ESV move more toward the middle, as does the NIV^2 (2011), while the NJB, REB and NLT [the revision of the Living Bible] also have moved more toward the middle from their originals).

Formal Equivalence (literal)				Functional Equivalence (dynamic)				Free
1. KJV	NASB	RSV	NIV^1	NAB	GNB	JB	NEB	LB
2. NKJV	HCSB	NRSV ESV	NIV^2	NJB	REB	NLT		The Message

Our view is that the best theory of translation is the one that remains as faithful as possible to *both* the original and receptor languages, but that when something has to "give," it should be in favor of the receptor language—without losing the meaning of the original language, of course—since the very reason for translation is to make these ancient texts accessible to the English-speaking person who does not know the original languages.

But note well: If the best translational theory is functional equivalence, a translation that adheres to formal equivalence is often helpful as a *second* source; it can give the reader some confidence as to what the Hebrew or Greek actually looked like. A free translation also can be helpful—to stimulate thinking about the possible meaning of a text. But the basic translation for reading and studying should be something in the NIV/NRSV range.

The problem with a formal-equivalent translation is that it keeps distance at the wrong places—in language and grammar. Thus the translator often renders the Greek or Hebrew into English that currently is never written or spoken that way. It is like translating *maison blanche* from French to English as "house white." For example, no native English-speaking person, even in the sixteenth century, would *ever* have said "coals of fire" (Rom 12:20 KJV). That is a literal rendering of the Greek construction, but what it *means* in English is "burning coals" (NIV) or "live coals" (REB).

A second problem with a literal translation is that it often makes the English ambiguous, where the Greek or Hebrew was quite clear to the original recipients. For example, in 2 Corinthians 5:16 the Greek phrase *kata sarka* can be translated literally "[to know] according to the flesh" (as in the NASB). But this is not an ordinary way of speaking in English. Furthermore, the phrase is ambiguous. Is it the person who is *being known* who is "according to the flesh," which seems to be implied in the NASB, and which in this case would mean something like "by their outward appearance"? Or is the person who *is* "*knowing*" doing so "according to the flesh," which would mean "from a worldly point of view"? In this case, however, the context is clear, which the NIV correctly renders: "So from now on [since we have been raised to a new life, v. 15] we regard no one from a worldly point of view."

The problem with a free translation, on the other hand, especially for study purposes, is that the translator updates the original author too much. In the second half of the twentieth century, three "free translations" served succeeding generations of Christians: Phillips (by J. B. Phillips), the Living Bible (by Ken Taylor, who "translated" into language for the young not the Greek Bible but the KJV), and The Message (by Eugene Peterson). On the one hand, these renditions sometimes have especially fresh and vivid ways of expressing some old truths and have thus each served to stimulate contemporary Christians to take a new look at their

Bibles. On the other hand, such a "translation" often comes very close to being a commentary, but without other options made available to the reader. Therefore, as stimulating as these can sometimes be, they are never intended to be one's only Bible, as even these translators would be quick to admit. Thus the reader needs regularly to check these rather eye-catching moments against another translation or a commentary to make sure that not too much freedom has been taken.

SOME PROBLEM AREAS

The way various translations handle the problem of "historical distance" can best be noted by illustrating several of the kinds of problems involved.

1. *Weights, measures, money.* This is a particularly difficult area. Does one transliterate the Hebrew and Greek terms ("ephah," "homer," etc.), or try to find their English equivalents? If one chooses to go with equivalents in weights and measures, does one use the standard "pounds" and "feet" still in vogue in the United States (but not Canada), or does one follow the rest of the English-speaking world and translate "liters" and "meters"? Inflation can make a mockery of monetary equivalents in a few years. The problem is further complicated by the fact that exaggerated measures or money are often used to suggest contrasts or startling results, as in Matthew 18:24–28 or Isaiah 5:10. To transliterate in these cases would likely cause an English reader to miss the point of the passages altogether.

The KJV, followed closely by the NKJV and NRSV, was inconsistent in these matters. For the most part they transliterated, so that we got "baths," "ephahs," "homers," "shekels," and "talents." Yet the Hebrew *'ammāh* was translated "cubit," the *zeret* a "span," and the Greek *mna* ("mina") became the British "pound," while the *dēnarion* became a mere "penny." For most North Americans all of these have the effect of being meaningless or misleading.

The NASB uses "cubit" and "span"—both of which, according to modern dictionaries, represent "an ancient linear unit"—but otherwise consistently transliterates and then puts an English equivalent in the margin (except for John 2:6 [where the NASB had put the transliteration in the margin!]). This is the way the original NIV also chose to go (except for Genesis 6–7, where "cubits" were turned into feet), while the marginal notes are given both in English standards and in metric equivalents. The apparent reason for this is that the "cubit" was just flexible enough in length so as to preclude precision in English—especially when translating the measurements of structures.

On the matter of monetary equivalents translations are sometimes puzzling, but in fairness the difficulties here are enormous. Take, for example, the first occurrence of *talantōn* and *dēnarion* in the New Testament (Matt 18:23–34, the parable of the unmerciful servant). The *talantōn* was a Greek monetary unit of a varying, but very large, amount. Traditionally it was transliterated into English as "talent," which you will immediately recognize as quite problematic, since that word has changed meaning over time in English to connote "ability." The *dēnarion*, on the other hand, was a Roman monetary unit of a modest amount, basically the daily wage of a day laborer. So what to do with these words? In the parable they are intentionally not precise amounts but are purposely hyperbolic contrasts (see ch. 8). The NIV, therefore, rightly translates "ten thousand talents" as "ten thousand bags of gold" and "a hundred denarii" as "a hundred silver coins," and then explains the words in a footnote.

On the other hand, when a precise amount is in view or the coin itself is being spoken about, most contemporary formal- and functional-equivalent translations have moved toward transliterating "*denarius*" but are still ambivalent about the "*talent*."

We would argue that either equivalents or transliterations with marginal notes are a good procedure with most weights and measurements. However, the use of equivalents is surely to be preferred in passages like Isaiah 5:10 and the Matthew parable noted above. Note, for example, how much more meaningfully—though with some liberties as to precision—the GNB renders the purposeful contrasts in Isaiah 5:10 than does the NKJV (cf. NASB):

Isaiah 5:10

NKJV: "For ten acres of vineyard shall yield one bath, and a homer of seed shall yield one ephah."

GNB: "The grapevines growing on five acres of land will yield only five gallons of wine. Ten bushels of seed will produce only one bushel of grain."

2. *Euphemisms.* Almost all languages have euphemisms for matters of sex and toilet. A translator has one of three choices in such matters: (1) translate literally but perhaps leave an English-speaking reader bewildered or guessing, (2) translate the *formal equivalent* but perhaps offend or shock the reader, or (3) translate with a *functionally equivalent euphemism.*

Option 3 is probably the best, if there is an appropriate euphemism. Otherwise it is better to go with option 2, especially for matters that generally no longer require euphemisms in English. Thus to have Rachel say, "I am having my monthly period" (Gen 31:35 GNB; cf. NIV) is to be preferred to the literal "the manner of women is upon me" (NASB, cf. KJV, RSV). For the same idiom earlier in Genesis (18:11) the GNB is consistent ("Sarah had stopped having her monthly periods"), while the NIV is much freer, having the public reading of Scripture in mind ("Sarah was past the age of childbearing"). Similarly, "[he] forced her, and lay with her" (2 Sam 13:14 KJV) becomes simply "he raped her" in the NIV and GNB.

There can be dangers in this, however, especially when translators themselves miss the meaning of the idiom, as can be seen in the original NIV, GNB, and LB renderings of the first assertion addressed in 1 Corinthians 7:1 "It is good for a man not to marry," which unfortunately is both wrong and misleading. The idiom "to touch a woman" in every other case in antiquity means to have sexual intercourse with a woman, and never means anything close to "to marry." Here the NAB has found an equivalent euphemism: "A man is better off having no relations with a woman"; but this has the possibility of being misunderstood or misconstrued to mean no relations whatsoever—including friendly ones. So the NIV has eliminated the euphemism altogether: " 'It is good for a man not to have sexual relations with a woman,' " which it also correctly puts in quotes as something being put forward in Corinth, to which Paul will eventually answer with both a "yes" and "no," qualified by the circumstances.

3. *Vocabulary.* When most people think of translation, this is the area they usually have in mind. It seems like such a simple task: find the English word that means the same as the Hebrew or Greek word. But finding precisely the right word is what makes translation so difficult. Part of the difficulty is not only in the choosing of an appropriate English word but also in the choosing of a word that will not already be filled with connotations that are foreign to the original language.

The problem is further complicated by the fact that some Hebrew or Greek words have ranges of meaning different from anything available in English. In addition, some words can have several shades of meaning, as well as two or more considerably different meanings. And a deliberate play on words borders on being nearly impossible to translate from one language to another.

We have already noted how various translations have chosen to interpret "virgin" in 1 Corinthians 7:36. In chapter 1 we also noted the difficulty in rendering Paul's use of the word *sarx* ("flesh"). In most cases, almost anything is better than the literal "flesh." The NIV handles this word especially well: "sinful nature" when Paul is contrasting "flesh" and "spirit"; "human nature" in Romans 1:3 where it refers to Jesus' Davidic descent; "from a worldly point of view" in 2 Corinthians 5:16 noted above (cf. 1 Cor 1:26 "by human standards"); and "body" when it means that, as in Colossians 1:22.

This kind of example can be illustrated many times over and is one of the reasons why a translation by functional equivalence is much to be preferred to a more literal one, since the latter has the frequent possibility of misleading the English-speaking reader, and thus misses the reason for translation.

4. *Wordplays.* Wordplays tend to abound in most languages, but they are always unique to the original language and can seldom, if ever, be translated into a receptor language. The same is true with wordplays in the Bible, which abound in the poetry of the Old Testament and can be found throughout the New Testament as well. So what does the translator do?

Take, for example, the play on the sounds for the words "summer" and "end" in Amos 8:1–2, where even though the Hebrew consonants are *qyṣ* and *qṣ* respectively, the two words themselves were pronounced virtually alike in Amos's day. Translations that tend toward formal equivalence translate in a straightforward manner:

> NRSV: "[God] said, 'Amos, what do you see?' And I said, 'A basket of summer [*qyṣ*] fruit.' Then the LORD said to me, 'The end [*qṣ*] has come upon my people Israel.'"

Translations that move toward functional equivalence try to work with the wordplay, even when doing so may alter the meaning somewhat:

NIV: " 'What do you see, Amos,' [God] asked. 'A basket of
ripe [*qyṣ*] fruit,' I answered. Then the LORD said to
me, 'The time is ripe [*qṣ*] for my people Israel.' "

An example of the same difficulty can be found in some instances of Paul's use of the word "flesh," noted above and in the previous chapter (p. 23). This happens especially in Galatians 3:3, where Paul says (NASB): "Having begun by the Spirit, are you now being perfected by the flesh?" Lying behind this rhetoric is the issue of Gentile believers yielding to Jewish-Christian pressure to submit to circumcision (of the literal flesh!). But it is clear from the full argument of Galatians that Paul here means more than just circumcision when referring to "by the flesh." In Galatians 5 the "flesh" has to do with living in a self-centered, ungodly way as opposed to living "by the Spirit." So what does the functional-equivalent translator do in 3:3? The 1984 NIV renders it "by human effort" (cf. NLT) and the GNB "by your own power"; but in doing so they must lose the "Spirit/flesh" contrast that is picked up again later (4:28 and 5:13–26). Both ways of translating are "right," of course, in keeping with the respective theories of translation; but in both cases something is lost, simply because these particular wordplays are not available in English. And this is yet another reason why you should frequently use more than one translation, especially when "reading" borders on "studying."

5. *Grammar and Syntax.* Even though most Indo-European languages have a great many similarities, each language has its own preferred structures as to how words and ideas are related to each other in sentences. It is at these points especially where translation by functional equivalence is to be preferred. A formal-equivalent translation tends to abuse or override the ordinary structures of the receptor language by directly transferring into it the syntax and grammar of the original language. Such direct transfers are often *possible* in the receptor language, but they are seldom *preferable*. From hundreds of examples, we choose two as illustrations, one from Greek and one from Hebrew.

a. One of the characteristics of Greek is its fondness for what are known as genitive constructions. The genitive is the ordinary case of possession, as in "my book." Such a true possessive can also, but only very awkwardly, be rendered "the book of me." However, other possessives in English, such as "God's grace," do not so much mean, for example, that God owns the grace as that he gives it, or that it comes from him. Such "non-true" possessives can always be translated into English as "the grace *of* God."

The Greek language has a great profusion of these latter kinds of genitives, which are used, for example, as descriptive adjectives to express source or to connote special relationships between two nouns. A "literal" translation almost invariably transfers these into English with an "*of*" phrase, but frequently with strange results, such as the "coals of fire" noted above, or "the word of His power" (Heb 1:3 NKJV). Both of these are clearly adjectival or descriptive genitives, which in the NIV are more accurately rendered "burning coals" and "his powerful word." Similarly the NASB's "steadfast-ness of hope" (1 Thess 1:3) and "joy of the Holy Spirit" (1:6) are translated in the NIV as "endurance inspired by hope" and "joy given by the Holy Spirit." These are not only to be preferred; they are, in fact, more accurate because they give a genuine English equivalent rather than a literal, Greek way of expressing things that in English would be nearly meaningless.

Interestingly enough, in one of the few places where the KJV (followed by the RSV but not the NASB) offered something of an equivalent (1 Cor 3:9), the translators missed the meaning of the genitive altogether. Apparently they were led astray by the word "fellow-workers" and thus translated, "For we are labourers together with God: ye are God's husbandry, ye are God's build-ing." But in Paul's sentence each occurrence of "God" is clearly a *possessive* genitive, with an emphasis on both *we* (Paul and Apollos) and *you* (the church as God's field and building) as belonging to him. This is correctly translated in the 2011 NIV as, "For we are God's co-workers; you are God's field, God's building." Paul's point is made even more clearly in the NAB, where they have ren-dered "field" as "cultivation."

But the still greater problem exists with the first of these Greek sentences, which is regularly rendered "God's co-workers." In almost anyone's understanding of English this would mean co-workers *with* God, as it has in fact been so often understood. But Paul's genitive is almost certainly intended as a "possessive," meaning "co-workers in God's service" as the 2011 NIV renders it, not working "alongside God," as the standard rendering seems to imply and is thus frequently misunderstood and misused

b. Thousands of times in the Old Testament the KJV translators woodenly followed the Hebrew word order in a way that does not produce normal idiomatic English. One common example is how often verses (with each verse a paragraph!) begin with the word "and." For example, in Genesis 1 every verse, without exception, begins with "and"—a total of thirty times. Even the NKJV translators had difficulty with this idiom; nonetheless they still rendered the Hebrew "and" in almost every case (using "and," "then," "so," etc.). Now compare the NIV. It reduces the number of occurrences of "and" to fifteen, while at the same time improving the flow of the language so that it sounds more natural to the ear.

The NIV translators produced an improved English version by taking seriously the fact that the vast majority of prose sentences in Old Testament Hebrew begin with one of the two Hebrew forms for the word "and." The word for "and" appears even when there is absolutely nothing preceding it to which the sentence logically connects. In fact, six books of the Old Testament (Joshua, Judges, 1 Samuel, Ezra, Ruth, and Esther) begin in Hebrew with the word "and," though these obviously do not follow any previous statement. Accordingly, it is now recognized by Hebrew grammarians that "and" at the beginning of a sentence is virtually the equivalent of the use of capitalization at the beginning of English sentences. This does not mean that the Hebrew "and" should *never* be translated by the English "and"; it simply means that "and" is only *sometimes,* and certainly not a majority of the time, the best rendering in English. A simple English sentence beginning with a capital letter will do nicely in most cases.

Another example is the KJV's repeated "and it came to pass," which is frequently retained in the NKJV, even though this is never used in normal English anymore. Indeed, it was rare even in the seventeenth century when the KJV was undertaken. Because the Hebrew narrative verb form that lies behind it was followed literally and woodenly, the resulting translation, "and it came to pass," occupied a prominent position in Old Testament style but nowhere else in English speech. We once heard a sermon on the concept that all things are temporary and shall eventually pass away (cf. 1 Cor 13:8–10) based on the frequency of the clause "and it came to pass," which the preacher misunderstood to mean, "And it came *in order to* pass away." In fact, the NIV translators (rightly) do not give expression to the Hebrew clause as such. Judiciously rendering Hebrew into English requires an equivalent *meaning,* not an equivalent word or clause pattern.

6. *Matters of Gender*. When this book first appeared in 1981, the problem of using masculine language where women are included or are in view was just beginning to become an issue for translators. By the time the second edition appeared in 1993, one revision (NRSV) of a well-established translation (RSV) had already appeared, which became deliberately inclusive in all such instances in both the Old and New Testaments. In the following decade all the other leading translations have followed suit to a greater or lesser degree, while at least one revision (ESV) came into existence to "stem this tide," as it were, so that in effect it is deliberately exclusive of women in many places where it is quite unnecessary to do so. Indeed, there can be no question that standard usage in both Great Britain and North America has now shifted strongly toward inclusiveness when both men and women are being addressed or are in view. Recent surveys show that a majority of people up to age seventy (!) will consider a statement like "Let him who is without sin cast the first stone" to refer only to men or boys, not to women or girls.

But this also presents some agonizing decisions on the part of translators. There is very little difficulty, for example, in translating Paul's vocative "brothers" as "brothers and sisters," since in almost all cases it is clear that women are also in view—and in any case some Christian traditions (Pentecostals, for example) have been using this inclusive vocative for several generations. But other cases are more problematic. Two examples will suffice.

In order to avoid excluding women from passages that are spoken to or about people in general, it has been deemed necessary by some to make certain clauses plural that are expressed in the singular (although this usually does not have significance in itself). Psalm 1:1 ("Blessed is the man" [RSV]) is an example, where many revisions of existing translations have moved to the plural in order to avoid unnecessarily excluding women from this psalm, since the generic use of "man" as a way of saying "person" has generally fallen out of current usage. To render this as "person" here would require the translator to follow up with either masculine pronouns (v. 2 "his delight") or with some kind of awkwardness ("his or her") that would distort the poetry.

Although there have been a variety of attempts to resolve this problem in contemporary English versions, the present NIV seems to have done so quite successfully, by recasting to "one" in verse

1, to "the person" in verse 3, and simply "the wicked" and "the righteous" for the concluding contrasts in verses 4–6. Here, functional equivalence rules, since the only item lost in the poem is the author's own move from speaking first in the singular and then the plural. What is lost in terms of actual meaning is usually relatively small in these sorts of cases. It should be noted that "pluralizing" is not usually particularly harmful, and the issue is more a matter of getting used to a shift in English grammar. In gnomic sayings that begin with "If anyone" or "Whoever" or "When someone," the standard English rule learned by the authors as schoolboys was that these must be followed by a singular pronoun, which of course was always masculine. But that was not everyone's rule, since it turns out that several well-known authors of nineteenth-century English novels frequently used a "singular" *them, their,* or *they* in such sentences. Again, this is now becoming standard English, at least in the print and spoken media, so that one can regularly hear, "If anyone …, let them …" For one of the authors of this book the issue was settled a couple years back, when a TV advertisement used "anyone …, … they" in the sentence.

ON CHOOSING A TRANSLATION

We have been trying to help you choose a translation. We conclude with a few summary remarks about several translations.

First, it should be noted that we have not tried to be exhaustive. There are still other translations of the whole Bible that we have not included in our discussion, not to mention over eighty others of the New Testament alone that have appeared since the beginning of the twentieth century. Several of the latter were excellent (e.g., Weymouth, 1903; Helen Montgomery, 1924; Williams, 1937) but now tend to be quite outdated in their use of English.

Among the whole-Bible translations not discussed are some that are theologically biased, such as the Jehovah's Witnesses' New World Translation (1961). This is an extremely literal translation into which have been worked the heretical doctrines of this cult. Others of these translations are eccentric, such as that by George Lamsa (1940), who believed that a Syriac translation from around AD 400 held the keys to everything. One should probably also include here The Amplified Bible, which had a run of popularity far beyond its worth. It is far better to use several translations, note where they differ, and then check out these differences in another source than to be led to believe that a word can mean one of several things in any given sentence, with the reader left to choose whatever best strikes his or her fancy.

Which translation, then, should one read? We would venture to suggest that the current NIV (2011), a committee translation by the best scholarship in the evangelical tradition is as good a translation as you can get. The GNB, HCSB and NAB are also especially good. One would do well to have some or all of these. The NAB is a committee translation by the best scholarship in the American Catholic tradition. The HCSB is a committee translation by evangelical scholars holding to the inerrancy of Scripture. The GNB is an outstanding translation by a single scholar, Robert G. Bratcher, who regularly consulted with others and whose expertise in linguistics has brought the concept of dynamic equivalence to translation in a thoroughgoing way.

Along with one or more of these, readers would also do well to use one or more of the following: the NASB or the NRSV. Both translations are attempts to update the KJV. The translators used superior original texts and thereby eliminated most of what in the KJV did not exist in the original languages. At the same time they tried to adhere as closely as possible to the *language* of the KJV, with some modernization. The NRSV is by far the better translation; the NASB is much more like the KJV and therefore far more literal—to the point of being wooden.

Along with one or more of these, we recommend you also consult either the REB or NJB—or both. Both of these are committee translations. The REB is the product of the best of British scholarship and therefore includes many British idioms not always familiar to North American readers. The NJB is an English translation from the French *Bible de Jerusalem*. Both of these translations tend to be freer at times than the others described here as functionally equivalent. But both of them also have some outstanding features and are well worth using in conjunction with the others.

In the following chapters we will follow the NIV 2011 unless otherwise noted. If you were regularly to read this translation, and then consult at least one from three other categories (NRSV/NASB; GNB/NAB; REB/NJB), you would be giving yourself the best possible start to an intelligent reading and study of the Bible.

CHAPTER 3

The Epistles: Learning to Think Contextually

We start our discussion of the various biblical genres by looking at the New Testament Epistles. Our reasons for doing this are twofold: First, along with the Gospels they are the most familiar portions of the Bible for most people, and second, for many readers they appear to be generally easy to interpret. After all, who needs special help to understand that "all have sinned" (Rom 3:23), that "the wages of sin is death" (Rom 6:23), and that "by grace you have been saved, through faith" (Eph 2:8), or the imperatives "walk by the Spirit" (Gal 5:16) and "walk in the way of love" (Eph 5:2)?

On the other hand, the "ease" of interpreting Epistles can be quite deceptive. This is especially so at the level of hermeneutics. One might try leading a group of Christians through 1 Corinthians, for example, and see how many are the difficulties. "How is Paul's opinion about 'virgins' at the beginning of his long discussion of 'the married' and 'the not yet, or unmarried' in 1 Corinthians (7:25–40) to be taken as God's Word?" some will ask, especially when they personally dislike some of the implications of this opinion. And the questions continue. How does the excommunication of the brother earlier in the letter (ch. 5) relate to the contemporary church, especially when he can simply go down the street to another church? What is the point of the corrections of the abuses of Spirit-gifting (chs. 12–14), if one is in a local church where the gifts of the Spirit mentioned here are not accepted as valid for the twenty-first century? How do we get around the implication that women should wear a head covering when praying and prophesying (11:2–16)—or the clear implication that they do in fact pray and prophesy in the community gathered to worship?

It becomes clear that Epistles are *not* as easy to interpret as is often thought. Thus, because of their importance to the Christian faith and because so many of the important hermeneutical issues are raised here, we are going to let them serve as models for the exegetical and hermeneutical questions we want to raise throughout the book.

THE NATURE OF THE EPISTLES

Before we look specifically at 1 Corinthians as a model for exegeting Epistles, some general words are in order about the whole collection of Epistles (all the New Testament except the four gospels, Acts, and Revelation).

First, it is necessary to note that the Epistles themselves are not a homogeneous lot. Many years ago Adolf Deissmann, on the basis of the vast papyrus discoveries, made a distinction between letters and epistles. The former, the "real letters," as he called them, were nonliterary, that is, they were not written for the public and posterity but were intended only for the person or persons to whom they were addressed. In contrast to the letter, the epistle was an artistic literary form or a species of literature that was intended for the public. Deissmann himself considered all the Pauline Epistles as well as 2 and 3 John to be "real letters." Although some other scholars have cautioned that one should not reduce all the letters of the New Testament to one or the other of these categories—in some instances it seems to be a question of more or less—the distinction is nevertheless a valid one. Romans and Philemon differ from one another not only in content but also to the degree that one is far more personal than the other. And in contrast to any of Paul's letters, 2 Peter and 1 John are far more like epistles.

The validity of this distinction may be seen by noting the *form* of ancient letters. Just as there is a standard form to our letters (date, salutation, body, closing, and signature), so there was for theirs. Thousands of ancient letters have been found, and most of them have a form exactly like those in the New Testament (cf. the letter of the Jerusalem council in Acts 15:23–29). The form consists of six parts:

1. name of the writer (e.g., Paul)
2. name of the recipient (e.g., to the church of God in Corinth)
3. greeting (e.g., Grace to you and peace from God our Father ...)
4. prayer wish or thanksgiving (e.g., I always thank God for you ...)
5. body
6. final greeting and farewell (e.g., The grace of the Lord Jesus be with you.)

The one variable element in this form is number 4, which in most of the ancient letters either takes the form of a prayer wish (almost exactly like 3 John 2), or else is missing altogether (as in Galatians, 1 Timothy, Titus), although at times one finds a thanksgiving and prayer (as often in Paul's letters). In three of the New Testament Epistles this thanksgiving turns into a doxology (2 Corinthians, Ephesians, 1 Peter; cf. Rev 1:5–6).

It will be noted that New Testament Epistles that lack either formal elements 1–3 or 6 are those that fail to be true letters, although they are partially epistolary in form. Hebrews, for example, which has been described as three parts tract and one part letter, was indeed sent to a specific group of people, as two passages (10:32–34 and 13:1–25) make clear. Note especially the letter form at the end (13:22–25). Yet the first ten chapters are little like a letter; indeed, they are in fact an eloquent homily in which the argument as to Christ's total superiority to all that has preceded is interspersed with urgent words of exhortation that the readers hold fast to their faith in Christ (2:1–4; 3:7–19; 5:11–6:20; 10:19–25). In fact, at the end, the author himself calls it his "word of exhortation" (13:22).

The apostle John's first letter is similar in some ways, except that it has *none* of the formal elements of a letter. Nonetheless, it was clearly written for a specific group of people (e.g., 2:7, 12–14, 19, 26) and looks very much like the body of a letter with all the formal elements shorn off. In any case this suggests that it is not simply a theological treatise for the church at large.

James and 2 Peter, on the other hand, are both addressed as letters, but they lack the familiar final greeting and farewell, not to mention lacking specific addressees, as well as any personal notations by the writers. These are the closest writings in the New

Testament to "epistles" (that is, tracts for the whole church), although 2 Peter seems to have been called forth by some who were denying Christ's second coming (3:1–7). James, on the other hand, so completely lacks an overall argument that it looks more like a collection of "sermon notes" on a variety of ethical topics than a letter.

Despite this variety of kinds, however, there is one item that all of the Epistles have in common, and this is *the* crucial item to note in reading and interpreting them: They are all what are technically called *occasional documents* (i.e., arising out of and intended for a specific occasion), and they are *all* from the *first century*. Although inspired by the Holy Spirit and thus belonging to all time, they were first written out of the context of the author to the context of the original recipients. It is precisely these factors—that they are occasional and that they belong to the first century—that make their interpretation difficult at times.

Above all else, their *occasional* nature must be taken seriously. This means that they were occasioned, or called forth, by some specific circumstance, either from the reader's side or the author's. Almost all of the New Testament letters were occasioned from the reader's side (Philemon and probably James and Romans appear to be exceptions). Usually the occasion was some kind of behavior that needed correcting, or a doctrinal error that needed setting right, or a misunderstanding that needed further light.

Most of our problems in interpreting the Epistles are due to this fact of their being occasional. We have the answers, but we do not always know what the questions or problems were—or even if there was a problem. It is much like hearing one end of a telephone conversation and trying to figure out who is on the other end and what that unseen party is saying (an experience from life for one of the authors; when informed, everything made "perfectly good sense"!). Yet in many cases it is especially important for us to try to hear "the other end" so that we know to what our passage is a response.

One further point here: The occasional nature of the Epistles also means that they are *not* first of all theological treatises, nor are they summaries of Paul's or Peter's theology. There is theology implied, but it is always "task theology"—theology being written for or brought to bear on the task at hand. This is true even of Romans, which is a fuller and more systematic statement of Paul's theology than one finds elsewhere. But it is only *some* of his theology; in this case it is theology born out of his own special task as apostle to the Gentiles. It is his special struggle for Jew and Gentile to become one people of God, based on grace alone and apart from the law, that causes the discussion to take the special form it does in Romans and that causes "justification" to be used there as the primary metaphor for salvation. After all, the word "justify," which predominates in Romans (fifteen times) and Galatians (eight times), occurs only two other times in all of Paul's other letters (1 Cor 6:11; Titus 3:7).

Thus one will go to the Epistles again and again for Christian theology; they are loaded with it. But one must always keep in mind that they were not primarily written to expound Christian theology. It is always theology applied to or directed toward a particular need. We will note the implications of this for hermeneutics in our next chapter.

Given these important preliminaries, how then does one go about the exegesis, or an informed exegetical reading, of an epistle? From here on, we will proceed with a case study of 1 Corinthians. We are well aware that not every epistle will be like this one, but nearly all the questions one needs to ask of any epistle are raised here.

THE HISTORICAL CONTEXT

The first thing one must try to do with any of the Epistles is to form a tentative but informed reconstruction of the situation to which the author is speaking. What was going on in Corinth that caused Paul to write 1 Corinthians? How does he come to learn of their situation? What kind of relationship and former contacts has he had with them? What attitudes do they and he reflect in this letter? These are the kinds of questions to which you want answers. So what do you do?

First, you need to consult your Bible dictionary or the introduction to your commentary to find out as much as possible about Corinth and its people. Among other important things, you should note that by ancient standards it was a relatively young city—only ninety-four years old when Paul first visited it. Yet because of its strategic location for commerce, it was cosmopolitan, wealthy, a patron of the arts, religious (at least twenty-six temples and shrines), and well-known for its sensuality. With a little reading and imagination one can see that it was a bit of New York, Los Angeles, and Las Vegas, all wrapped up in one place. Therefore, it will hardly be a letter to the community church in Rural Corners, USA. All of this will need to be kept in mind as you read in order to note how it will affect your understanding on nearly every page.

Second, and now especially for study purposes, you need to develop the habit of reading the whole letter through in one sitting, and preferably aloud, so that mouth and ear join the eye. You may well be surprised by how much more you retain when you learn to read this way. You will need to block out an hour or more to do this, but nothing can ever substitute for reading the whole letter through at one time. It is the way one reads every other letter. A letter in the Bible should be no different. There are some things you should be looking for as you read, but you are not, at this point, trying to grasp the meaning of every word or sentence. It is the big view that counts first.

We cannot stress enough the importance of reading and rereading. Once you have divided the letter into its logical parts or sections, you will want to begin the study of every section precisely the same way. Read and reread; and keep your eyes open! And again, learn to read aloud whenever you can—to hear as well as see the Word of God.

As you read through the whole letter, you may find it helpful to jot down a few *very brief* notes with references if you have a hard time making mental notes. What things should you note as you read for the big picture? Remember, the purpose here is first of all to reconstruct the problem. Thus we suggest four kinds of notes:

1. what you notice about the recipients themselves (e.g., whether Jew or Greek, whether wealthy or slave; their problems, attitudes, etc.)
2. Paul's attitudes
3. any specific things mentioned as to the specific occasion of the letter
4. the letter's natural, logical divisions

If all of this is too much for one sitting and causes you to lose the value of reading it through, then read first and afterwards quickly go back through the letter with a skim reading to pick up these items. Here are the kinds of things you may have noticed, grouped according to the four suggested categories:

1. The Corinthian believers are chiefly Gentiles, although there are also some Jews (see 6:9–11; 8:10; 12:2, 13). They obviously love wisdom and knowledge (1:18–2:5; 4:10; 8:1–13; hence the irony in 6:5); they are proud and arrogant (4:18; 5:2, 6) even to the point of judging Paul (4:1–5; 9:1–18), yet they have a large number of internal problems.

2. Paul's response to all of this fluctuates between rebuke (4:8–21; 5:2; 6:1–8), appeal (4:14–17; 16:10–11), and exhortation (6:18–20; 16:12–14).

3. Concerning the occasion of the letter, you may have noted that early on (1:10–12) Paul says he has been *informed* by people from Chloe's household; the beginning of the next major section (5:1) also refers to reported information. About a third of the way through he says, "Now for the matters you wrote about" (7:1), which means he has also received a letter from the church. Did you also notice the repetition of "now about" in what follows (7:25; 8:1; 12:1; 16:1; and 16:12)? Probably these all refer to items from their letter that he is taking up one at a time. One further observation: Did you notice the "arrival" of Stephanas, Fortunatus, and Achaicus at the end (16:17)? Since Stephanas is to be "submitted to" (v. 16), it is certain that these men (or Stephanas, at least) are leaders in the church. Probably they brought the letter to Paul as a kind of official delegation.

If you did not catch all of these things, do not give up. We have gone over this material a lot of times, and it is all familiar turf. The important step is to learn to read with your eyes open to picking up these kinds of clues.

4. We come now to the important matter of having a working outline of the letter. This is especially important for 1 Corinthians because it is easier to study or read the letter in convenient "packages." Not all of Paul's letters are made up of so many separate items, but such a working outline is nonetheless always useful.

The place to begin is with the obvious major divisions. In this case, the beginning of chapter 7 is the big clue. Since here Paul first mentions their letter to him, and since earlier on (1:10–12 and 5:1) he mentions items reported to him, we may initially assume that the matters that have preceded (chs. 1–6) are all responses to what has been reported to him. Introductory phrases and subject matter are the clues to all other divisions in the letter. There are four in the first six chapters:

- the problem of division in the church (1:10–4:21)
- the problem of the incestuous man (5:1–13)
- the problem of lawsuits among believers (6:1–11)
- the problem of sexual immorality (6:12–20)

We have already noted the clues to dividing most of chapters 7–16 on the basis of the introductory formula "now about." The items not introduced by this formula are three: 11:2–16; 11:17–34; and 15:1–58. Probably the items in chapter 11 (at least 11:17–34) were also reported to him but are included here because everything from chapters 8 to 14 deals with worship in some way or another. It is difficult to know whether chapter 15 is a response to the report or to the letter. The phrase "how can some of you say" in verse 12 does not help much because Paul could be quoting either a report or their letter. In any case the rest of Paul's letter can easily be outlined:

- about behavior within marriage (7:1–24)
- about virgins (7:25–40)
- about food sacrificed to idols (8:1–11:1)
- the covering of women's heads in worship (11:2–16)
- an abuse of the Lord's Supper (11:17–34)
- about spiritual gifts (12–14)
- the bodily resurrection of believers (15:1–58)
- about the collection (16:1–11)
- about the return of Apollos (16:12)
- concluding exhortations and greetings (16:13–24)

It may be that by following the headings in the NIV you divided chapters 1–4, 8–10, and 12–14 into smaller groupings. But do you also see that these are complete units? For example, note how thoroughly chapter 13 belongs to the whole argument of chapters 12 to 14 by the mention of specific giftings of the Spirit (vv. 1–2 and 8).

Before we go on, you should note carefully two things. (1) The only other place in Paul's letters where he takes up a succession of independent items like this is his first letter to the Thessalonians (chs. 4–5). For the most part, the other letters basically form one long argument—although sometimes the argument has several distinct parts to it. (2) This is only a tentative outline. We know what occasioned the letter only at the surface—a report and a letter. But what we really want to know is *the precise nature of each of the problems in Corinth* that called forth each specific response from Paul. For our purposes here, therefore, we will spend the rest of our time zeroing in on only the first item—the problem of division within the church (chs. 1–4).

THE HISTORICAL CONTEXT OF 1 CORINTHIANS 1–4

As you approach each of the smaller sections of the letter, you will need to repeat much of what we have just done. If we were giving you an assignment for each lesson, it would look like this: (1) Read 1 Corinthians 1–4 through at least two times (preferably in two different translations). Again, you are reading to get the big picture, to get a "feel" for the whole argument. After you have read it through the second time (or even the third or fourth if you want to read it in each of your translations), go back and (2) list in a notebook everything you can find that tells you something about the recipients and their problem. Try to be thorough here and list everything, even if after a closer look you want to go back and scratch off some items as not entirely relevant. (3) Then make another list of key words and repeated phrases that indicate the subject matter of Paul's answer.

One of the reasons for choosing this section as a model is not only because it is so crucial to much of 1 Corinthians but also, frankly, because it is a difficult one. If you have read the whole section with care and with an eye for the problem, you may have noted—or even been frustrated by—the fact that, although Paul begins by specifically spelling out the problem (1:10–12), the beginning of his answer (1:18–3:4) does not seem to speak to the problem at all. In fact, one may initially think these opening sections to be a digression, except that Paul does not argue as a man off on a tangent. Moreover, in the conclusion (3:18–23) "wisdom" and "foolishness" (key ideas in 1:18–3:4) are joined with "boasting about human leaders" and references to Paul, Apollos, and Cephas. The crucial matter for discovering the issue at hand, then, is to see how all this may fit together.

The place to begin is by making note of what Paul specifically says. At the outset (1:10–12) he says they are divided in the name of their leaders (cf. 3:4–9; 3:21–22; 4:6). But did you also notice that the division is not merely a matter of differences of opinion among them? They are in fact quarreling (1:12; 3:3) and "puffed up in being a follower of one of us *over against* the other" (4:6, emphasis added; cf. 3:21).

All of this seems clear enough. But a careful reading with an eye for the problem should cause two other things to surface.

1. There appears to be some bad blood between the church and Paul himself. This becomes especially clear at the beginning and end of our chapter 4 (vv. 1–5 and 18–21). With that in mind, one may legitimately see the quarreling and division to be not simply a matter of some of them *preferring* Apollos to Paul but of their actually being *opposed to* Paul.

2. One of the key words in this section is "wisdom" or "wise" (twenty-six times in chs. 1–3, and only eighteen more times in all of Paul's letters!). In this case it is also clear that this is more often a pejorative term than a favorable one. God is out to set aside the wisdom of this world (1:18–22, 27–28; 3:18–20), having done so in three ways: by the cross (1:18–25), by his choice of the Corinthian believers (1:26–31), and by the weakness of Paul's preaching (2:1–5). Christ, through the cross, has "become for us wisdom from God" (1:30), and *this* wisdom is revealed *by* the Spirit to those who *have* the Spirit (2:10–16). The use of "wisdom" in this way in Paul's argument makes it almost certain that this, too, is a part of the problem of division. But how? At the least, we can suspect that they are carrying on their division over leaders and their opposition to Paul in the name of wisdom, whatever form that may have taken for them.

Anything we say beyond this will lie in the area of speculation, or educated guessing. Since the term "wisdom" is a semitechnical one for philosophy as well, and since itinerant philosophers of all kinds abounded in the Greek world of Paul's time, we suggest that the Corinthian believers were beginning to think of their new Christian faith as a new "divine wisdom," which in turn caused them to evaluate their leaders in merely human terms as they might any of the itinerant philosophers. But note, as helpful as this "guess" may be, it goes beyond what can be said for certain according to what Paul actually describes here.

On the basis of his response here, three important items can be said with the highest level of certainty: (1) On the basis of 3:5–23 it is clear that the Corinthians have seriously misunderstood the nature and function of leadership in the church. (2) Similarly, on the basis of what precedes (1:18–3:4) they seem also to have misunderstood the basic nature of the gospel. (3) It is clear at the end (4:1–21) that they also are wrong in their judgments on Paul and need to reevaluate their relationship to him. You will notice that with this we have also begun to move to an analysis of Paul's answer.

THE LITERARY CONTEXT

The next step in studying the letter is to learn to trace Paul's argument as an answer to the problem of division tentatively set out above. You will recall from chapter 1 that this, too, is something you can do without initial dependence on scholars.

If we were to give you an assignment for this part of the lesson, it would look like this: Trace the argument of 1 Corinthians 1:10–4:21, paragraph by paragraph, and in a sentence or two explain the point of each paragraph for the argument as a whole — or explain how it functions as a part of Paul's response to the problem of division.

We simply cannot stress enough the importance of learning to THINK PARAGRAPHS, and not just as natural units of thought but as the absolutely necessary key to understanding the argument in the various epistles. You will recall that the one question you need to learn to ask over and again is *what's the point?* Therefore, you want to be able to do two things: (1) In a compact way state the *content* of each paragraph. *What* does Paul say in this paragraph? (2) In another sentence or two try to explain *why* you think Paul says this right at this point. How does this content contribute to the argument?

Since we cannot do this here for all of this passage, let us go into some detail with the three crucial paragraphs in the second part of Paul's answer: 3:5–17. Up to this point Paul, under the inspiration of the Spirit, has responded to inadequate understanding of the gospel by pointing out that the heart of the gospel — a crucified Messiah — stands in contradiction to human wisdom (1:18–25), as does God's choice of those who make up the new people of God (1:26–31) — as though Paul had said to them, "So you think the gospel is a new kind of wisdom, do you? How can this be so? Who in the name of wisdom would have chosen *you* to become the new people of God?" Paul's own preaching also serves as an illustration of the divine contradiction (2:1–5). Now all of this is indeed wisdom, Paul goes on to assure them (2:6–16), but it is wisdom revealed by the Spirit to God's new people—those who have the Spirit. Since the Corinthians *do* have the Spirit, he continues now by way of transition, they should stop acting like those who do *not* (3:1–4). That they are still acting "like mere human beings" is evidenced by their quarreling over Paul and Apollos.

How, then, do the next three paragraphs function in this argument? First, note how the content of the first paragraph (vv. 5–9) deals with the nature and function of the leaders over whom they are quarreling. Paul emphasizes that they are merely servants, not lords, as the Corinthian slogans seem to be making them. Next (vv. 6–9), by means of an analogy from agriculture, he makes two points about his and Apollos's servant status, both of which are crucial to the Corinthian misunderstanding: (1) Both he and Apollos are one in a common cause, even though their tasks differ and each will receive his own "pay." (2) Everything and everyone belongs to God—the church, the servants, the growth.

Notice how crucial these two points are to the problem. They are dividing the church on the basis of its leaders. But these leaders are not *lords* to whom one belongs. They are servants who, even though they have differing ministries, are one in the same cause. And these servants belong to God, just as the Corinthians themselves do.

The following paragraph (3:10–15) has especially been wrongly interpreted because of the failure to think in paragraphs. Note two things: (1) At the end of the preceding paragraph (v. 9) Paul shifts the metaphor from agriculture to architecture, which will be the metaphor used from here on. (2) The particulars in both metaphors are the same (Paul plants/lays the foundation; Apollos waters/builds on the foundation; the Corinthian church is the field/building; God owns the field/building). However, the *point* of each paragraph differs. The point now is clearly expressed at the beginning (v. 10), "But each one should build with care." And it is also clear from Paul's elaboration of the metaphor that one can build well or poorly, with differing final results. Note that what is being built throughout is the church; there is not even a hint that Paul is referring to how each individual Christian builds his or her life on Christ, which, in fact, is totally irrelevant to the argument. What Paul does here is to turn the argument slightly, to warn those who lead the church that they must do so with great care because a day of testing is coming. Building the church with human wisdom or eloquent speech that circumvents the cross is building with wood, hay, and straw.

The question that begins the following paragraph (3:16–17) has also frequently been misapplied, partly because many are well aware that a little later (6:19) Paul calls the Christian's body "the temple of the Holy Spirit." Thus the direct confrontation in 3:5–17, too, has been individualized to refer to one's abuse of the body or to the neglect of one's spiritual life. Elsewhere, however, Paul uses the temple metaphor in a collective sense to refer to the church as God's temple (2 Cor 6:16; Eph 2:19–22). This is surely his intention here, which the NIV tries to bring out by rendering it "you yourselves are God's temple."

What, then, is Paul's point in this context? The Corinthian church was to be *God's* temple in Corinth—over against all the other temples in the city. To put it in our words, they were God's people in Corinth, his alternative to the Corinthian lifestyle. What made them God's temple was the presence of the Spirit in their midst. But by their divisions they were destroying God's temple. Those responsible for so destroying the church, Paul says, will themselves be destroyed by God, because the church in Corinth was precious (i.e., sacred) to him.

Paul's argument has now come full circle. He began by exposing the Corinthians' inadequate understanding of the gospel, a gospel that is in no way based on human wisdom but in every way stands as the contradiction to it. Then he turns to expose their inadequate understanding of leadership in the church and at the same time warns both the leaders and the church itself of God's judgment on those who promote division. At the end of the chapter (3:18–23) he brings these two themes together in a concluding statement. Human wisdom is folly; therefore, "no more boasting about human leaders!"

Notice as we summarize this analysis: (1) the exegesis is self-contained; that is, we have not once had to go outside the text to understand what Paul is getting at; (2) there is nothing in the paragraph that does not fit into the argument; and (3) all of this makes perfectly good sense of everything. This, then, is what exegesis is all about. This was God's word *to them*. You may have further questions about specific points of content, for which you can consult your commentary. *But all of what we have done here, you can do.* It may take practice—in some cases even some hard work of thinking—but you can do it, and the rewards are great.

ONE MORE TIME

Before we conclude this chapter, let us go through the process of exegesis one more time for practice, and this time in a somewhat easier passage in a later letter, but one that also deals with internal tensions in the church, namely, Philippians 1:27–2:18.

Read Philippians 1:12–2:18 several times. Note that Paul's argument to this point has gone something like this: *The occasion* is that Paul is in prison (1:13, 17) and the Philippian church has sent him a gift through a member named Epaphroditus (see 2:25, 30; 4:14–18). Apparently Epaphroditus contracted an illness that ordinarily ended in death, and the church had heard of it and was saddened (2:26). But God spared him, so now Paul is sending him back (2:25–30) with this letter in order to (1) tell them how things are with him (1:12–26), (2) thank them for their gift (4:10, 14–19), and (3) exhort them on a couple of matters: to live in harmony (1:27–2:18; 4:2–3) and to avoid the Judaizing heresy (3:1–4:1).

Paul has just completed the section (1:12–26) where he has told them how he is getting along in his imprisonment. The new section (1:27–2:18), where our interest lies, is the first part of the exhortation. Notice, for example, how he is no longer talking about himself, as before (vv. 12–26). Did you notice the clear shift from I/me/my to you/your at the beginning of the next paragraph (verse 27)?

What, then, is the point of each paragraph in this section?

The first paragraph, 1:27–30, begins the exhortation. The point seems to be what we read at the outset, that they should "stand firm in the one Spirit." This is (1) an exhortation to unity, especially because (2) in Philippi they are facing opposition. (Note: If we decide that v. 27 is really the point of the paragraph, then we have to ask, what is the point of vv. 28–30 and the emphasis on opposition and suffering? Notice how he tried to answer this.)

How then does what follows (2:1–4) relate to unity? First, Paul repeats the exhortation (vv. 1–2, which now makes us sure we were right about the first paragraph). But the point now is that humility is the proper attitude for the believers to have unity.

Now you try it with the next paragraph (2:5–11). What is the point? Why this appeal to the humiliation and exaltation of Christ Jesus? Your answer does not have to be in our words but surely should include the following: Jesus in his incarnation and death is the supreme example of the humility Paul wants them to have. (You will notice that when you ask the questions this way, the point of the paragraph is *not* to teach us something new about Christ. Rather, Paul is appealing to these great truths about Christ to get the Philippians to *have the same mind-set Christ had*, not simply to *know about him*.)

Go on to the next paragraph (vv. 12–13). Now what is the point? Notice how "therefore" clearly signals that this is the conclusion. Given Christ's example, they are now to obey Paul; but, in what? Surely it is in having unity, which also requires humility.

Finally, ask yourself how what follows (vv. 14–18) fits into this argument, and how it relates to the problem as noted above: disharmony in the church while they are facing opposition in Philippi.

At the end, you might note, from the way Paul deals here with the problem of disunity, that the similar problem in Corinth was surely of a much more serious and complex nature. This should further help to confirm our reconstruction of the problem there.

THE PROBLEM PASSAGES

We have purposely led you through two passages where we are convinced you could have done most of this kind of exegesis on your own, given that you have learned to think in paragraphs and to ask the right historical and contextual questions. But we are well aware that there are all those other texts—the kinds of texts the authors are repeatedly asked about: the meaning of "because of the angels" in 1 Corinthians 11:10, or "baptized for the dead" in 1 Corinthians 15:29, or Christ's preaching to the "imprisoned spirits" in 1 Peter 3:19, or "the man of lawlessness" in 2 Thessalonians 2:3. In short, how do we go about finding the meaning of the problem passages?

Here are some guidelines:

1. In many cases the reason the problem passages are so difficult for us is that, frankly, they were not written to us. That is, the original author and his readers are on a similar wavelength that allows the inspired author to assume a great deal on the part of his readers. Thus, for example, when Paul tells the Thessalonians that they are to recall that he "used to tell [them] these things," and therefore "you know what is holding him back" (2 Thess 2:5–6), we may need to learn to be content with our lack of knowledge. What he had told them orally they could now fit into what he was saying by letter. Our lack of the oral communication makes the written one especially difficult. But we take it as a truism: What God wants us to know has been communicated to us; what God has not told us may still hold our interest, but our uncertainty at these points should make us hesitant about being dogmatic.

2. Despite some uncertainty as to some of the precise details, one needs to learn to ask what can be said for certain about a given passage and what is merely possible but not certain. Look, for an example, at the puzzling words in the rhetorical question that begins a new phase of Paul's argument with the Corinthian believers regarding the *bodily* resurrection of the dead (1 Cor 15:29). What can be said for certain? Some of the Corinthians really were being "baptized for the dead," whether we like to admit it or not. Moreover, Paul neither condemns nor condones their practice; he simply refers to it—for a totally different reason from the actual practice itself. But we do not know and probably never will know *who* was doing it, *for whom* they were doing it, and *why* they were doing it. The details and the meaning of the practice, therefore, are probably forever lost to us.

3. Nonetheless, as we have suggested before, even if one cannot have full certainty about some of the details, very often the point of the whole passage is still within one's grasp. Whatever it was the Corinthians were doing in baptizing for the dead, we do know why Paul referred to this practice of theirs. Their own action was a kind of "proof from experience" that they were not consistent in their rejecting a future *bodily* resurrection of believers.

4. On such passages as this one you will need to consult a good commentary. As we point out in the appendix, it is the handling of just such a passage that separates the better commentaries from all the others. The good ones will list and at least briefly discuss the

various options that have been suggested as solutions, including the reasons for and against. You may not always go along with the individual commentator's choices, but you do need to be informed about the variety of options—and the better commentaries will do this for you.

Finally, we suggest that even scholars do not have all the answers. You can more or less count on it that, where there are four to fourteen viable options as to what a given passage meant, even the scholars are guessing! Texts like 1 Corinthians 15:29 (on which there are at least forty different guesses) should serve to give us proper humility.

What we have done in this chapter is only half the task. It is the essential first half, but now we want to go on to ask how these various texts apply to *us*. We have learned to hear God's word to *them*. What about his word to *us*? This is the concern of the next chapter.

CHAPTER 4

The Epistles: The Hermeneutical Questions

We come now to what we referred to previously as hermeneutical questions. What do these texts mean to *us*? This is the crux of everything, and compared with this task, exegesis is relatively easy. At least in exegesis, even if there are disagreements at particular points, most people agree as to the parameters of meaning; there are limitations of possibilities set by the historical and literary contexts. Paul, for example, cannot have meant something that he and his readers had never heard of. His meaning at least has to have been a first-century possibility.

However, no such consensus of parameters seems to exist for hermeneutics (learning to hear the meaning in the contexts of our own day). *All* people "do" hermeneutics, even if they know nothing about exegesis and don't have a clue as to the meaning of these two words! It is no wonder that there are so many differences among Christians; what might be a cause for wonder is that there are not far more differences than actually exist. The reason for this is that there is, in fact, a common ground of hermeneutics among us, even if we have not always spelled it out.

What we want to do in this chapter is first of all to delineate the common hermeneutics of most believers, show its strengths and weaknesses, and then offer and discuss guidelines for several areas where this common hermeneutics seems inadequate.

The big issue among Christians committed to Scripture as God's word has to do with the problems of cultural relativity — what is cultural and therefore belongs to the first century alone and what transcends culture and is thus a word for all seasons.

This problem will therefore receive a considerable amount of attention.

OUR COMMON HERMENEUTICS

Even if you are among those who have asked, "Herman who?" when confronted with the word "hermeneutics," you are in fact involved in hermeneutics all the time. What is it that all of us do as we read an epistle? Very simply, we bring our own form of common sense to the text and apply what we can to our own situation. What does not seem to apply is simply left in the first century.

None of us, for example, has ever felt called by the Holy Spirit to take a pilgrimage to Troas in order to carry Paul's cloak from Carpus's house to his Roman prison (2 Tim 4:13), even though the passage is clearly a command to do that. Yet from that same letter most Christians believe that God tells us in times of stress that we are to "join ... in suffering, like a good soldier of Christ Jesus" (2:3), another word to Timothy that does seem applicable to ourselves. None of us would ever think to question what has been done with either of these passages — although many of us may have moments of struggle in graciously obeying the latter.

Let it be emphasized here that most of the matters in the Epistles fit nicely into this commonsense hermeneutics. For most texts it is not a matter of whether one *should* or not; it is more a matter of "to stir you up by way of reminder" (2 Pet 1:13 NASB).

Our problems — and differences — are generated by those moments that lie somewhere in between these two, where some of us think we should obey exactly what is stated and others of us are not so sure. Our hermeneutical difficulties here are several, but they are all related to one issue — a general lack of consistency. This is the great flaw in our common hermeneutics. Without necessarily intending to, we bring our theological heritage, our church traditions, our cultural norms, or our existential concerns to the Epistles as we read them. And this results in all kinds of selectivity or "getting around" certain passages.

It is interesting to note, for example, that almost everyone in American evangelicalism or fundamentalism would agree with our common stance on two passages in 2 Timothy (2:3 and 4:13). However, the cultural milieu of most of the same Christians causes them to argue against obedience to an earlier passage in 1 Timothy: "Stop drinking only water, and use a little wine because of your stomach and your frequent illnesses" (5:23). That had only to do with Timothy, not with us, we are told, because water was unsafe to drink back then. Or else, it is even argued that "wine" really meant "grape juice"—although one wonders how that could have happened when Welch's processing and refrigeration were not available! But why is this personal word limited to Timothy, while the exhortation to continue in the Word (2 Tim 3:14–16), which is also an imperative addressed only to Timothy, becomes an imperative for all people at all times? Mind you, one may well be right in bypassing "use a little wine" as not having personal or universal application, but on what hermeneutical grounds?

Or take the problems that many traditional churchgoers had with the "Jesus people" in the late 1960s and early 1970s. Long hair on boys had already become the symbol of a new era in the hippie culture of the 1960s. For Christians to wear this symbol, especially in light of what Paul argues with the believers in Corinth, "Does not nature itself teach you that for a man to wear long hair is degrading to him?" (1 Cor 11:14, RSV), seemed like an open defiance of God himself. Yet most who quoted this text against the youth culture allowed for Christian women to cut their hair short (despite v. 15), did not insist on women's heads being covered in worship, and never considered that "nature" came about by a very *un*natural means—a haircut.

These two examples simply illustrate how one's own culture tends to dictate what is common sense regarding present application. But other things also dictate common sense—ecclesiastical traditions, for example. How is it that in many evangelical churches women are forbidden to speak in church on the basis of a probably spurious moment in 1 Corinthians 14:34–35 (spurious because it is a marginal gloss found in two different locations in the manuscript tradition, and clearly contradicts 11:2–3), yet in many of the same churches everything else in chapter 14 is argued *against*, as not belonging to the twenty-first century? How is it that verses 34–35 belong to all times and cultures, while verses 1–5, 26–33, and 39–40, which give regulations for prophesying and speaking in tongues, belong only to the first-century church?

Notice further how easy it is for twenty-first-century Christians to read their own tradition of church order into 1 Timothy and

Titus. Yet very few churches have the plural leadership that seems clearly to be in view there (1 Tim 5:17; Titus 1:5 [Timothy was *not* the pastor; he was Paul's temporary delegate to set things in order and to correct abuses]). And still fewer churches actually enroll widows under the guidelines of 1 Timothy 5:3–15.

And have you noticed how our prior theological commitments cause many of us to read such commitments into some texts while we read around others? It comes as a total surprise to some believers when they find out that other Christians find support for infant baptism in such texts as 1 Corinthians 1:16; 7:14; or Colossians 2:11–12, or that others find evidence for a two-stage second coming in 2 Thessalonians 2:1, or that still others find evidence for sanctification as a second work of grace in Titus 3:5. For many in the Arminian tradition, who emphasize the believer's free will and responsibility, texts like Romans 8:30; 9:18–24; Galatians 1:15; and Ephesians 1:4–5 are something of an embarrassment. Likewise many Calvinists have their own ways of getting around what is said quite plainly in passages like 1 Corinthians 10:1–13; 2 Peter 2:20–22; and Hebrews 6:4–6. Indeed our experience as teachers is that students from these traditions seldom ask what these texts mean; they want only to know "how to get around" what these various passages seem clearly to affirm!

After the last few paragraphs, we may well have lost a lot of friends, but we are trying to illustrate how thoroughgoing the problem is and how Christians need to carry on more genteel conversation with one another in this crucial area. What kinds of guidelines, then, are needed in order to establish more consistent hermeneutics for the Epistles?

THE BASIC RULE

You will recall from chapter 1 that we set out as a basic rule the premise that *a text cannot mean what it never could have meant to its author or readers.* This is why exegesis must always come first. It is especially important that we repeat this "basic rule" here, for this at least establishes some absolute parameters with regard to meaning. This rule, of course, does not always help one find out what a given passage means, but it does help to set limits as to what it *cannot* mean.

For example, the most frequent justification for disregarding the imperatives about seeking spiritual gifts in 1 Corinthians 14 is a particular interpretation of a preceding moment, which states that "when the perfect comes, the partial will be done away" (1 Cor 13:10, NASB). We are told that the perfect *has* come, in the form of the New Testament, and therefore the imperfect (prophecy and tongues) have ceased to function in the church. *But this is one thing the text cannot mean* because good exegesis quite disallows it. There is no way Paul could *possibly* have meant this; after all, the Corinthians did not know there was going to be a New Testament, and the Holy Spirit would not likely have inspired Paul to write something to them that would be totally incomprehensible.

THE SECOND RULE

The second basic rule is actually a slightly different way of expressing our common hermeneutics. It goes like this: *Whenever we share comparable particulars (i.e., similar specific life situations) with the first-century hearers, God's word to us is the same as his word to them.* It is this rule that causes most of the theological texts and the community-directed ethical imperatives in the Epistles to give modern-day Christians a sense of immediacy with the first century. It is still true that "all have sinned" (Rom 3:23) and that "by grace [we] have been saved, through faith" (Eph 2:8). Clothing ourselves with "compassion, kindness, humility, gentleness and patience" (Col 3:12) is still God's word to those who are believers. Our problems here are not with understanding as such, but with understanding quite well and then failing to "wear the clothing."

The two longer passages we worked through in the preceding chapter (1 Cor 1–4; Phil 1:27–2:18) seem to be of this kind. Once we have done our exegesis and have discovered God's word to them, we have immediately brought ourselves under that same word. We still have local churches, which still have leaders who need to hear the Word and take care how they build the church. It appears that the church has too often been built with wood, hay, and straw rather than with gold, silver, and costly stones, and such work when tried by fire has been found wanting. We would argue that Paul's warnings to the Corinthians about their "destroying God's temple," the church (see 1 Cor 3:16–17), is still God's word to us as to our responsibilities to the local church. It must be a place where the Spirit is known to dwell, and which therefore stands as God's alternative to the sin and alienation of worldly society.

The great caution here is that we do our exegesis well so that we have confidence that our situations and particulars are genuinely comparable to theirs. This is why the careful reconstruction of their problem is so important. For example, it is significant for our hermeneutics to note that the lawsuit in 1 Corinthians 6:1–11 was between two Christian brothers before a pagan judge out in the open marketplace in Corinth. We would argue that the point of the text does not change if the judge happens to be a Christian or because the trial takes place in a courthouse. The wrong is for two brothers to go to law outside the church, instead of handling things internally, as Paul's own rhetoric (vv. 6–11) makes perfectly clear. On the other hand, one could rightly ask whether this would still apply to a Christian suing a corporation in modern-day America, for in this case not all the particulars would remain the same—although one's decision should surely take Paul's appeal to the non-retaliation ethic of Jesus (v. 7) into account.

All of what has been said thus far seems easy enough. But the question as to how a text such as a case-specific matter like the lawsuit among believers (6:1–11) may apply *beyond* its specific particulars is but one of the several kinds of questions that need to be discussed. The rest of this chapter addresses four such problems.

THE PROBLEM OF EXTENDED APPLICATION

We first take up the issue just mentioned. When there are comparable particulars and comparable contexts in today's church, is it legitimate to extend the application of the text to other contexts, or to make a first-century case-specific matter apply to a context totally foreign to its first-century setting?

For example, it might be argued that even though Paul's warning about destroying God's temple in Corinth (1 Cor 3:16–17) addresses the local church, it also presents the principle that what God has set aside for himself by the Holy Spirit's indwelling is sacred and whoever destroys that will come under God's awful judgment. May not this principle now be applied to the individual Christian to teach that God will judge the person who abuses his or her body? Similarly, in 1 Corinthians 3:10–15 Paul is addressing those with building responsibilities in the church and warns of the loss they who build poorly will suffer. Since the text speaks of judgment and salvation "as by fire" (KJV), is it legitimate to use this text to illustrate the security of the believer?

If these were deemed legitimate applications, then we would seem to have good reason to be concerned. For inherent in such application is the bypassing of exegesis altogether. After all, to apply 1 Corinthians 3:16–17 to the individual believer is precisely what many in the church have erroneously done for centuries. Why do exegesis at all? Why not simply take any passage at "face value," as it were, and begin with the here and now — and thus perpetuate centuries of misunderstanding?

We would argue, therefore, that when there are comparable situations and comparable particulars (that is, the particulars in the text are similar to ours), God's word *to us* in such texts should be limited to its original intent. Furthermore, it should be noted that the extended application is usually seen to be legitimate because it is true, that is, it is clearly spelled out in other passages where that is the *intent* of the passage. If that be the case, then one should ask whether what one learns *only* by extended application can truly be the word of God for all times and settings.

A more difficult case is presented by an imperative in Paul's next letter to the believers in Corinth, "Do not be yoked together with unbelievers" (2 Cor 6:14). Traditionally, picking up a more contemporary metaphor, this has been interpreted as forbidding marriage between a Christian and non-Christian. However, the metaphor of a yoke is rarely used in antiquity to refer to marriage, and there is nothing whatsoever in the context that remotely suggests that marriage is in view here.

Our problem is that we cannot be certain as to what the original text is forbidding. Most likely it has something to do with idolatry, perhaps as a further prohibition of attendance at the idol feasts (cf. 1 Cor 10:14–22). Can we not, therefore, legitimately "extend" the principle of this text, since we cannot be sure of its original meaning? Probably so, but again, precisely because it is indeed a biblical principle that can be sustained apart from this single text.

THE PROBLEM OF PARTICULARS THAT ARE NOT COMPARABLE

The next problem has to do with two kinds of passages in the Epistles: those that speak to first-century issues that for the most part are without any twenty-first-century counterparts, and those that speak to problems that could happen also in the twenty-first century but are highly unlikely to do so. What does one do with such texts, and how do they address us? Or do they?

An example of the first kind of passage is found in 1 Corinthians 8–10, where Paul speaks to three kinds of issues: (1) Christians who are arguing for the privilege of continuing to join their pagan neighbors at their feasts in the idol temples (see 8:10; 10:14–22); (2) the Corinthians' calling into question Paul's apostolic authority (see 9:1–23); and (3) food sacrificed to idols and sold in the open market (10:23–11:1).

Sound exegesis of these passages indicates that Paul answers these problems as follows: (1) They are absolutely forbidden to attend the temple feasts on three grounds: the stumbling-block principle (8:7–13), such eating is incompatible with life in Christ as it is experienced at his table (10:16–17), and it means to participate in the demonic (10:19–22). (2) Paul defends his right to financial support as an apostle, even though he has given up that right; he also defends his actions in matters of indifference (9:19–23). (3) Idol food previously presented to an idol and now sold in the marketplace may be purchased and eaten; such food may also be freely eaten in someone else's home. In the latter context it may also be refused if it could potentially create a problem for someone else. Believers may eat anything to the glory of God; but one should not do something that deliberately offends.

To be sure, these passages are still very existential for Christians in many Asian cultures; but in Western cultures this kind of idolatry is largely unknown, so that problems 1 and 3 are not common—unless one regularly eats at a restaurant run by a cult that dedicates its food to a "god" as it is prepared. Moreover, regarding problem 2, we no longer have apostles in Paul's sense of those who have actually encountered the risen Lord (9:1; cf. 15:8) and who have founded and have authority over new churches (9:1–2; cf. 2 Cor 10:16).

The second kind of passage may be illustrated by the incestuous believer in 1 Corinthians 5:1–11, or by the "haves" abusing the "have-nots" by their meals eaten in conjunction with the Lord's Table (1 Cor 11:17–22), or by people wanting to force circumcision on Gentile Christians (Gal 6:12). These things could happen but are highly improbable in our culture.

The question is, how do the apostle's answers to these noncontemporary problems speak to twenty-first-century Christians? We suggest that proper hermeneutics here should legitimately take two steps.

First, we must do our exegesis with particular care so that we hear what God's word to them really was. In very many cases a clear *principle* has been articulated, which usually will transcend the historical particularity to which it was being applied.

Second, and here is the important point, the "principle" does not now become timeless to be applied at random or whim to any and every kind of situation. We would argue that it *must be applied to genuinely comparable situations.*

To illustrate both of these points: First, Paul forbids participation in the temple meals on the basis of the stumbling-block principle. But note that this does not refer to something that merely offends another believer. The stumbling-block principle refers to something that one believer feels can be done in good conscience and then, by their action or persuasion, they try to induce another believer to do, who cannot do so in good conscience. After all, Paul's language is intensive: the other believer is "destroyed" by *emulating* another's action; they are not merely offended by it. The principle would seem to apply, therefore, only to truly comparable situations. In any case, this principle is especially abused when long-standing believers use it to condemn younger believers for their actions!

Second, Paul finally absolutely forbids participation in the temple meals because it means to participate in the demonic. To be sure, some followers of Jesus have at times been confused as to what constitutes demonic activity. Nonetheless, this seems to be a normative prohibition for Christians against all forms of spiritism, witchcraft, astrology, etc.

Again, we may not have apostles, and most Protestants do not think of their ministers as standing in the apostolic succession. But the principle that "those who preach the gospel should receive their living from the gospel" (1 Cor 9:14) certainly seems applicable to contemporary ministries, since it is corroborated elsewhere in Scripture (e.g., 1 Tim 5:17–18).

The problem of eating marketplace idol food (1 Cor 10:23–11:1) presents an especially difficult dimension of this hermeneutical problem. The food itself was a matter of indifference — both to God and to Paul. But because of prior beliefs and associations, it was not so to others. The same was true of food and drink and the observance of days (Rom 14), as well as various similar matters in his letter to the believers in Colosse (Col 2:16–23).

The problem for us at a much later moment in history is how to distinguish matters of indifference from matters that count. This problem is especially intensified for us because these things change from culture to culture and from one Christian group to another, just as they appear to have done in the first century. In twentieth-century America alone the list of such matters included clothing (length of dresses, ties, women's slacks), dyed hair, body piercing, tattoos, cosmetics, jewelry, entertainment and recreation (movies, TV, cards, dancing, mixed swimming), athletics, food, and drink. The ongoing problem for many contemporary believers is that just as with those who judged Paul's freedom on the matter of idol food, so it always is that those who think abstinence from any one of these constitutes holiness before God do *not* think of them as matters of indifference.

What, then, makes something a matter of indifference? We suggest the following as guidelines:

1. What the Epistles specifically indicate as matters of indifference may still be regarded as such: food, drink, observance of days, etc.

2. Matters of indifference are not inherently moral but are cultural — even if they stem from *religious* culture. Matters that tend to differ from culture to culture, therefore, even among genuine believers, may usually be considered to be matters of indifference (e.g., wine and nonwine cultures).

3. It is especially important to note that the sin-lists in the Epistles (e.g., Rom 1:29–30; 1 Cor 5:11; 6:9–10; 2 Tim 3:2–4) never include the first-century equivalents of the items we have listed above. Moreover, such matters of indifference are never included among the various lists of Christian imperatives (e.g., Rom 12; Eph 5; Col 3; etc.).

We know that not all will agree with our assessment. However, according to Romans 14, people on both sides of any of these matters are neither to judge nor disparage one another. The free person is not to flaunt their freedom; the person for whom such matters are a deep personal conviction is not to condemn someone else.

THE PROBLEM OF CULTURAL RELATIVITY

This is the area where most present-day difficulties — and differences — lie. It is the place where the problem of God's *eternal word* having been given in *historical particularity* comes most sharply into focus. The problem has the following steps: (1) Epistles are occasional documents of the first century, conditioned by the language and culture of the first century, which spoke to specific situations in the first-century church. (2) Many of the specific situations in the Epistles are so completely conditioned by their first-century setting that all recognize that they have little or no personal application as a word for today, except perhaps in the most distant sense of one's deriving some principle from them (e.g., bringing Paul's cloak from Carpus's house in Troas). (3) Other passages are also thoroughly conditioned by their first-century settings, but the word contained in them may be "translated" into new but comparable settings. (4) Is it not possible, therefore, that still other texts, although they appear to have comparable particulars, are also conditioned by their first-century setting and need to be translated into new settings, or simply left in the first century?

Nearly all Christians, at least to a limited degree, do translate biblical texts into new settings. Without articulating it in precisely this way, twenty-first-century evangelicals use this principle to leave "a little wine for thy stomach's sake" in the first century, to not insist on head coverings or long hair for women today, and to not practice the "holy kiss." Many of the same evangelicals, however, wince when a woman's teaching in the church (when men are present) is also defended on these grounds, and they become downright indignant when someone tries to defend same-sex partnerships on the same grounds.

Frequently there have been some who have tried to reject the idea of cultural relativity altogether, which has led them more or less to argue for a wholesale adoption of first-century culture as the divine norm. But such a rejection is usually only moderately successful. They may keep their daughters home, deny them an education, and have the father arrange for their marriage, but they usually allow them to learn to read and go out in public. The point is that it is extremely difficult to be consistent here, precisely because there is no such thing as a divinely ordained culture; cultures are in fact different, not only from the first to the twenty-first century, but in every conceivable way in the twenty-first century itself.

Rather than rejection, we suggest that the recognition of a degree of cultural relativity is a valid hermeneutical procedure and is an inevitable corollary of the occasional nature of the Epistles. But we also believe that to be valid, one's hermeneutics must operate within recognizable guidelines.

We suggest the following guidelines, therefore, for distinguishing between items that are culturally relative on the one hand and those that transcend their original setting on the other hand and are thus normative for all Christians of all times. We do not contend for these guidelines as "once for all given to the saints," but they do reflect our current thinking, and we would encourage further discussion and interaction (many of these have been worked out in conjunction with our former colleague, David M. Scholer).

1. One should first distinguish between the central core of the message of the Bible and what is dependent on or peripheral to it. This is not to argue for a canon within the canon (i.e., to elevate certain parts of the New Testament as the norm for reading other parts); it is to safeguard the gospel from being turned into law through culture or religious custom on the one hand and to keep the gospel itself from changing to reflect every conceivable cultural expression on the other hand.

Thus the fallenness of all humanity, redemption from that fallenness as God's gracious activity through Christ's death and resurrection, the consummation of that redemptive work by the return of Christ, etc., are clearly part of this central core. But the holy kiss, women's head coverings, and charismatic ministries and gifts would seem to be less so.

2. Similarly, one should be prepared to distinguish between what the New Testament itself sees as inherently moral and what is not. Those items that are inherently moral are therefore absolute and abide for every culture; those that are not inherently moral are therefore cultural expressions and may change from culture to culture.

Paul's sin-lists, for example, never contain cultural items. Some of the sins may indeed be more prevalent in one culture than another, but there are never situations in which they may be considered *Christian* attitudes or actions. Thus sexual immorality, adultery, idolatry, drunkenness, homosexual practice, thievery, greed, and the like (1 Cor 6:9–10) are *always* wrong. This does not mean that Christians have not from time to time been guilty of any of these. But they are not viable moral choices. After all, Paul goes on to say, "That is what some of you *were*. But you were washed …" (v. 11, emphasis added).

On the other hand, foot washing, exchanging the holy kiss, eating marketplace idol food, women having a head covering when praying or prophesying, Paul's personal preference for celibacy, or a woman's teaching in the church are not *inherently* moral matters. They become so only by their use or abuse in given contexts, when such use or abuse involves disobedience or lack of love.

3. One must make special note of items where the New Testament itself has a uniform and consistent witness and where it reflects differences. The following are examples of matters on which the New Testament bears uniform witness: love as the Christian's basic ethical response, a nonretaliation personal ethic, the wrongness of strife, hatred, murder, stealing, practicing homosexuality, drunkenness, and sexual immorality of all kinds.

On the other hand, the New Testament does not appear to be uniform on such matters as women's ministries in the church (see Rom 16:1–2, where Phoebe is a "deacon" in Cenchrea; Rom 16:7, where Junia—*not* Junias, which is an unknown masculine name—is named among the apostles; Rom 16:3, where Priscilla is Paul's coworker [cf. Phil 4:2–3]—the same word used of Apollos in 1 Cor 3:9; and 1 Cor 11:5 over against 1 Tim 2:12 [and 1 Cor 14:34–35, which is suspect textually]); the political evaluation of Rome (see Rom 13:1–5 and 1 Pet 2:13–14 over against Rev 13–18); the retention of one's wealth (Luke 12:33; 18:22 over against 1 Tim 6:17–19); or eating food offered to idols (1 Cor 10:23–29 over against Acts 15:29; Rev 2:14, 20). By the way, if any of these suggestions cause an emotional reaction on your part, you may ask yourself why, since in each case the New Testament evidence is *not* uniform, whether we like that or not.

Sound exegesis may cause us to see greater uniformity than appears to be the case now. For example, in the matter of food offered to idols, one can make a good exegetical case for the Greek word in Acts and Revelation to refer to going to the temple to eat such food. In this case the attitude would be consistent with Paul's in 1 Corinthians 10:14–22. However, precisely because these other matters appear to be more cultural than moral, one should not be disturbed by a lack of uniformity. Likewise, one should not pursue exegesis only as a means of finding uniformity, even at the cost of common sense or the plain meaning of the text.

4. It is important to be able to distinguish within the New Testament itself between principle and specific application. It is possible for a New Testament writer to support a relative application by an absolute principle and in so doing not make the application absolute. Thus in 1 Corinthians 11:2–16, for example, Paul appeals (apparently) to the divine order of creation and redemption (v. 3) and establishes the principle that one should do nothing to distract from the glory of God (especially by breaking convention) when the community is at worship (vv. 7, 10). The specific application, however, seems to be relative, since Paul repeatedly appeals to "practice" or "nature" (vv. 6, 13–14, 16).

This leads us to suggest that one may legitimately ask at such specific applications: would this have been an issue for us had we never encountered it in the New Testament documents? In Western cultures, the failure to cover a woman's head (especially her hair) with a full-length veil would probably create no difficulties at all. In fact, if she were literally to obey the text in most American churches, she would thereby almost certainly abuse the spirit of the text by drawing attention to herself. But with a little thinking, one can imagine some kinds of dress—both male and female—that would be so out of place as to create the same kind of disruption of worship (a man in his swimsuit, for example, would be so noticeable as to distract others).

5. It might also be important, as much as one is able to do this with care, to determine the cultural options open to any New Testament writer. The degree to which a New Testament writer agrees with a cultural situation in which there is *only one option* increases the possibility of the cultural relativity of such a position. Thus, for example, homosexual activity was both affirmed and condemned by writers in antiquity, yet the New Testament takes a singular position against it. On the other hand, attitudes toward slavery as a system or toward the status and role of women were

basically singular; no one denounced slavery as an evil, and women were consistently held to be basically inferior to men by the philosophers. The New Testament writers also do not denounce slavery as an evil—although they undercut it by urging that the householder and his slaves were brother and sister in Christ (see Phlm 16; cf. Eph 6:9). On the other hand, they generally move well beyond the attitudes toward women held by their contemporaries. But in either case, to the degree to which they reflect the prevalent cultural attitudes in these matters, they are thereby reflecting the only cultural option in the world around them.

6. One must keep alert to possible cultural differences between the first and twenty-first centuries that are sometimes not immediately obvious. For example, to determine the role of women in the twenty-first-century church, one should take into account that there were few educational opportunities for women in the first century, whereas such education is the expected norm in our society. This may affect our understanding of such moments as the one on women's dress and demeanor in Paul's first letter to Timothy (2:9–15). Likewise, a participatory democracy is radically different from the government of which Paul speaks in his admonition to the believers in Rome (13:1–7). It is expected in a participatory democracy that bad laws are to be changed and bad officials are to be ousted. These differences should surely affect how one brings such a moment into twenty-first-century English-speaking North America.

7. One must finally exercise Christian charity at this point. Christians need to recognize the difficulties, open the lines of communication with one another, start by trying to define some principles, and above all else have love for and a willingness to ask forgiveness from those with whom they differ.

Before we conclude this discussion, it may be helpful to see how these guidelines apply to two current issues: the ministry of women and homosexual activity—especially since some who are arguing for women's ministries are using some of the same arguments to support same-sex partnerships as a valid Christian alternative.

We begin with the question of women's role in the church as teachers or proclaimers of the Word. This issue has basically focused on two unrelated passages (1 Cor 14:34–35 and 1 Tim 2:11–12). But the first passage is highly suspect as being anything

Paul wrote, since it is the only place in the entire transmission of Scripture that a passage like this occurs in two different places in the Greek manuscripts and was most likely brought in as a marginal gloss from someone who was not quite satisfied with Paul's affirmation of women both praying and prophesying in worship (as in 11:2–5). In the second case silence and submission or a quiet demeanor are enjoined—although in neither case is the submission necessarily to her husband—and in 1 Timothy 2 she is not permitted to teach or to "assume authority over" a man. Full compliance with this text in the twenty-first century would seem to rule out not only a woman's preaching and teaching in the local church, but it also would seem to forbid her writing books on biblical subjects that men might read, teaching Bible or related subjects (including religious education) in Christian colleges or Bible institutes where men are in her classes, and teaching men in missionary situations. But those who argue against women teaching in the contemporary church seldom carry the interpretation this far. And almost always they make the matters about clothing in the preceding verse (1 Tim 2:9) to be culturally relative.

On the other hand, that the passage in 1 Timothy might be culturally relative can be supported first of all by exegesis of all three of the Pastoral Epistles. Certain women were troublesome in the church at Ephesus (1 Tim 5:11–15; 2 Tim 3:6–9), and they appear to have been a major part of the cause of the false teachers making headway there. Since women are found teaching (Acts 18:26) and prophesying (Acts 21:9; 1 Cor 11:5) elsewhere in the New Testament, it is altogether likely that the 1 Timothy passage spoke to a local problem. In any case, the guidelines above support the possibility that this singular (uncertain) prohibition is culturally relative.

The question of homosexuality, however, is considerably different. In this case the guidelines stand against its being culturally relative. The whole Bible has a consistent witness against homosexual activity as being morally wrong.

In recent years some people have argued that the homosexuality against which the New Testament speaks is that in which people abuse others, and that private monogamous homosexuality between consenting adults is a different matter. They argue that it cannot be proved on exegetical grounds that such homosexual activity is forbidden. It is also argued that these are twenty-first-century cultural options not available in the first century. Therefore, they would propose that some of our guidelines (e.g., 5 and 6) open the possibility that the New Testament prohibitions against homosexuality are also culturally relative, and they would further argue that some of the guidelines are not true or not relevant.

The problem with this argument, however, is that it does not hold up either exegetically or historically. The homosexuality Paul had in view early on in his letter to the believers in Rome (1:24–28) is clearly *not* of the "abusive" type; it is homosexuality of choice between men or women. Furthermore, Paul's word "homosexual" in 1 Corinthians 6:9 literally means genital homosexuality between males. Since the Bible as a whole witnesses against homosexuality and invariably includes it in moral contexts, and since it simply has not been proved that the options for homosexual practice differ today from those of the first century, there seem to be no valid grounds for seeing it as a culturally relative matter for Paul. One may not like what Paul says, but to re-create him to fit present culture is an infraction of the highest order.

THE PROBLEM OF TASK THEOLOGY

We noted in the last chapter that much of the theology in the Epistles is task oriented and therefore is not systematically presented. However, this must not be taken to mean that one cannot in fact systematically present the theology that is either expressed in or derived from statements in the Epistles. To the contrary, this is one of the mandatory tasks of the Bible student. One must always be forming—and "reforming"—a biblical theology on the basis of sound exegesis. And very often, we readily acknowledge, a given biblical writer's theology is found in his presuppositions and implications as well as in his explicit statements.

All we want to do here is to raise some cautions as one goes about the task of theology, cautions that are the direct result of the occasional nature of the Epistles.

1. Because the Epistles are "occasioned" either by the author or the recipients, we must be content at times with some limitations to our theological understanding. For example, to get the Corinthians to see how absurd it was for them to have two brothers going to the pagan court for a judgment, Paul states that Chris-

tians will someday judge both the world and angels (1 Cor 6:2–3). But beyond this the texts say nothing. Thus we may affirm as a part of Christian eschatology (our understanding of final events) that Christians will in fact exercise judgments at the eschaton (the end time). But we know very little as to what this means or how it is going to be worked out. *Everything beyond the affirmation itself is mere speculation.*

Similarly, Paul argues from the nature of the Corinthians' own participation in the Lord's Supper that they may not likewise participate in the meals at the idol temple (1 Cor 10:16–21). What Paul says about that participation seems indeed to go beyond the theology of the Supper found in most of evangelical Protestantism. Here is not mere remembrance but actual participation in the Lord himself. From other New Testament texts we may further argue that the participation was by means of the Spirit and that the benefits came by faith. But even here we are going outside the immediate texts to express Paul's understanding in a theological way, and many will probably not agree with our choice of outside texts. But our point is that we simply are not told what the precise nature of this participation is or how the benefits come to the believer. We may all *want* to know, but our knowledge is defective precisely because of the occasional nature of the statements. What is said beyond what the texts themselves reveal cannot have the same biblical or hermeneutical import as what can be said on the basis of solid exegesis. We are merely affirming, therefore, that in Scripture, God has given us all we *need* but not necessarily all we *want*.

2. Sometimes our theological problems with the Epistles derive from the fact that we are asking *our* questions of texts that by their occasional nature are answering *their* questions only. When we ask the texts to speak directly to the question of abortion, or of remarriage, or of infant baptism, we want them to answer the questions of a later time. Sometimes they may do so, even if at times indirectly, but often they will not because the question simply had not been raised back then.

There is a clear example of this in the New Testament itself. On the question of divorce Paul says, "not I, but the Lord" (1 Cor 7:10), meaning Jesus himself spoke to this question. But to the question raised in a Greek environment as to whether a believer should divorce a pagan partner, Jesus apparently had no occasion to speak. The problem simply lay outside his own Jewish culture. But Paul did feel the need to speak to it, so he said "I, not the Lord" (v. 12). One of the problems, of course, is that we ourselves possess neither Paul's apostolic authority nor his inspiration. The only way we can speak to such questions is on the basis of a whole biblical theology that includes our understanding of creation, the fall, redemption, and the final consummation. That is, we must attempt to bring a biblical worldview to the problem. But no proof texting when there are no immediately relevant texts!

These, then, are some of our hermeneutical suggestions for reading and interpreting the Epistles. Our immediate aim is for greater precision and consistency; our larger aim is to call us all to greater obedience to what we do hear and understand—and to an openness and charity toward others when they differ with us. Perhaps if we were truly to do so, the world might pay more attention to our Savior.

CHAPTER 5

The Old Testament Narratives: Their Proper Use

The single most common type of literature in the Bible is narrative. In fact, over 40 percent of the Old Testament is narrative—and the Old Testament itself constitutes three-quarters of the bulk of the Bible. The following Old Testament books are largely or entirely composed of narrative material: Genesis, Joshua, Judges, Ruth, 1 and 2 Samuel, 1 and 2 Kings, 1 and 2 Chronicles, Ezra, Nehemiah, Daniel, Jonah, and Haggai. Moreover, Exodus, Numbers, Jeremiah, Ezekiel, Isaiah, and Job also contain substantial narrative portions. Although a goodly portion of the New Testament is also narrative (the Gospels, Acts), our interest in this chapter is specifically with Hebrew narrative—the special way that the Old Testament people were inspired of the Holy Spirit to tell their story.

Our concern in this chapter is to guide you toward a good understanding of how Hebrew narrative "works," so that you may read your Bibles more knowledgeably and with greater appreciation for God's story. Unfortunately, failure to understand both the reason for and the character of Hebrew narrative has caused many Christians in the past to read the Old Testament story poorly. If you are a Christian, the Old Testament is *your* spiritual history. The promises and calling of God to Israel are *your* historical promises and calling. Yet, in our experience, people force incorrect interpretations and applications on narrative portions of the Bible as much as or more than they do on any other parts. Their intended value and meaning are replaced with ideas read into rather than out of the text. So we will pay extra attention in this chapter to describing the literary nature of narratives in general, as well as pointing out the most dangerous pitfalls to avoid as you read.

THE NATURE OF NARRATIVES
What Narratives Are

Narratives are stories—purposeful stories retelling the *historical events* of the past that are intended to give meaning and direction for a given people *in the present*. This has always been so for all peoples in all cultures; and in this regard the biblical narratives are no different from other such stories. Nonetheless, there is a crucial difference between the biblical narratives and all others because, inspired by the Holy Spirit as they are, the story they tell is not so much our story as it is God's story—and it becomes ours as he "writes" us into it. The biblical narratives thus tell the ultimate story—a story that, even though often complex, is altogether true and crucially important. Indeed, it is a magnificent story, grander than the greatest epic, richer in plot and more significant in its characters and descriptions than any humanly composed story could ever be. But to appreciate this story you will need to know some basic things about narratives—what they are, and how they work.

At their basic level Bible narratives tell us about things that happened in the past. All narratives have three basic parts: characters, plot, and plot resolution. That is, most narratives presuppose some kind of conflict or tension that needs resolving. In traditional literary terms, the characters are the "protagonist" (the primary person in the story), the "antagonist" (the person who brings about the conflict or tension), and (sometimes) the "agonist(s)" (the other major characters in the story who get involved in the struggle).

In the biblical story God is the protagonist, Satan (or opposing people/powers) are the antagonists, and God's people are the agonists. The basic "plot" of the biblical story is that the creator God has created a people for his name—in his own "image"—who as his image bearers were to be his stewards over the earth that he created for their benefit. But an enemy entered the picture who persuaded the people to bear *his* "image" instead, and thus to become God's enemies. The plot resolution is the long story of "redemption," how God rescues his people from the enemy's clutches, restores them back into his image, and (finally) will restore them "in a new heaven and new earth."

Three Levels of Narrative

It should help you as you read and study Old Testament narratives to realize that the story is being told, in effect, on three levels. The top ("third") level is the one we have just described. Often called the "metanarrative," this level has to do with the whole universal plan of God worked out through his creation, and focusing primarily on God's chosen people. Key aspects of the plot at this top level are the initial creation itself, the fall of humanity, the power and ubiquity of sin, the need for redemption, and Christ's incarnation and sacrifice. Sometimes this top level is also referred to as the "story of redemption" or "redemptive history" (see *How to 2*, pp. 14–20).

The second level is the story of God's redeeming a people for his name. These people are constituted twice—by a former covenant and a "new" covenant (see ch. 9 below). Our interest in this chapter is with the story of the first covenant, the story of the people of Israel: the call of Abraham; the establishment of an Abrahamic lineage through the patriarchs; the enslaving of the Israelites in Egypt; God's delivering them from bondage; God's making covenant with them at Sinai, followed by the conquest of the promised land of Canaan; the Israelites' frequent sins and increasing disloyalty; God's patient protection of and pleading with them; the ultimate destruction of northern Israel and then of Judah; and the restoration of the holy people after the exile (see further, *How to 2*, pp. 21–23).

Finally, there is the "first" level. Here are found all the hundreds of individual narratives that make up the other two levels. This includes both compound narratives—for example, the Genesis narrative(s) of Abraham, Isaac, Jacob, or Joseph, as a whole—and the smaller units that make up the larger narrative. Our interest in this chapter is primarily in helping you read and understand these first-level narratives. But it is especially important that you always be asking yourself how these first-level narratives fit into the second and third levels of the biblical story.

An awareness of this "hierarchy of narrative" should help you in your understanding and application of Old Testament narratives.

Thus, when Jesus taught that the Scriptures "testify about me" (John 5:39), he was speaking of the ultimate, top level of the narrative, in which his atonement was the central act, and the subjection of all creation to him is the climax of its plot. He obviously was *not* speaking about every short individual passage of the Old Testament. True, the individual passages, including narratives, that are messianic or otherwise identified in the New Testament as typological of Christ (cf. 1 Cor 10:4) are an important part of the Old Testament; but these constitute only a small portion of its total revelation. What Jesus was saying was that the Scriptures in their entirety bear witness to him and focus toward his loving lordship.

What Narratives Are Not

Because the Old Testament narratives have frequently been used in some unfortunate ways in the church, we need here to remind you how the Old Testament narratives are *not* to be understood.

1. Old Testament narratives are *not allegories or stories filled with hidden meanings*. While there may be aspects of narratives that are not easy to understand, you should always assume that they had meaning for their original hearers. But whatever else, they are not allegories. The account of Moses going up and down Mount Sinai in Exodus 19–34 is not an allegory of the descent and ascent of the soul to God. Elijah's battle with the priests of Baal on Mount Carmel (1 Kings 18) is not an allegory of Jesus' triumph over evil spirits in the New Testament. The story of Abraham's securing a bride for Isaac (Gen 24) is not an allegory about Christ (Isaac) securing a bride (the church/Rebekah) through the Holy Spirit (the servant).

2. Individual Old Testament narratives are *not intended to teach moral lessons*. The purpose of the various individual narratives is to tell what God did in the history of Israel, not to offer moral examples of right or wrong behavior. Very often you will hear people say, "What we can learn from this story is that we are not to do [or say] ..." But unless the biblical narrator makes that point, on what grounds do we make it? We may rightly recognize from the story of Jacob and Esau the negative results of parental favoritism. But this is not the reason for the presence of this narrative in Genesis. Rather, it serves to tell us how Abraham's family line was carried on through Jacob and not Esau; it is one more illustration of God's not doing it "right," according to prevailing cultural norms,

in not choosing the firstborn to carry on the family line. While the narrative may incidentally illustrate the outcome of parental rivalry, this has little to do with the intent of the narrative as such.

3. However, even though the Old Testament narratives do not necessarily teach moral values directly, they often illustrate what is taught explicitly and categorically elsewhere. This represents an *implicit* kind of teaching by illustrating the corresponding *explicit* teachings of Scripture. For example, in the narrative of David's adultery with Bathsheba (2 Sam 11), you will not find any such statement as, "In committing adultery David did wrong." You are expected to know that adultery is wrong because this is taught explicitly already in the Ten Commandments (Exod 20:14), which David would have known very well. The narrative illustrates the harmful consequences of his adultery to the personal life of King David and to his ability to rule. The narrative does not systematically teach about adultery and could not be used as the sole basis for such teaching. But as one illustration of the effects of adultery in a particular case, it conveys a powerful message that can imprint itself on the mind of the careful reader in a way that direct, categorical teaching may not.

THE CHARACTERISTICS OF HEBREW NARRATIVE

Hebrew narratives have some distinctive features that, if looked for and recognized, can greatly enhance one's ability to hear the story from the perspective of the divinely inspired narrator. We will illustrate these characteristics by using the story of Joseph, as skillfully narrated by Moses (Gen 37–50). This, in fact, except for the insertions of the story of Judah and Tamar (ch. 38), of the genealogy (46:8–27), and of Jacob's blessing his sons (49:1–28), is the longest single-focused narrative in the Bible. And in its present form in Genesis, the "inserted" items are especially significant to the entire narrative. For an excellent commentary on Genesis that takes all of these narrative features as an essential part of "commenting" on the text, we highly recommend Bruce K. Waltke's *Genesis: A Commentary* (Grand Rapids: Zondervan, 2001).

The Narrator

We begin by paying attention to the one party who is not mentioned directly in the unfolding of the narrative: the narrator himself. For you to understand how narrative works, you need to be aware of two important things about the narrator's role in the unfolding of the story.

First, since he is the one who chooses what to include in the story, he is comparatively "omniscient"; that is, he is everywhere and knows everything about the story he tells. But he never shares all he knows, nor does he usually comment, explain, or evaluate during the unfolding of the narrative itself. His role is to tell the story in such a way that you are drawn into the narrative so that you will see things for yourself.

Second, the narrator is responsible for the "point of view" of the story, that is, the perspective from which the story is told. In the end, of course, he thus presents the divine point of view. Sometimes God's point of view is disclosed directly, as in the repeated "the LORD was with Joseph" (Gen 39:2, 3, 21, 23); note how this fourfold repetition happens early on in the narrative when Joseph is first in Egypt. Very often the point of view comes by way of one of the characters. So note how at the end of the narrative (50:20) it is Joseph who tells the reader the divine perspective for the whole narrative: "You intended to harm me, but God intended it for good to accomplish what is now being done, the saving of many lives"!

As you read the various narratives, be constantly on the lookout for how the inspired narrator discloses the point of view from which you are to understand the story.

The Scene(s)

Rather than build the story around the "character" of any of the characters, the predominant mode of narration in Hebrew narrative is "scenic." The action is moved along by a series of scenes that together make up the whole. This has been likened to the way a movie or a television drama tells a story through a succession of scenes. Each scene has its own integrity, yet it is the progressive combination of scenes that makes up the story as a whole.

Note, for example, how this happens in the opening episode narrated in Genesis 37. In the opening scene Joseph squeals on his brothers (v. 2), after which you are informed of the basic reason his brothers hate him: parental favoritism—again (vv. 3–4)! The scene quickly shifts to two scenes in which Joseph recounts two dreams (vv. 5–11), which sets you up for the next scene

(vv. 12–17) where Joseph searches for his brothers but does not find them. This scene serves as a kind of pause in the story to make sure you understand that the "timing" of the crucial scene—the arrival of Joseph, the plot to kill, and the arrival of the Midianites—is divinely ordained. The next three scenes (the plot to kill and the intercession by Reuben, the role of Judah in "rescuing" Joseph by selling him, the grief of Reuben and Jacob) are interwoven with consummate skill; but the point comes in the last verse, where Joseph ends up in Egypt as the servant of a well-placed Egyptian official (v. 36).

It is the "scenes," separately and together, that make the narrative work. Another feature of the scenic nature of the narrative is that in most scenes only two or three characters (or groups) are in place. More than that would intrude on the main plot of the story.

The Characters

In the scenic nature of Hebrew narrative, the characters are the absolutely central element. But you will also note that "characterization" has very little to do with physical appearance—so much so, that if such a thing ever does appear (e.g., Ehud's being "left-handed," Judg 3:15), you need always to ask why. Hebrew narrative is simply not interested in creating a "visual image" of the characters. More important are matters of status (wise, wealthy, etc.) or profession ("captain of the guard," Gen 37:36; "wife," "cupbearer," "baker" chs. 39–40) or tribal designation ("Midianites," 37:36).

Two features of characterization stand out: (1) Characters often appear either in contrast or in parallel. When they are contrasted, which is most often, they must be understood in relationship to each other. In our narrative the contrast between Joseph and his brothers that begins in chapter 37 lies at the heart of the unfolding subsequent narrative in chapters 42–45 (especially the "changes" that have taken place in both Joseph and Judah) and a bit later (50:15–21). Characters in parallel usually happen at the second level of narrative; for example, John the Baptist is a "reenactment" of Elijah, and Mary's story (Luke 1–2) is a clear echo of the story of Hannah (1 Sam 1–2).

(2) The predominant mode of characterization occurs in the characters' words and actions, not in the narrator's own descriptions. In our narrative this happens especially with the main char-

acter, Joseph, and with the most significant secondary character, Judah. In particular, how Joseph's moral character develops from negative to positive is a main theme. At the beginning, Joseph, as part of a notably dysfunctional family, is depicted as "spoiled brat, talebearer, braggart" (Waltke, p. 498). His moral character comes alive in the incident with Potiphar's wife, made explicit by the dialogue (see below), and his faithfulness to sexual morality lands him in prison (ch. 39). But the crucial matter is the loving but firm way he handles his brothers in chapters 42–45; he weeps for them but will not reveal himself to them until they are tested and proved to be changed themselves.

Likewise, the narrator shows special interest in Judah. Judah is the one who argues for selling rather than killing Joseph (37:26–27); yet his own moral life is highly questionable (ch. 38—a story that is also told in part because Judah will assume the "rights of the firstborn" through whom Israel's eventual king will come [49:10], and because his offspring continue the motif of the choice of the younger son [38:27–30]). But the narrator's primary interest in Judah is in his radical change of character that emerges a bit later in the story (42–45).

Dialogue

Dialogue is a crucial feature of Hebrew narrative, and one of the chief methods of characterization. Indeed, a significantly large part of all narratives is carried on by the "rhythm" between narrative and dialogue. There are three things to look for here:

First, *the first point of dialogue is often a significant clue both to the story plot and to the character of the speaker.* Look, for example, how this happens in the brief scenes at the beginning of the story of Joseph (Gen 37:5–11). Joseph's narration of his dreams reflects straightforward arrogance (vv. 6–7); his brothers' (and father's) response both sets the plot itself in motion ("Will you actually rule us?") and is expressly brought to conclusion by way of narrative at the end (50:18). But in contrast to his brothers' hatred, his father "kept the matter in mind" (37:11, a narrative clue for the reader to do the same).

Second, *contrastive dialogue often functions as a way of characterization as well.* Note the length of Joseph's reply (39:8–9) to the very brief invitation of Potiphar's wife (v. 7). You will see a different kind of contrastive dialogue with the final speeches of

Judah and Joseph (44:18–34 and 45:4–13), by which the first plot resolution is achieved.

Third, *very often the narrator will emphasize the crucial parts of the narrative by having one of the characters repeat or summarize the narrative in a speech.* This happens particularly in the speeches of the brothers (42:30–34) and of Judah (44:18–34). So don't yield to the temptation to speed read through these repetitions; they often tell you very important things about the point of view of the narrative.

Plot

A narrative cannot function without a plot and plot resolution. This means, of course, that the narrative must have a beginning, middle, and end, which together focus on a buildup of dramatic tension that is eventually released. Usually the plot is thrust forward by some form of conflict, which generates interest in the resolution. Plots can be either simple (as the inserted story of Judah and Tamar in Gen 38) or complex, as is the whole of the Joseph narrative, where several subplots vie for attention during the unfolding of the major plot: how the conflict between Joseph and his brothers brought Israel to Egypt—which in turn prepares the way for the next major part of the story of Israel (the exodus from Egypt).

You will find that the plot in Hebrew narrative moves at a much faster pace than most modern narration—even that of the "short story" genre. So as you look for the major plot and its resolution in any narrative, be alert to the various devices the narrator uses to slow the pace of his story. This usually happens by dialogue, the sudden elaboration of detail, or by other forms of repetition. Very often a slowed pace is a signal pointing to the narrator's focus or point of view, so again, don't yield to the temptation to skim read.

Features of Structure

In ways that most of us in modern settings can hardly appreciate, Hebrew narrative uses a whole series of structural features to catch the hearer's attention and keep him or her fastened on the narrative. The reason for these features is something that often escapes us and thus causes us to overlook them, namely, that these narratives, even when written down, were designed primarily for *hearers, not readers.* In a time when our senses are bombarded by dozens of images in a brief thirty-second television commercial, taking the time to "hear" a text read is virtually a lost art. Yet, these texts were composed altogether with the hearer in view and thus contain structural features designed to make the narrative memorable. We have already noted some of these. Here we isolate them and add others so you will be constantly on the lookout for them.

Repetition. Repetition, which pervades Hebrew narrative, can take several forms. We point out only a few. The first, and probably most important, is repetition of *key words*. For example, can you notice the emphasis on "brother" in chapter 37, a word that occurs fifteen times in the narrative? Note also how the conflict dimension of the plot is carried forward by the repetition of "hated" (37:4, 5, 8; cf. "jealous" in 37:11).

Repetition also happens as a form of *resuming* the narrative after an interruption or detour; note, for example, how the concluding moment when Joseph is sold by his brothers (37:36) is repeated at the resumption of the Joseph narrative (39:1). At other times repetition takes the form of *stereotyped patterns*, as in the cycles of the judges or the introductions and conclusions to the stories of each of Israel's kings.

Inclusion. "Inclusion" is a technical term for the form of repetition where a narrative is begun and brought to conclusion on the same note or in the same way. We have already noted this in the theme of Joseph's brothers' bowing to him (37:6–8 and 50:18). A frequent, and special, form of inclusion is known as *chiasm,* in which whole books or smaller narratives are structured in some form of an A B C B A pattern. In *How to 2* (pp. 55–62), we point out how the entire book of Deuteronomy is structured in this way. Another way this happens is called *foreshadowing*, where something that is briefly noted in an early part of a narrative is picked up in detail later on (e.g., the births of Perez and Zerah in 38:27–30 anticipate their appearance in the genealogy in 46:12, and especially the role of Perez as the "firstborn" later in the Old Testament story).

Besides the features of biblical narrative we have included here, you will find still other, sometimes more complex, rhetorical features noted in the better commentaries. For some of these, see Waltke's *Genesis* (pp. 31–43). But these are enough to give you plenty to think about as you read any Hebrew narrative, be it short or long.

A Final Word

As our own form of inclusion, we conclude this section by remind-ing you that the one crucial item to keep in mind as you read any Hebrew narrative is the presence of God in the narrative. In any biblical narrative, God is the *ultimate* character, the supreme hero of the story. Sometimes this is indicated in bold terms: "The LORD was with Joseph" (39:2; etc.); "interpretations [of dreams] belong to God" (40:8; etc.); "God sent me ahead of you to pre-serve for you a remnant on earth and to save your lives by a great deliverance" (45:7); "God intended it for good" (50:20). Thus the whole story climaxes with Joseph's prophecy, "God will surely come to your aid and take you up out of this land" (50:24, note the repetition in verse 25, which then foreshadows Exod 13:19 and Josh 24:32!).

To miss this dimension of the narrative is to miss the perspec-tive of the narrative altogether; and precisely because of these explicit statements about God's presence in the narrative, one should constantly be aware of God's presence in more implicit ways (e.g., the source of Joseph's dreams in ch. 37; the timing in the narrative that brought Joseph, his brothers, and the Midianites together in 37:25–28; etc.).

ON READING "BETWEEN THE LINES"

We turn to the book of Ruth for another narrative to illustrate fur-ther how much one can learn from what is *implicit* in narrative—parts the narrator has embedded in the story that you might miss on a first, or otherwise casual, reading of the book. The Ruth narrative is a good candidate for this task since it is brief and self-contained; and an initial careful reading of the text will point out its essential features with regard to its being a marvelous expres-sion of Hebrew narrative. Whatever else, the book of Ruth is not a "love story"; rather it is the story of God's "kindness" (1:8—first point of dialogue; 2:20; 3:10) being played out in the lives of three people who are the central characters in the plot; and it is filled with several subplots as well (e.g., the foreigner who showed kind-ness assumes a place in the royal lineage of King David).

To remind you again: Implicit teaching is that which is clearly present in the story but not stated in so many words. At issue here is the fact that the narrator and his implied hearers/readers share the same presuppositions, and therefore he does not make explicit many things he assumes they will know simply by the way he tells the story. Rather than looking for hidden meanings, you must try to discover these shared assumptions that make the story work easily for them but that can otherwise leave us on the outside of the narrative. What you want to find is what is thus *implied* in the story, that which can't be read right off the page. Being able to distinguish what is explicitly taught can be fairly easy. Being able to distinguish what is implicitly taught can be more difficult. It requires skill, hard work, caution, and a prayerful respect for the Holy Spirit's care in inspiring the text. After all, you want to read things *out of* the narrative rather than *into* it.

Ruth's story may be summarized as follows. The widow Ruth, a Moabite, emigrates from Moab to Bethlehem with her Israelite mother-in-law, Naomi, who is also a widow (Ruth 1). Ruth gleans leftover grain in the field of Boaz, who befriends her, having heard of her faith and her kindness to Naomi, who is a relative of his (Ruth 2). At Naomi's suggestion, Ruth lets Boaz know that she hopes he would be willing to marry her (Ruth 3). Boaz undertakes the legal procedures necessary to marry Ruth and to protect the family property rights of her late husband, Mahlon. The birth of Ruth and Boaz's first son, Obed, is a great consolation to Naomi. Eventually, Obed's grandson turned out to be King David (Ruth 4).

If you are not familiar with the Ruth narrative, we suggest that you read the book through at least twice. Then go back and take particular note of the following *implicit* points that the narrative makes.

1. The narrative tells us that *Ruth converted* to faith in the Lord, the God of Israel. It does this by reporting Ruth's words to Naomi, "Your people will be my people and your God my God" (1:16) rather than by telling us "Ruth was converted." We are expected to be able to recognize this by the content of this first piece of dialogue spoken by Ruth (verse 10 is spoken by both daughters-in-law). Moreover, the genuineness of her conversion is implicitly confirmed by her next words: "May the LORD deal with me, be it ever so severely, if . . ." (1:17), an oath taken in the name of Israel's God. You can be sure that the original hearers/readers well understood this.

2. The narrative tells us implicitly that *Boaz was a righteous Israelite* who kept the Mosaic law, though many other Israelites

did not. Look carefully at four specific moments in the narrative (2:3–13, 22; 3:10–12; and 4:9–10). Again, by means of dialogue, the narrator makes clear to his readers that Boaz is faithful to the Lord because he keeps the law. As with Boaz, they would know the law of gleaning set forth in Leviticus (19:9–10). In this case one might note that Ruth fits both categories of this law—she is poor *and* a foreigner, not to mention a widow. Original readers would know, too, the law of redemption decreed later in Leviticus (25:23–24). Also implied is the fact that not all Israelites were so loyal to the law—indeed it was dangerous to glean in the fields of people who did not obey the law's gleaning obligations (2:22). Again, we get a lot of important information *implicitly* from the narrative, which is not *explicitly* given.

3. The narrative tells us implicitly that *a foreign woman belongs to the ancestry of King David*—and by extension, therefore, to Jesus Christ. Look at how this unfolds at the conclusion of the narrative (4:17–21). The brief genealogy with which it begins (v. 17) and the fuller genealogy that follows (vv. 18–21) both end with the name David. This David is obviously the focus—the endpoint—of this portion of the narrative. We know from several other genealogical lists in the Bible that this David is King David, the founder of Israel as a nation on the larger political scene, and thus the first great Israelite king. We also know from the New Testament genealogies that Jesus, humanly speaking, was descended from David. Ruth, then, was David's great-grandmother and an ancestor of Jesus! This is an important part of the teaching of the entire narrative. It is a story not just about Ruth and Boaz in terms of their faithfulness to Yahweh but also in terms of their place in Israel's history. They had no way of knowing it, but these were people whom God would use in the ancestry of David and "David's son" Jesus.

4. The narrative tells us implicitly that *Bethlehem was an exceptional town* during the period of the judges by reason of the faithfulness of its citizenry. To spot this implicit thrust in the narrative is not easy or automatic. It requires a careful reading of the whole narrative, with special attention to the words and actions of all the participants in the story. It also requires knowledge of what things were generally like in other parts of Israel in those days in contrast to what they were like specifically in Bethlehem. The latter knowledge depends on a familiarity with the main events and themes

of the book of Judges, since Ruth is directly related to that time period by the narrator (1:1).

If you have had the opportunity to read Judges carefully (see *How to 2,* pp. 70–77), you will have noticed that the judges' period (about 1240–1030 BC) was generally marked by such practices as widespread idolatry, syncretism (mixing features of pagan religions with those of Israel's true faith), social injustice, social turmoil, intertribal rivalries, sexual immorality, and other indications of unfaithfulness to Yahweh. Indeed, the picture presented to us in the book of Judges is hardly a happy one, though there are individual cases where God in his mercy benefits Israel, or tribes within Israel, in spite of the general pattern of rebellion against him.

What in the book of Ruth tells us that Bethlehem is an exception to this general picture of unfaithfulness? Practically everything except for one sentence in the narrative (2:22), and even that one gives the reader a hint as to the troublesome nature of the time. What is implied is that not all Bethlehemites were practicing the gleaning laws as they should. Otherwise, the picture is remarkably consistent. The words of the characters themselves show just how consciously the people of this town manifest their allegiance to the Lord.

Remember that all the characters mentioned in the narrative, except for Ruth and her sister-in-law Orpah, are citizens of Bethlehem. Consider Naomi: whether in times of great bitterness (1:8–9, 13, 20–21) or in times of happiness (1:6; 2:19–20), she recognizes and submits to the Lord's will. Moreover, Boaz consistently shows himself by his words to be a worshiper and follower of Yahweh (2:11–12; 3:10, 13), and his actions throughout confirm his words.

Even the way people greet one another shows a high degree of conscious allegiance to their God (2:4). Likewise, the elders of the town in their blessings on the marriage and its offspring (4:11–12) and the women of the town in their blessing on Naomi (4:14) show their faith. Their acceptance of the converted Moabite, Ruth, is further implicit testimony to their faith.

The point is that one cannot read the narrative carefully (and in comparison with Judges) and not see again and again how exceptional Bethlehem was! Nowhere does the narrative actually say, "Bethlehem was a town remarkable for its piety in those days."

But this is exactly what the narrative does tell us—in ways just as forceful and convincing as the outright words could ever be.

These examples, we hope, will demonstrate that careful attention to details and to the overall movement of a narrative and its context are necessary if its full meaning is to be obtained. What is implicit can be every bit as significant as what is explicit.

Warning! Implicit does not mean secret! You will get into all sorts of trouble if you try to find meanings in the text that you think God has "hidden" in the narrative. This is not at all what is meant by implicit. "Implicit" means that a dimension of the message is capable of being understood from what is said, though it is not stated in so many words. Your task is not to ferret out things that cannot be understood by everyone. Your task, rather, is to take note of all that the narrative actually tells you—directly and indirectly but *never* mystically or privately. If you are not able confidently to express to others something taught implicitly so that they, too, can understand it and get the point, you probably are misreading the text. What the Holy Spirit has inspired is of benefit for all believers. Discern and relay what the story recognizably has in it; do not make up a new story (2 Pet 2:3)!

SOME FINAL CAUTIONS

It is our conviction that the primary reason Christians have often read the Old Testament narratives so poorly, finding things that are not really there, is the one we mentioned at the outset of this book: the tendency to "flatten" everything because they assume that everything God has said in his Word is thereby a direct word to them. Thus they wrongly expect that everything in the Bible applies directly as instruction for their own individual lives. The Bible, of course, *is* a great resource. It contains all that a believer really needs in terms of guidance from God for living. And we have assumed throughout that the Old Testament narratives are indeed a rich source for our hearing from God. But this does not mean that each individual narrative is somehow to be understood as a direct word from God for each of us separately or as teaching us moral lessons by examples.

So that you might avoid this tendency, we list here several of the most common errors of interpretation that individuals commit when reading the biblical narratives, although many of these errors are not limited to narratives.

Allegorizing. Instead of concentrating on the clear meaning of the narrative, some relegate the text to merely reflecting another meaning beyond the text. There are allegorical portions of Scripture (e.g., Ezek 23 and parts of Revelation), but no historical narrative is ever intended at the same time to be an allegory.

Decontextualizing. Ignoring the full historical and literary contexts, and often the individual narrative, some people concentrate on small units only and thus miss interpretational clues. If you take things out of context enough, you can make almost any part of Scripture say anything you want it to. But at that moment you are no longer *reading* the Bible, you are abusing it.

Selectivity. This is similar to decontextualizing. It involves picking and choosing specific words and phrases to concentrate on while ignoring the others and ignoring the overall sweep of the narrative being studied. Instead of listening to the whole to see how God was working in Israel's history, it ignores some of the parts and the whole entirely.

Moralizing. This is the assumption that principles for living can be derived from all passages. The moralizing reader, in effect, asks the question, what is the moral of this story? at the end of every individual narrative. An example would be: what can we learn about handling adversity from how the Israelites endured their years as slaves in Egypt? The fallacy of this approach is that it ignores the fact that the narratives were written to show the progress of God's history of redemption, not to illustrate principles. They are historical narratives, not illustrative narratives.

Personalizing. Also known as individualizing, this refers to reading Scripture in the way suggested above, supposing that any or all parts apply to you or your group in a way that they do not apply to everyone else. This is, in fact, a self-centered reading of the Bible. Examples of personalizing would be, "The story of Balaam's talking donkey reminds me that I talk too much." Or, "The story of the building of the temple is God's way of telling us that we have to construct a new church building."

Misappropriation. This is closely related to personalizing. It is to appropriate a narrative for purposes that are quite foreign to its reason for being there. This is what is happening when, on the basis of the Gideon narrative (Judg 6:36–40), people "fleece" God as a way of finding God's will! This, of course, is both misappropriation and decontextualizing, since the narrator is pointing out that God saved Israel through Gideon despite his lack of trust in God's word. It is yet another account of God's mercy, not a method of finding God's will!

False appropriation. This is another form of decontextualizing. It is to read into a biblical narrative suggestions or ideas that come from contemporary culture that are simultaneously foreign to the narrator's purpose and contradictory to his point of view. A prime example is to find the "hint" of a homosexual relationship between David and Jonathan in the language, "[Jonathan] loved him as he loved himself" (1 Sam. 20:17), followed by, "they kissed each other" (v. 41)—which of course in that culture was not on the lips! But such a "hint" not only is not in the text, it stands completely outside the narrator's point of view: Their "love" is covenantal and is likened to God's love (vv. 14 and 42); moreover the author is narrating the story of Israel's greatest king, and he presupposes Israel's law, which forbids such behavior.

False combination. This approach combines elements from here and there in a passage and makes a point out of their combination, even though the elements themselves are not directly connected in the passage itself. An example of this all-too-common interpretational error is the conclusion that the account of David's capturing Jerusalem (2 Sam 5:6–7) must have been a *recapturing* of that city, since Judges 1:8, an earlier part of the same grand narrative that runs all the way from Joshua through 2 Kings, says that the Israelites had already captured it. What you need to know (i.e., what the narrator and his original audience knew) is that there were two Jerusalems—a "greater" Jerusalem and, within it, the walled city of Jerusalem (also known as Zion). The account in Judges refers to the capture of the former; David captured the latter, finally completing the conquest hundreds of years after it started and then faltered, finally fulfilling promises going all the way back to Abraham (Gen 15:18–21).

Redefinition. When the plain meaning of the text leaves people cold, producing no immediate spiritual delight, or says something other than what they wish it said, they are often tempted to redefine it to mean something else. An example is the use often made of God's promise to Solomon as it is narrated in Chronicles (2 Chron 7:14–15). The context of this narrative clearly relates the promise to "this place" (the temple in Jerusalem) and "their land" (Israel, the land of Solomon and the Israelites). Understandably many modern Christians yearn for it to be true of *their* land wherever they live in the modern world—and so they tend to ignore the fact that God's promise that he will "hear from heaven and will forgive their sin and will heal their land" was about the only earthly land God's people could ever claim as "theirs," the Old Testament land of Israel. In the new covenant, God's people have no earthly country that is "their land"—despite the tendency of some American Christians to think otherwise about the world. The country all believers now most truly belong to is a heavenly one (Heb 11:16).

Perhaps the single most useful bit of caution we can give you about reading and learning from narratives is this: Do not be a monkey-see-monkey-do reader of the Bible. No Bible narrative was written specifically about *you*. The Joseph narrative is about Joseph, and specifically about how God carried out the divine purposes through him—it is not a narrative directly about us. The Ruth narrative glorifies God's protection of and benefit for Ruth and the Bethlehemites—not us. We can always learn a great deal from these narratives, and from all the Bible's narratives, but you can never assume that God expects you to do exactly the same thing that Bible characters did or to have the same things happen to you that happened to them. For further discussion on this point, see chapter 6.

Bible characters are sometimes good and sometimes evil, sometimes wise and sometimes foolish. They are sometimes punished and sometimes shown mercy, sometimes well-off and sometimes miserable. Our task is to learn God's word from the narratives about them, not to try to do everything that was done in the Bible. Just because someone in a Bible story did something, it does not mean a modern reader has either permission or obligation to do it too.

What we can and should do is obey what God in Scripture actually commands Christian believers to do. Narratives are precious to us because they so vividly *demonstrate* God's involvement in the world and *illustrate* his principles and calling. They thus teach us a lot—but what they directly teach us does not systematically include personal ethics. For this area of life, we must turn elsewhere in the Scriptures—to the various places where personal ethics are actually taught categorically and explicitly. The richness and variety of the Scriptures must be understood as our ally—a welcome resource, and never a complicated burden.

PRINCIPLES FOR INTERPRETING NARRATIVES

We conclude this chapter by isolating ten summarizing principles for interpreting Old Testament narratives that should also help a reader avoid certain pitfalls as one reads.

1. An Old Testament narrative usually does not directly teach a doctrine.
2. An Old Testament narrative usually illustrates a doctrine or doctrines taught propositionally elsewhere.
3. Narratives record what happened—not necessarily what should have happened or what ought to happen every time. Therefore, not every narrative has an individual identifiable moral application.
4. What people do in narratives is not necessarily a good example for us. Frequently, it is just the opposite.
5. Many (if not most) of the characters in Old Testament narratives are far from perfect—as are their actions as well.
6. We are not always told at the end of a narrative whether what happened was good or bad. We are expected to be able to judge this on the basis of what God has taught us directly and categorically elsewhere in Scripture.
7. All narratives are selective and incomplete. Not all the relevant details are always given (cf. John 21:25). What does appear in the narrative is everything that the inspired author thought important for us to know.
8. Narratives are not written to answer all our theological questions. They have particular, specific, limited purposes and deal with certain issues, leaving others to be dealt with elsewhere in other ways.
9. Narratives may teach either explicitly (by clearly stating something) or implicitly (by clearly implying something without actually stating it).
10. In the final analysis, God is the hero of all biblical narratives.

CHAPTER 6

Acts: The Question of Historical Precedent

In one sense a separate chapter on the Acts of the Apostles is a bit redundant, for almost everything that was said in the last chapter applies here as well. However, for a very practical hermeneutical reason, Acts requires a chapter of its own. The reason is simple: most Christians do not read Acts in the same way they read Judges or 2 Samuel, even if they are not fully aware of it.

When we read the Old Testament narratives, we tend to do the things mentioned in the last chapter—moralize, allegorize, personalize, and so on. Seldom do we think of these narratives as serving as patterns for Christian behavior or church life. Even in the case of those few we do treat this way—for example, putting out a fleece to find God's will—we never do exactly what they did. That is, we never put out an actual fleece for God to make wet or dry. Rather we "fleece" God by setting up a set, or sets, of circumstances. "If someone from California calls us this week, then we'll let that be God's way of telling us that the move to California is the one he wants us to make." And never once in using this "pattern" do we consider that Gideon's action was really not a good one inasmuch as it first of all demonstrated his lack of trust in God's word that had already been given to him.

Thus we seldom think of the Old Testament histories as setting biblical precedents for our own lives. On the other hand, this has been a normal way for Christians to read Acts. It not only tells us the history of the early church, but it also serves as the normative model for the church of all times. And this is precisely our hermeneutical difficulty.

Many sectors of evangelical Protestantism have a "restoration" mentality. We regularly look back to the church and Christian experience in the first century either as the norm to be restored or the ideal to be approximated. Thus we often say things like, "Acts plainly teaches us that ..." However, it seems obvious that not all of the "plain teaching" is equally plain to all.

In fact it is our lack of hermeneutical precision as to what Acts is trying to teach that has led to a lot of the division one finds in the church. Such diverse practices as the baptism of infants or of believers only, congregational and episcopalian church polity, the necessity of observing the Lord's Supper every Sunday, the choice of deacons by congregational vote, the selling of possessions and having all things in common, and even ritual snake handling (!) have been supported in whole or in part on the basis of Acts.

The main purpose of this chapter is to offer some hermeneutical suggestions for the problem of biblical precedent. What is said here, therefore, will also apply to all the historical narratives in Scripture, including some of the material in the Gospels. Before that, however, we need to address how to read and study Acts itself.

In the discussion that follows, we will have occasion regularly to refer to Luke's intention or purpose in writing Acts. It must be emphasized that we always mean that the Holy Spirit lies behind Luke's intention. In the same way that "God works in [us]" as we "continue to work out [our] salvation" (Phil 2:12–13), so Luke had certain interests and concerns in writing Luke-Acts. Yet behind it all, we believe, was the special superintending work of the Holy Spirit.

THE EXEGESIS OF ACTS

Although Acts is a readable book, it is also a difficult book for group Bible study. The reason is that people come to the book, and thus to its study, for a whole variety of reasons. Some are greatly interested in historical details, that is, what Acts can furnish about the history of the primitive church. The interest of others in the history is apologetic, proving the Bible to be true by showing Luke's accuracy as a historian. Most people, however, come to the book for purely religious or devotional reasons, wanting to know what the early Christians were like so that they may inspire us or serve as models.

The interest that brings people to Acts, therefore, causes a great deal of selectivity to take place as they read or study. For the person coming with devotional interests, for example, Gamaliel's speech (Acts 5:35–39) holds far less interest than Paul's conversion somewhat later (9:1–19) or Peter's miraculous escape from prison (12:1–19). Such reading or study usually causes people to skip over the chronological or historical questions. As you read the first eleven chapters, for example, it is difficult to imagine that what Luke has included there had in fact taken place during a time span of ten to fifteen years.

Our present interest, therefore, is to help you read and study the book alertly, to help you to look at the book in terms of *Luke's* interests, and to spur you to ask some new kinds of questions as you read.

Acts as History

Most of the exegetical suggestions given in the preceding chapter hold true for Acts. What is important here is that Luke was a Gentile, whose inspired narrative is at the same time an excellent example of Hellenistic historiography, a kind of history writing that had its roots in Thucydides (ca. 460–400 BC) and flourished during the Hellenistic period (ca. 300 BC–AD 200). Such history was not written simply to keep records or to chronicle the past. Rather, it was written both to encourage and/or entertain (i.e., to be good reading) and to inform, moralize, or offer an apologetic. At the same time, of course, Luke had been greatly influenced by his reading of, and living with, the Old Testament narratives, so that this kind of divinely inspired, religiously motivated history is also evident in his telling of the early Christian story.

Thus Luke's two volumes (Luke and Acts) fit both of these kinds of history well. On the one hand, they are especially good reading; on the other hand, in keeping with both the Old Testament histories and the best of Hellenistic historiography, Luke at the same time has interests that go far beyond simply informing or entertaining. There is a divine activity going on in this story, and Luke is especially concerned that his readers understand this. For him, the divine activity that began with Jesus and continues through the ministry of the Holy Spirit in the church is a continuation of God's story that began in the Old Testament. Therefore, making note of Luke's own theological interests is of special importance as you read or study Acts. Exegesis of Acts, therefore, includes not only the purely historical questions like what happened but also the theological ones such as, what was Luke's purpose in selecting and shaping the material in this way?

The question of Luke's intent is at once the most important and the most difficult. It is the most important because it is crucial to our hermeneutics. If it can be demonstrated that Luke's intent in Acts had been to lay down a pattern for the church at all times, then that pattern surely becomes normative, that is, it is what God requires of all Christians under any and all conditions. But if his intent is something else, then we need to ask the hermeneutical questions in a different way. To find Luke's intent, however, can also be difficult, partly because we do not know who Theophilus was or why Luke would have written to him, and partly because Luke himself seems to have so many different interests.

However, because of the significance of Luke's purpose for hermeneutics, it is especially important that you keep this question before you as you read or study at the exegetical level. In a way, this is much like thinking paragraphs when exegeting the Epistles. But in this case it moves beyond paragraphs to whole narratives and sections of the book.

Our exegetical interest, therefore, is both in *what* and *why*. As we have already learned, one must begin with *what* before asking *why*.

The First Step

As always, the first step one does is to read, preferably the whole book in one sitting. And as you read, learn to make observations and ask questions. The problem with making observations and asking questions as you read Acts, of course, is that the narrative is so engrossing that one frequently simply forgets to ask the exegetical questions.

So as before, if we were to give you an assignment here, it would look like this: (1) Read Acts all the way through in one or two sittings. (2) As you read, make mental notes of such things as key people and places, recurring motifs (what really interests Luke?), and natural divisions of the book. (3) Now go back and skim read, and jot down with references your previous observations. (4) Ask yourself, why did Luke write this book? And consider why *this* particular narrative has been included.

Since Acts is the only one of its kind in the New Testament, we will be more specific here in guiding your reading and study.

Acts: An Overview

Let us begin our quest of *what* by noting the natural divisions as Luke himself gives them to us. Acts has frequently been divided on the basis of Luke's interest in Peter (chs. 1–12) and Paul (chs. 13–28), or in the geographical expansion of the gospel suggested at the beginning (1:8 = chs. 1–7, Jerusalem; 8–10, Samaria and Judea; 11–28, to the ends of the earth). Although both of these divisions are recognizable in terms of actual content, there is another clue, given by Luke himself, that seems to tie everything together much better.

As you read, notice the several brief summary statements, whose first example reads: "So the word of God spread. The number of disciples in Jerusalem increased rapidly, and a large number of priests became obedient to the faith" (6:7; cf. 9:31; 12:24; 16:4; and 19:20). In each case the narrative seems to pause momentarily before it takes off in a new direction of some kind. On the basis of this clue, Acts can be seen to be composed of six sections (or panels) that give the narrative a continual forward movement from its Jewish setting based in Jerusalem, with Peter as its leading figure, toward a predominantly Gentile church, with Paul as the leading figure, and with Rome, the capital of the Gentile world, as the goal. Once Paul reaches Rome, where he once again turns to the Gentiles because they will listen (28:28), the narrative comes to an end.

You should notice, then, as you read, how each section contributes to this "movement." You may wish, in your own words, to describe each panel, both as to its content and its contribution to the forward movement. What seems to be the key to each new forward thrust? Here is our own attempt to do this:

1:1–6:7. A description of the primitive church in Jerusalem, its early preaching, its common life, its spread, and its initial opposition. What is especially noteworthy is how Jewish everything is, including the sermons, the opposition, and the fact that the early believers continue to have associations with the temple and the synagogues. This introductory panel concludes with a narrative indicating that a division had begun between Greek-speaking and Aramaic-speaking believers.

6:8– 9:31. A description of the first geographical expansion, carried out by the "Hellenists" (Greek-speaking Jewish Christians), to Greek-speaking Jews in the Diaspora or "nearly Jews" (Samaritans and a proselyte). Luke also includes the conversion of Paul, who was (1) a Hellenist, (2) a Jewish opponent of the gospel, and (3) the one who was going to be used to set in motion the specifically Gentile expansion. Stephen's martyrdom is the key to this initial expansion.

9:32– 12:24. A description of the first expansion to the Gentiles. The key moment here is the conversion of Cornelius, made clear because his story is told twice, once by way of Peter's vision and then followed by a full explanation. The significance of Cornelius is that his conversion was a direct act from God, who carried it out through Peter, the acknowledged leader of the Jewish-Christian mission (had God used the Hellenists, the event would have been even more suspect in Jerusalem). Also included is the story of the church in Antioch, whose significance is that Gentile conversion is now carried out by the Hellenists in a purposeful way.

12:25– 16:5. A description of the first geographical expansion into the Gentile world, with Paul now as the lead character in the narrative. Jews now regularly reject the gospel because it includes Gentiles. The church meets in council and does not reject its Gentile converts, nor does it lay Jewish religious requirements on them. The latter serves as the key to full expansion into the Gentile world.

16:6– 19:20. A description of the further, ever westward, expansion into the Gentile world, now into Europe. The singularly repeated motif is that the Diaspora Jews reject and the Gentiles welcome the gospel.

19:21– 28:30. A description of the events that move Paul and the gospel on to Rome, with a great deal of interest in Paul's trials, in which three times he is declared innocent of any wrongdoing.

Once you try reading Acts with this outline in view, this sense of movement, you will be able to see for yourself that this seems to capture what is going on. As you read you should also notice that our description of the content omits one crucial factor—indeed *the* crucial factor—namely, the role of the Holy Spirit in all of this. You will notice as you read that at every key juncture, in every key person, the Holy Spirit plays the absolutely leading role. According to Luke, all of this forward movement did not happen by human design; it happened because God willed it and the Holy Spirit carried it out.

Luke's Purpose

We must be careful that we do not move too glibly from this overview of what Luke did to an easy or dogmatic expression of what his inspired purpose in all of this was. But a few observations are in order in this case, partly based also on what Luke did *not* do.

1. The key to understanding Acts seems to be in Luke's interest in this movement of the gospel, orchestrated by the Holy Spirit, from its Jerusalem-based, Judaism-oriented beginnings to its becoming a worldwide, Gentile-predominant phenomenon. Once the primary advocate of Gentile conversion arrives at the capital of the Gentile world (Rome itself), Luke quickly brings his narrative to conclusion. Thus on the basis of structure and content alone, any statement of purpose that does not include the Gentile mission and the Holy Spirit's role in that mission will surely have missed the point of the book.

2. This interest in "movement" is further substantiated by what Luke does *not* tell us. First, he has no interest in the "lives," that is, biographies, of the apostles. Indeed, James (the son of Zebedee) is the only one about whose death we know (12:2). Once the movement to the Gentiles gets underway, Peter drops from sight except in chapter 15, where he certifies the Gentile mission. Apart from John, the other apostles are not even mentioned, and Luke's interest in Paul is almost completely in terms of the Gentile mission.

Second, he has little or no interest in church organization or polity. The "seven" in chapter 6 are not called deacons, and in any case they soon leave Jerusalem. Luke never tells us why or how it happened that the church in Jerusalem passed from the leadership of Peter and the apostles to James, the brother of Jesus (12:17; 15:13; 21:18); nor does he ever explain how any local church was organized in terms of polity or leadership, except to say that elders were appointed (14:23).

Third, there is no word about other geographical expansion except in the one direct line from Jerusalem to Rome. There is no mention of Crete (Titus 1:5), Illyricum (Rom 15:19—modern Croatia and Yugoslavia), or Pontus, Cappadocia, and Bithynia (1 Pet 1:1), not to mention the church's expansion eastward toward Mesopotamia or southward toward Egypt.

All of this together indicates that church history per se was simply not Luke's primary reason for writing.

3. Luke's interest also does not seem to be in standardizing things, bringing everything into uniformity. When he records individual conversions there are usually two elements included: the gift of the Spirit and water baptism. But these can be noted in reverse order, with or without the laying on of hands, with or without the mention of tongues, and scarcely ever with a specific mention of repentance, even after what Peter says in his opening address in the book (2:38–39). Similarly, Luke neither says nor implies that the Gentile churches experienced a communal life similar to that in Jerusalem, which he mentions twice (2:42–47 and 4:32–35). Such diversity should almost certainly be understood to say that no specific example is being set forth as *the* model of Christian experience or of church life.

But is this to say that Luke is not trying to tell us something by these various specific narratives? Not necessarily. The real question is, then, what was he trying to tell his first readers?

4. Nonetheless, we believe that much of Acts is intended by Luke to serve as a model. But the model is not so much in the specifics as in the overall picture. By the very way the Holy Spirit has moved him to structure and narrate this history it seems probable that we are to view this triumphant, joyful, forward-moving expansion of the gospel into the Gentile world, empowered by the Holy Spirit and resulting in changed lives and local communities, as God's intent for the continuing church. And precisely because this is God's intent for the church, nothing can hinder it, neither Sanhedrin nor synagogue, dissension nor narrow-mindedness, prison nor plot. Luke, therefore, probably intended that the ongoing church should be "like them," but in the larger sense of proclaiming the good news to the entire world, not by modeling itself on any specific example.

An Exegetical Sampling

With this overview of content and a provisional look at intent before us, let us examine two narratives (6:1–7 and 8:1–25) and note the kinds of exegetical questions one needs to learn to ask of the text of Acts.

As always, one begins by reading over and over the selected portion and its immediate context. As with the Epistles, the contextual questions one must repeatedly ask in Acts include: What is the point of this narrative or speech? How does it function in Luke's total narrative? Why has he included it here? You can usually answer these questions provisionally after one or two careful readings. Sometimes, however, especially in Acts, you will need to do some outside reading to answer some of the *content* questions before you can feel confident you are on the right track.

Let us begin with the narrative about the choosing of the seven (6:1–7). How does this section function in the overall picture? Two things can be said right away. First, it serves to conclude the first panel (1:1–6:7); second, it also serves as a transition to the second panel (6:8–9:31). Note how Luke does this. His interest at the outset (1:1–6:7) is to give us a picture both of the life of the primitive community and of its expansion *within Jerusalem.* The concluding moment of this narrative (6:1–7) includes both of these features. At the same time it also hints of the first tension within the community itself, a tension based on traditional lines within Judaism between Jerusalem (or Aramaic-speaking) Jews and the Diaspora (Greek-speaking) Jews. In the church this tension was overcome by an official recognition of the leadership that had begun to emerge among the Greek-speaking Jewish Christians.

We have put the last sentence in that particular way because at this point one should also do some outside work on the historical context. By a little digging (articles in Bible dictionaries on "deacons" and "Hellenists," commentaries, and background books like Joachim Jeremias, *Jerusalem in the Time of Jesus* [Philadelphia: Fortress, 1969]), you can discover the following important facts:

1. The Hellenists were almost certainly Greek-speaking Jews, that is, Jews from the Diaspora (descendants of the exiles noted in the Old Testament) who had returned to live in Jerusalem.

2. Many such Hellenists returned to Jerusalem in their later years to die there and thus be buried near Mount Zion. Since they were not native to Jerusalem, when a man died, his widow had no regular means of sustenance.

3. These widows were thus cared for by daily subsidies—care that caused a considerable economic strain in Jerusalem.

4. It is clear from the Stephen narrative (6:8–15) that the Hellenists had their own Greek-speaking synagogue of which both Stephen and Saul, who was from Tarsus (located in Greek-speaking Cilicia, v. 9), were members.

5. The evidence of the narrative in Acts 6 is that the early church had made considerable inroads into the synagogue — note the mention of "their widows" (v. 1), the fact that all seven chosen to handle this matter have Greek names, and the fact that the intense opposition to the church comes from the Diaspora synagogue.

6. Finally, it is also important to note that the seven men are never called deacons. They are simply "the Seven" (21:8), who, to be sure, are to oversee the daily food subsidies for the Greek-speaking widows; but who are also clearly ministers of the Word (Stephen, Philip).

This knowledge of content will especially help to make sense of what follows. For in the succeeding narrative (6:8–8:1) Luke focuses on one of the seven men as the key figure in the first expansion outside Jerusalem. He explicitly tells us that Stephen's martyrdom has this result (8:1–4). You should note also from this latter passage how important this Greek-speaking community of Christians in Jerusalem is to God's larger plan. They are forced to leave Jerusalem because of persecution; but since they were not native there anyway, they simply go out and share the Word "throughout Judea and Samaria" (8:1).

The opening narrative (6:1–7), therefore, is not given to tell us about the first organization of the church, and especially not about clergy and lay deacons. It functions to set the scene for the first expansion of the church outside its Jerusalem base.

The following narrative (8:5–25) is of a different kind. Here we have the actual story of the first known spread of the early church. This narrative is especially important for our present concerns because (1) it contains several exegetical difficulties and (2) it has frequently served as something of a hermeneutical battleground in the later church.

As always, we must begin by trying to do our exegesis with care, and again, there is no substitute for reading the text over and over, making observations and notes. In this case, to get at the *what* of the narrative, you might try to set it out in your own words. Our summary observations are as follows:

The story is straightforward enough. It tells us of Philip's initial ministry in Samaria, which was accompanied by healings and deliverances from demons (8:5–7). Many Samaritans apparently became "people of the way," inasmuch as they believed and were baptized. Indeed, the miracles were so powerful that even Simon, a notorious purveyor of black magic, came to believe (8:9–13). When the Jerusalem church heard of this phenomenon, they sent Peter and John, and only then did the Samaritans receive the Holy Spirit (8:14–17). Simon then wanted to have this power by buying what Peter and John had. Peter rebuked Simon, but it is not clear from his final response (8:24) whether he was repentant or was to be the recipient of the judgment Peter spoke over him (8:20–23).

The way Luke has woven this narrative together makes it clear that two interests clearly predominate: the conversion of the Samaritans and the Simon matter. Most of our later exegetical problems with these two matters basically stem from one's prior knowledge and convictions. We tend to think that things are just not supposed to happen this way. Since Paul has said in his letter to the believers in Rome (ch. 8) that without the Spirit one cannot be a Christian, how is it that these believers had not yet received the Spirit? And, what about Simon? Was he really a believer who "fell away," or did he merely profess without having saving faith?

But most likely the real problem for readers of a much later time stems from the fact that Luke himself makes no attempt to harmonize everything for us. It is difficult to listen to a passage like this without our prior biases getting in the way, and the authors of this book are not immune. Nonetheless, we shall try to hear it from Luke's point of view. What interests *him* in presenting this story? How does it function in *his* overall concern?

First, about the Samaritan conversions, two matters seem to be significant for him: (1) The mission to Samaria, which was the first geographical expansion of the gospel, was carried out by one of the seven men, a Hellenist, quite apart from any design or program on the part of the apostles in Jerusalem. (2) Nonetheless, it is important for Luke's readers to know that the mission had both divine and apostolic approval, as evidenced by the withholding of the Spirit until the laying on of the apostles' hands. It is in keeping with Luke's overall concern to show that the missionary work of the Hellenists was not a maverick movement, although it happened quite apart from any apostolic conference on church growth.

Second, although we cannot prove this—because the text does not tell us and it lies apart from Luke's concerns—it is likely that what was withheld until the coming of Peter and John was the visible, charismatic evidence of the Spirit's presence. Our reasons for suggesting this are three: (1) All of what is said about the Samaritans before the coming of Peter and John are said elsewhere in Acts to describe genuine Christian experience. Therefore, they must have, in fact, begun the Christian life. (2) Elsewhere in Acts the presence of the Spirit—as here—is the crucial element in the Christian life. How then could they have begun Christian life without the crucial element? (3) For Luke, in Acts, the presence of the Spirit means power (1:8; 6:8; 10:38), which is usually manifested by some visible evidence. Therefore it is probably this powerful, visible manifestation of the Spirit's presence that had not yet occurred in Samaria and that Luke equates with the "coming" or "receiving" of the Spirit.

The role of Simon in this narrative is equally complex. However, there is plenty of outside evidence that this Simon became a well-known opponent of the early Christians. Luke probably includes this material, therefore, to explain Simon's tenuous relationship with the Christian community and to indicate to his readers that Simon did not have divine or apostolic approval. Simon's final word seems ambiguous only if one is interested in early conversion stories. The whole of Luke's narrative, in fact, has a negative attitude toward Simon. Whether he was really saved or not is of no ultimate interest to the account. That he had a short time of contact with the church, at least as a professing believer, is of interest. But Peter's speech seems to reflect Luke's own judgment on Simon's Christianity—it was false!

We grant that exegesis of this kind, which pursues the *what* and *why* of Luke's narrative, is not necessarily devotionally exciting, but we would argue that it is the mandatory first step to the proper hearing of Acts as God's Word. Not every sentence in every narrative or speech is necessarily trying to tell *us* something. But every sentence in every narrative or speech contributes to what God is trying to say as a whole through Acts. In the process we can learn from the individual narratives about the variety of ways and people God uses to get his task accomplished.

THE HERMENEUTICS OF ACTS

As noted previously, our concern here is with one question: How do the individual narratives in Acts, or any other biblical narrative for that matter, function as precedents for the later church, or do they? Or to put it another way, does the book of Acts provide information that not only *describes* the primitive church but *speaks as a norm* to the church at all times? If so, how does one discover it or set up principles to aid in understanding it? If not, then what do we do with the concept of precedent? In short, just exactly what role does historical precedent play in Christian doctrine or in the understanding of Christian experience?

It must be noted at the outset that almost all biblical Christians tend to treat precedent as having normative authority to some degree or another. But it is seldom done with consistency. On the one hand, people tend to follow some narratives as establishing obligatory patterns while neglecting others; on the other hand, they sometimes tend to make one pattern mandatory when there is a complexity of patterns in Acts itself.

The following suggestions are not proposed as something absolute, but we hope they will help you come to grips with this hermeneutical problem.

Some General Principles

The crucial hermeneutical question here is whether biblical narratives that describe *what happened* in the early church also function as norms intended to delineate *what should or must happen* in the ongoing church. Are there instances from Acts of which one may appropriately say, "We *must* do this," or should one merely say, "We *may* do this"?

Our assumption, shared by many others, is this: *Unless Scripture explicitly tells us we must do something, what is only narrated or described does not function in a normative (i.e. obligatory) way—unless it can be demonstrated on other grounds that the author intended it to function in this way.* There are good reasons for making this assumption.

In general, doctrinal statements derived from Scripture fall into three (or four) categories: (1) Christian theology (what Christians *believe*), (2) Christian ethics (how Christians ought to *live* in relation to God and others), (3) Christian experience and Christian practice (what Christians *do* as religious/spiritual people). Within these categories one might further distinguish two levels of statements, which we will call primary and secondary. At the primary level are those doctrinal statements derived from the explicit propositions or imperatives of Scripture (i.e., what Scripture *intends* to teach). At the secondary level are those statements derived only incidentally, by implication or by precedent.

For example, in the category of Christian theology, such statements as God is one, God is love, all have sinned, Christ died for our sins, salvation is by grace, and Jesus Christ is divine are derived from passages where they are taught by intent and are therefore primary. At the secondary level are those statements that are the logical outflow of the primary statements or are derived by implication from Scripture. Thus the fact of the deity of Christ is primary; *how* the two natures (deity and humanity) concur in unity is secondary.

A similar distinction may be made with regard to the doctrine of Scripture. That it is the inspired Word of God is primary, based on a variety of affirmations within Scripture itself; the precise nature of this inspiration is secondary. This is not to say that the secondary statements are unimportant. Often they will have significant bearing on one's faith with regard to the primary statements. In fact, their ultimate theological value may be related to how well they preserve the integrity of the primary statements.

What is important to note here is that almost everything Christians derive from Scripture by way of precedent is in our third category—Christian experience or practice—and always at the secondary level. For example, that the Lord's Supper should be a continuing practice in the church is a primary-level statement. Jesus himself commands it; the Epistles and Acts bear witness to it. But the frequency of its observance—a place where Christians differ—is based on tradition and precedent; surely it is not binding. Scripture itself simply does not speak directly to this question. This also, we would argue, is the case with the necessity of baptism (primary) and its mode (secondary), or the practice of Christians "meeting together" (primary) and the frequency or the day of the week (secondary). Again, this is not to say that the secondary statements are unimportant. For example, one is surely hard-pressed to prove whether the day Christians meet to worship must be Saturday or Sunday, but in either case one is saying something of theological significance by one's practice.

Closely related to this discussion is the concept of intentionality. It is common among us to say, "Scripture teaches us that ..." Ordinarily people mean by this to say that something is "taught" by explicit statements. Problems with this arise when people move to the area of biblical history. Is something taught simply because it is recorded—even when it is recorded in what appears to be a favorable way?

It is a general maxim of hermeneutics that God's word is to be found in the *intent* of the Scripture. This is an especially crucial matter to the hermeneutics of the historical narratives. It is one thing for the historian to include an event because it serves the greater purpose of his work, and yet another thing for the interpreter to take that incident as having teaching value apart from the historian's larger intent.

Although Luke's inspired broader intent may be a moot point for some, it is our hypothesis, based on the preceding exegesis, that he was trying to show how the church emerged as a chiefly Gentile, worldwide phenomenon from its origins as a Jerusalem-based, Judaism-oriented sect of Jewish believers, and how the Holy Spirit was directly responsible for this phenomenon of universal salvation based on grace alone. The recurring motif that nothing can hinder this forward movement of the church empowered by the Holy Spirit makes us think that Luke also intended his readers to see this as a model for their existence. And the fact that Acts is in the canon further makes us think that surely this is the way the church was always intended to be—evangelistic, communal, joyful, empowered by the Holy Spirit.

But what of the specific details in these narratives, which only when taken all together help us to see Luke's larger intent? Do these details have the same teaching value? Do they also serve as normative models? We think not, basically because most such details are *incidental* to the main point of the narrative and because of the *ambiguity* of details from narrative to narrative.

Thus when we examined the narrative in Acts 6:1–7, we saw how it functioned in Luke's overall plan as a conclusion to his first major section, which at the same time served to introduce the Hellenists. It might also have been a part of his intent to show the amicable resolution of the first tension within the Christian community; in any case it is easy for us to read it in that way.

From this narrative we may also incidentally learn several other things. For example, one may learn that a good way to help a minority group in the church is to let that group have its own leadership, selected within. This is in fact what they did. *Must* we do it? Not necessarily, since Luke does not tell us so, nor is there any reason to believe that he had this in mind when he recorded the narrative. On the other hand, such a procedure makes such good sense one wonders why anyone would fight it.

Our point is that whatever else anyone gleans from such a story, such gleanings are incidental to Luke's intent. This does not mean that what is incidental has no theological value; it does mean that God's word *for us* in that narrative is primarily related to what it was *intended* to teach.

On the basis of this discussion the following principles emerge with regard to the hermeneutics of historical narrative:

1. The word of God in Acts that may be regarded as normative for Christians is related primarily to what any given narrative was *intended* to teach.

2. What is incidental to the primary intent of the narrative may indeed reflect an inspired authorial understanding, but it does not have the same teaching value as what the narrative was intended to teach. This does not negate what is incidental or imply that it has no relevance for us. What it does suggest is that what is incidental must not become primary, although it may always serve as additional support to what is unequivocally taught elsewhere.

3. Historical precedent, to have normative value, must be related to intent. That is, if it can be shown that the purpose of a given narrative is to *establish* precedent, then such precedent should be regarded as normative. For example, if it were to be demonstrated on exegetical grounds that Luke's intent in Acts 6:1–7 was to give the church a precedent for selecting its leaders, then such a selection process should be followed by later Christians. But if the establishing of precedent was not the intent of the narrative, then its value as a precedent for later Christians should be treated according to the specific principles suggested in our next section.

The problem with all of this, of course, is that it tends to leave us with little that is normative for two broad areas of concern—Christian experience and Christian practice. There is no express teaching on such matters as the *mode* of baptism, the *age* of those who are to be baptized, which charismatic phenomenon is to be in evidence when one receives the Spirit, or the frequency of the Lord's Supper, to cite but a few examples. Yet these are precisely the areas where there is so much division among Christians. Invariably, in such cases people argue that this is what *the earliest believers* did, whether such practices are merely described in the narratives of Acts or found by implication from what is said in the Epistles.

Scripture simply does not expressly command that baptism must be by immersion, or that infants are to be baptized, or that all genuine conversions must be as dramatic as Paul's, or that Christians are to be baptized in the Spirit evidenced by tongues as a second work of grace, or that the Lord's Supper is to be celebrated every Sunday. What do we do, then, with something like baptism by immersion? What *does* Scripture say? In this case it can be argued from the meaning of the word itself, from the one description of baptism in Acts of going "down into the water" and coming "up out of the water" (8:38–39), and from Paul's analogy of baptism as death, *burial*, and resurrection (Rom 6:1–3) that immersion was the *presupposition* of baptism in the early church. It was nowhere commanded precisely because it was presupposed.

On the other hand, it can be pointed out that without a baptismal tank in the local church in Samaria (!), the people who were baptized there would have had great difficulty being immersed. Geographically, there simply is no known supply of water there to have made immersion a viable option. Did they pour water over them, as an early church manual, the *Didache* (ca. AD 100), suggests should be done where there is not enough cold, running water or tepid, still water for immersion? We simply do not know, of course. The *Didache* makes it abundantly clear that immersion was the norm, but it also makes it clear that the act itself is far more important than the mode. Even though the *Didache* is not a biblical document, it is a very early, orthodox Christian document, and it may help us by showing how the early church made pragmatic adjustments in this area where Scripture is not explicit. The normal (regular) practice served as the norm. But because it was only *normal*, it did not become *normative*. We would probably do well to follow this lead and not confuse normalcy with normativeness in the sense that all Christians must do a given thing or else they are disobedient to God's Word.

Some Specific Principles

With these general observations and principles in view, we offer the following suggestions as to the hermeneutics of biblical precedents:

1. It is probably never valid to use an analogy based on biblical precedent as giving biblical authority for present-day actions. For example, Gideon's fleece has repeatedly been used as an analogy for finding God's will. Since God graciously condescended to Gideon's lack of trust, he may to others' as well, but there is no biblical authority or encouragement for such actions.

Likewise, on the basis of the narrative of Jesus' reception of the Spirit at his baptism, two different analogies have been drawn that move in quite different directions. Some see this as evidence for the believer's reception of the Spirit at baptism and thus as support by way of analogy for baptismal regeneration; by contrast, others see it as evidence for a baptism of the Holy Spirit subsequent to salvation (since Jesus had been earlier born of the Spirit).

There can be little question that Luke himself saw the event as the moment of empowering for Jesus' public ministry (cf. Luke 4:1, 14, 18; with Acts 10:38). But it is doubtful whether the narrative also functions well as an analogy for either of the later theological positions, especially when it is taken beyond mere analogy to become biblical support for either doctrine. Although Jesus' life is in many ways exemplary for later believers, not everything in his life can be normative for us. Thus while we are expected to live by taking up a cross, we are not expected to die by crucifixion and be raised three days later.

2. Although it may not have been the author's primary purpose, biblical narratives do have illustrative and (sometimes) "pattern" value. In fact, this is how the New Testament people occasionally used certain historical precedents from the Old Testament. Paul, for example, used some Old Testament examples as warnings to those who had a false security in their divine election (1 Cor 10:1–13), and Jesus used the example of David as an historical precedent to justify his disciples' Sabbath actions (Matt 12:1–8 // Mark 2:23–28 // Luke 6:1–5).

But none of us have God's authority to reproduce the sort of exegesis and analogical analyses that the New Testament authors occasionally applied to the Old Testament. It should be noted, especially in cases where the precedent justifies a present action, that *the precedent does not establish a norm for specific action*. People are not to eat regularly of the showbread or to pluck grain on the Sabbath to show that the Sabbath was made for people. Rather, the precedent illustrates a principle with regard to the Sabbath.

A warning is in order here. If one wishes to use a biblical precedent to justify some present action, one is on safer ground if the principle of the action is taught elsewhere, where it is the primary intent so to teach. For example, to use Jesus' cleansing of the temple to justify one's so-called righteous indignation—usually a euphemism for selfish anger—is to abuse this principle. On the other hand, one may properly base the present-day experience of speaking in tongues not only on the precedent of repeated occurrences (in Acts) but also on the teaching about spiritual gifts in 1 Corinthians 12–14.

3. In matters of Christian experience, and even more so of Christian practice, biblical precedents may sometimes be regarded as *repeatable patterns*—even if they are not understood to be normative. That is, for many practices there seems to be full justification for the later church's repeating of biblical patterns; but it is moot to argue that all Christians in every place and every time *must* repeat the pattern or they are disobedient to God's Word. This is especially true when the practice itself is mandatory but the mode is not. (It should be noted that not all Christians would be fully in agreement with this way of stating things. Some movements and denominations were founded partly on the premise that virtually all New Testament patterns should be restored as fully as possible in modern times; over the years they have developed a considerable hermeneutic of the mandatory nature of much that is only narrated in Acts. Others, similarly, would argue that Luke himself intended, for example, for the reception of the Spirit to be evidenced by the accompanying gift of tongues. But in both these cases the question rests finally not so much on the rightness or wrongness of the present principle but on the interpretation of Acts and of Luke's overall—as well as specific—intent in his telling of the story.)

The decision as to whether certain practices or patterns are repeatable should be guided by the following considerations. First, the strongest possible case can be made when only one pattern is found (although one must be careful not to make too much of silence), and when this pattern is repeated within the New Testament itself. Second, when there is an ambiguity of patterns or when a pattern occurs but once, it is repeatable for later Christians only if it appears to have divine approbation or is in harmony with what is taught elsewhere in Scripture. Third, what is culturally conditioned is either not repeatable at all or must be translated into the new or differing culture.

Thus, on the basis of these principles, one can make a very strong case for immersion as the mode of baptism, a weaker case for the observance of the Lord's Supper each Sunday, but almost no case at all for infant baptism (this may, of course, be argued from historical precedent in the church but not so easily from biblical precedent, which is the issue here). By the same token, the Christian minister's function as a priest (on the basis of Old Testament analogy!) fails on all counts in terms of its biblical base.

We do not imagine ourselves hereby to have solved all the problems, but we think these are workable suggestions, and we hope they will cause you to think exegetically and with greater hermeneutical precision as you read the biblical narratives.

CHAPTER 7

The Gospels: One Story, Many Dimensions

As with the Epistles and Acts, the Gospels seem at first glance easy enough to interpret. Since the materials in the Gospels may be divided roughly into sayings and narratives, that is, teachings *of* Jesus and stories *about* Jesus, one should theoretically be able to follow the principles for interpreting the Epistles for the one and the principles for historical narratives for the other.

In a sense this is true. However, it is not quite that easy. The four gospels form a unique literary genre for which there are few real analogies. Their uniqueness, which we will examine momentarily, is what presents most of our exegetical problems. But there are some hermeneutical difficulties as well. Some of these, of course, take the form of those several "hard sayings" in the Gospels. But the major hermeneutical difficulty lies with understanding "the kingdom of God," a term that is absolutely crucial to the whole of Jesus' ministry, yet at the same time is presented in the language and concepts of first-century Judaism. The problem is how to translate these ideas into more contemporary cultural settings.

THE NATURE OF THE GOSPELS

Almost all the difficulties one encounters in interpreting the Gospels stem from two obvious facts: (1) Jesus himself did not write a gospel; they were written by others, and thus do not come directly from him. (2) There are four gospels, three of which have remarkable similarities, while that by John tells the story in a quite different way.

1. The fact that the four gospels do not come from Jesus himself is a very important consideration. Had he written something, of course, it would probably have looked less like our Gospels and more like the Old Testament Prophetic Books, such as Amos for example—a collection of spoken oracles and sayings, plus a few brief personal narratives (Amos 7:10–17). Our Gospels do indeed contain collections of sayings, but these are always woven, as an integral part, into a historical narrative of Jesus' life and ministry. Thus they are not books *by* Jesus but books *about* Jesus, which at the same time contain a large collection of various sayings and teachings.

The difficulty this presents to us should not be overstated, but it is there and needs to be addressed. The nature of this difficulty might best be seen by noting an analogy from Paul in Acts and his epistles. If we did not have Acts, for example, we could piece together some of the elements of Paul's life from the epistles, but such a presentation would be meager. Likewise, if we did not have his epistles, our understanding of Paul's theology based solely on his speeches in Acts would likewise be meager—and somewhat out of balance. For key items in Paul's life, therefore, we read Acts and feed into this the information found in his epistles. For his teaching we do not first go to Acts but to the epistles, and to Acts as an additional source.

But the Gospels are *not* like Acts, for here we have both a narrative of Jesus' life and large blocks of his sayings (teachings) as an absolutely basic part of that life. But the sayings were not *written* by him, as the epistles were by Paul. Jesus' native tongue was Aramaic, which appears only once, in his cry from the cross; his teachings thus come to us only in Greek. Moreover, the same saying frequently occurs in two or three of the gospels, and even when it occurs in the exact chronological sequence or historical setting, it is seldom found with exactly the same wording in each.

To some this reality can be threatening, but it need not be. It is true, of course, that certain kinds of scholarship have distorted this reality in such a way as to suggest that nothing in the four gospels is trustworthy. But this is a historically problematic conclusion. Equally good scholarship has demonstrated the historical reliability of the gospel materials.

Our point here is a simple one: God gave us what we know about Jesus' earthly ministry in *this* way, not in another way that might better suit someone's mechanistic, tape-recorder mentality. And in any case the fact that the Gospels were not written by Jesus but about him, including many things said by him, is a part of their genius, we would argue, not their weakness.

2. Then there are four of them. How did this happen, and why? After all, we do not have four Acts of the Apostles. Moreover, the materials in the first three gospels are so often alike we call them the Synoptic ("common-view") Gospels. Indeed, one might wonder why retain Mark at all, since the amount of material found exclusively in his gospel would scarcely fill two pages of print. But again, the fact that there are four, we believe, is a part of their genius.

So what is the nature of the Gospels, and why is their unique nature part of their genius? This can best be answered by first speaking to the question, why four? From our distance we can hardly give an absolutely certain answer to this, but at least one of the reasons is a simple and pragmatic one: different Christian communities each had need for a book about Jesus. For a variety of reasons the gospel written for one community or group of believers did not necessarily meet all the needs in another community. So one was written first (Mark in the most widely accepted view), and that gospel was "rewritten" twice (Matthew and Luke) for considerably different reasons, to meet considerably different needs. Independently of them (again, in the most widely accepted view) John wrote a gospel of a different kind for still another set of reasons. All of this, we believe, was orchestrated by the Holy Spirit.

For the later church, none of the four gospels supersedes the other, but each stands beside the others as equally valuable and equally authoritative. How so? Because in each case *the interest in Jesus is at two levels.* First, there was the purely historical concern that this is who Jesus was and this is what he said and did; and *this* is the Jesus—crucified and raised from the dead—whom we now worship as the risen and exalted Lord. Second, there was the existential concern of retelling this story for the needs of later communities that did not speak Aramaic but Greek, and that did not live in a basically rural, agricultural, and Jewish setting, but in Rome, or Ephesus, or Antioch, where the gospel was encountering an urban, pagan environment.

In a certain sense, therefore, the four gospels are already functioning as hermeneutical models for us, insisting by their very nature that we, too, retell the same story in our own twenty-first-century contexts.

Thus these books, which tell us virtually all we know about Jesus, are nonetheless not biographies—although they are partly biographical. Nor are they like the contemporary lives of great men—although they record the life of the greatest man of all time. They are, to use the phrase of the second-century church father Justin Martyr, "the memoirs of the apostles." Four biographies could not stand side by side as of equal value; these books stand side by side because at one and the same time they record the facts *about* Jesus, recall the teaching *of* Jesus, and bear witness *to* Jesus. This is their nature and their genius, and this is important both for exegesis and for hermeneutics.

Exegesis of the four gospels, therefore, requires us to think both in terms of the historical setting of Jesus and the historical setting of the authors.

THE HISTORICAL CONTEXT

You will recall that the first task of exegesis is to have an awareness of the historical context. This means not only to know the historical context in general but also to form a tentative, but informed, reconstruction of the situation that the author is addressing. This can become complex at times because of the nature of the Gospels as two-level documents. Historical context first of all has to do with Jesus himself. This includes both an awareness of the culture and religion of the first century, Palestinian Judaism, in which he lived and taught, as well as an attempt to understand the particular context of a given saying or parable. But historical context also has to do with the individual authors (the evangelists) and their reasons for writing.

We are aware that trying to think about these various contexts can be an imposing task for the ordinary reader. Furthermore, we are aware that there is probably more speculative scholarship that goes on here than anywhere else in New Testament studies. Nonetheless, the *nature* of the Gospels is a given; they are two-level documents, whether one likes it or not. We do not begin to think that we can make you an expert in these matters. Our hope here is simply to raise your awareness level so that you will have a greater appreciation for what the Gospels are, as well as a good grasp of the kinds of questions you need to ask as you read them.

The Historical Context of Jesus — in General

It is imperative to the understanding of Jesus that a reader becomes immersed in the first-century Judaism of which Jesus was a part. And this means far more than knowing that the Sadducees did not believe in resurrection (and thus they were "sad, you see"). One needs to know *why* they did not believe and *why* Jesus had so little contact with them.

For this kind of background information there is simply no alternative to some good outside reading. Either one or both of the following books would be of great usefulness in this regard: Everett Ferguson, *Backgrounds of Early Christianity,* 2d edition (Grand Rapids: Eerdmans, 1993), pp. 373–546; Joachim Jeremias, *Jerusalem in the Time of Jesus* (Philadelphia: Fortress, 1969).

An important feature of this dimension of the historical context, but often overlooked, has to do with the *form* of Jesus' teaching. Everyone knows that Jesus frequently taught in parables. What people are less aware of is that he used a whole variety of such forms. For example, he was a master of purposeful overstatement (hyperbole). For instance, at one point Jesus tells his disciples to gouge out an offending eye or cut off an offending arm (Matt 5:29–30 // Mark 9:43–48). Now we all know that Jesus "did not really mean that." What he meant was that people are to do "surgery" on themselves regarding anything that causes them to sin. But how do we know that he did not really mean what he said? Because we can all recognize overstatement as a most effective teaching technique in which we are to take the teacher for what he means, not for what he says!

Jesus also made effective use of proverbs (e.g., Matt 6:21; Mark 3:24), similes and metaphors (e.g., Matt 10:16; 5:13), poetry (e.g., Matt 7:6–8; Luke 6:27–28), questions (e.g., Matt 17:25), and irony (e.g., Matt 16:2–3), to name a few. For further information on this as well as other matters in this chapter, you would do well to read Robert H. Stein's *The Method and Message of Jesus' Teaching* (Louisville, Ky.: Westminster John Knox, 1994).

The Historical Context of Jesus — in Particular

This is a more difficult aspect in the attempt to reconstruct the historical context of Jesus, mostly because so many of his teachings are presented in the four gospels with very little context.

The reason for this is that Jesus' words and deeds were handed on orally during a period of perhaps thirty years or more, during which time whole gospels did not yet exist. Rather, the content of the Gospels was being passed on in individual stories and sayings (called "pericopes," *pe-RI-co-pees*). Many of Jesus' sayings were also transmitted along with their original contexts. Scholars have come to call such pericopes "pronouncement stories," because the narrative itself exists only for the sake of the saying that concludes it. In a typical pronouncement story (Mark 12:13–17) the context is a question about paying taxes to the Romans. It concludes with Jesus' famous pronouncement, "Give back to Caesar what is Caesar's and to God what is God's." Can you imagine what we might have done in reconstructing an original context for that saying if it had not been transmitted with its original context?

The real difficulty, of course, comes with the fact that so many of Jesus' sayings and teachings were transmitted without their contexts. Paul himself bears witness to this reality. Three times he cites sayings of Jesus (1 Cor 7:10; 9:14; Acts 20:35) without alluding to their original historical contexts—nor should we have expected him to. Of these sayings, the two in 1 Corinthians are also found in the Gospels. The divorce saying is found in two different contexts (that of teaching disciples in Matt 5:31–32, and that of controversy in Matt 10:1–19 and Mark 10:1–12). The "right to remuneration" saying is found in Matthew 10:10 and its parallel in Luke 10:7 in the context of sending out the Twelve (Matthew) and the seventy-two (Luke). But the saying in Acts is not found in any of the Gospels, so for us it is totally without an original context.

It should not surprise us, therefore, to learn that many such sayings (without contexts) were available to the evangelists, and that it was the evangelists themselves, under their own guidance of the Spirit, who put the sayings in their present contexts. This is one of the reasons we often find the same saying or teaching in different contexts in the four gospels—and also why sayings with similar themes or the same subject matter are often grouped in a topical way.

Matthew, for example, has five large topical collections (each concludes with something like, "When Jesus had finished saying these things ..." 7:28): life in the kingdom (the so-called Sermon on the Mount, chs. 5–7); instructions for the ministers of the kingdom (10:5–42); parables of the kingdom at work in the world (13:1–52); teaching on relationships and discipline in the kingdom (18:1–35); and eschatology, or the consummation of the kingdom (chs. 23–25).

That these are Matthean collections can be illustrated in two ways from the collection in chapter 10. (1) The context is the historical mission of the Twelve and Jesus' instructions to them as he sent them out (vv. 5–12). The instructions that follow a bit later (vv. 16–20), however, are for a much later time, since earlier they had been told to go only to the lost sheep of Israel (vv. 5–6), while later Jesus speaks of their being brought before "governors and kings" and "the Gentiles," and none of these were included in the original mission of the Twelve. (2) These nicely arranged sayings in Matthew are found scattered all over Luke's gospel in this order: 9:2–5; 10:3; 21:12–17; 12:11–12; 6:40; 12:2–9; 12:51–53; 14:25–27; 17:33; 10:16. This suggests that Luke also had access to most of these sayings as separate units, which he then put in different contexts, as he was also being led by the Spirit.

Thus as you read the four gospels, one of the questions you will want to ask, even if it cannot be answered for certain, is whether Jesus' audience for a given teaching was his close disciples, the larger crowds, or his opponents. Discovering the historical context of Jesus, or who his audience was, will not necessarily affect the basic meaning of a given saying, but it will broaden your perspective and often help you understand *the point* of what Jesus said.

The Historical Context of the Evangelist

At this point we are not talking about the literary context in which each evangelist has placed his Jesus materials but about the historical context of each author that prompted him to write a gospel in the first place. Again we are involved in a certain amount of scholarly guesswork since the Gospels themselves are anonymous (in the sense that their authors are not identified by name) and we cannot be sure of their places of origin. But we can be fairly sure of each evangelist's interest and concerns by the way he selected, shaped, and arranged his materials.

Mark's gospel, for example, is especially interested in explaining the nature of Jesus' messiahship in light of Isaiah's "second exodus" motif (see *How to 2*, pp. 299–80). Although Mark knows that the Messiah is the strong Son of God (1:1), who moves through Galilee with power and compassion (1:1–8:26), he also knows that Jesus repeatedly kept his messiahship hidden (e.g., 1:34; 1:43; 3:12; 4:11; 5:43; 7:24; 7:36; 8:26; 8:30). The reason for this silence is that only Jesus understands the true nature of his messianic destiny—that of Isaiah's "Suffering Servant" who conquers through death. Although this is explained three times to the disciples, they too fail to understand (8:27–33; 9:30–32; 10:32–45). Like the twice-touched man (8:22–26), they need a second touch—the resurrection—for them to see clearly.

That Mark's concern is the suffering-servant nature of Jesus' messiahship is even more evident from the fact that he does not include any of Jesus' teaching on discipleship until after the first explanation of his own suffering (8:31–33). The implication, as well as the explicit teaching, is clear: the cross and servant-hood that Jesus experienced are also the marks of genuine discipleship. As the hymn by Horatius Bonar put it: "It is the way the Master went; should not the servant tread it still?"

All of this can be seen by a careful reading of Mark's gospel. This is his historical context in general. To place it specifically is more conjectural, but we see no reason not to follow the very ancient tradition that says that Mark's gospel reflects the "memoirs" of Peter and that it appeared in Rome shortly after the latter's martyrdom, at a time of great suffering among the Christians in Rome. In any case, such contextual reading and studying is as important for the Gospels as it is for the Epistles.

THE LITERARY CONTEXT

We have already touched on the literary context somewhat in the section "The Historical Context of Jesus—in Particular." The literary context has to do with the place of a given pericope in the context of any one of the gospels, that is, where the evangelists chose to put the deeds and teaching. To some extent this context was probably already fixed by its original historical context, which may have been known to the evangelist. But as we have already seen, many of the materials in the four gospels owe their present context to the evangelists themselves, according to their own inspiration by the Spirit.

Our concern here is twofold: (1) to help you read (or exegete) with understanding a given saying or narrative in its present context, and (2) to help you understand the nature of the composition of the gospels as wholes, and thus to interpret any one of the Gospels itself (as in *How to 2*), not just isolated facts about the life of Jesus.

Interpreting the Individual Pericopes

In discussing how to interpret the Epistles, we noted that one must learn to "think paragraphs." This is not quite so important with the Gospels, although it will still hold true from time to time, especially with the large blocks of teachings. As we noted at the outset, these teaching sections will indeed have some similarities to our approach with the Epistles. Because of the unique nature of the Gospels, however, you must do two things here: think horizontally, and think vertically.

This is simply our way of saying that, when interpreting or reading one of the gospels, one needs to keep in mind the two realities noted above: that there are four of them, and that they are "two-level" documents.

Think Horizontally

To think horizontally means that when studying a pericope in any one gospel, it is usually helpful to be aware of the parallels in the other gospels. To be sure, this point must not be overdrawn, since none of the evangelists intended his gospel to be read in parallel with the others. Nonetheless, the fact that God has provided four gospels in the canon means that they cannot be read totally in isolation from one another.

Our first word here is one of caution. The purpose of studying the Gospels in parallel is not to fill out the story in one gospel with details from the others. Usually such a reading of the Gospels tends to harmonize all the details and thus blur the very distinctives in each gospel that the Holy Spirit inspired. Such "filling out" may interest us at the level of the historical Jesus, but that is *not* the canonical level, which should be our first concern. Again, our interest lies at two levels: that of Jesus himself in his own context, and that of the author of the gospel, written with his original readers in view.

The basic reasons for thinking horizontally are two. First, the parallels will often give us an appreciation for the distinctives of any one of the gospels. After all, it is precisely their distinctives that are the reason for having four gospels in the first place. Second, the parallels will help us to be aware of the different kinds of contexts in which the same or similar materials lived in the ongoing church. We will illustrate each of these, but first consider this important word about presuppositions.

It is impossible to read the four gospels without having some kind of presupposition about their relationships to one another—even if you have never thought about it. The most common presupposition, but the one least likely to be true, is that each gospel was written independently of the others. There is simply too much clear evidence against this for it to be a live option for you as you read.

Take, for example, the fact that there is such a high degree of verbal similarity among Matthew, Mark, and Luke in their *narratives*, as well as in their recording of the sayings of Jesus. Remarkable verbal similarities should not surprise us about the *sayings* of the one who spoke as no one ever did (John 7:46). But for this to carry over to the narratives is something else again—especially so when one considers (1) that these stories were first told in Aramaic, yet we are talking about the use of Greek words; (2) that Greek word order is extremely free, yet often the similarities extend even to precise word order; and (3) that it is highly unlikely that three people in three different parts of the Roman Empire would tell the same story with the same words—even to such minor points of individual style as prepositions and conjunctions. Yet this is what happens over and again in the first three gospels.

This can easily be illustrated from the narrative of the feeding of the five thousand, which is one of the few stories found in all four gospels. Note the following statistics:

1. Number of words used to tell the story
   Matthew 157
   Mark   194
   Luke   153
   John   199
2. Number of words common to *all* of the first three gospels: 53
3. Number of words John has in common with all the others: 8 (five, two, five thousand, took loaves, twelve baskets of pieces)

4. Percentages of agreement

Matthew with Mark	59.0 percent
Matthew with Luke	44.0 percent
Luke with Mark	40.0 percent
John with Matthew	8.5 percent
John with Mark	8.5 percent
John with Luke	6.5 percent

The following conclusions seem inevitable: John represents a clearly *independent* telling of the story. He uses only those words absolutely necessary in order to tell the same story, and even uses a different Greek word for "fish"! The other three are just as clearly *interdependent*. Those who know Greek recognize how improbable it is for two people independently to tell the same story in narrative form and have a 60 percent agreement in the words used, let alone in the exact word order.

Take as a further example the words from Mark 13:14 and the parallel in Matthew 24:15. ("Let the reader understand"). These words can hardly have been a part of the *oral* tradition (it says "reader," not "hearer," and since in its earliest form [which is Mark's account] there is no mention of Daniel, it is unlikely that Jesus himself mentioned Daniel). The words were therefore inserted into the saying of Jesus by one of the evangelists (Matthew) for the sake of his readers. It seems highly improbable that exactly the same parenthesis would have been inserted independently at exactly the same point by two authors writing independently.

The best explanation of all the data is the one we suggested earlier—that Mark wrote his gospel first, probably in part at least from his recollection of Peter's preaching and teaching. Luke and Matthew had access to Mark's gospel and independently used it as the basic source for their own. But they also had access to all kinds of other material about Jesus, some of which they had in common. This common material, however, is scarcely ever presented in the same order in the two gospels, a fact suggesting that neither one had access to the other's writing. Finally, John wrote independently of the other three, and thus his gospel has little material in common with them. This, we would note, is *how* the Holy Spirit inspired the writing of the Gospels.

That this will help you interpret the Gospels can be seen from the following brief sample from the NRSV. Notice how the saying of Jesus on the "desolating sacrilege" appears when read in parallel columns:

Matthew 24:15–16	Mark 13:14	Luke 21:20–21
So when you see	But when you see	When you see Jerusalem surrounded by armies, then know that
the desolating	the desolating	its desolation has come near.
sacrilege standing in the holy place, as was spoken by the prophet Daniel	sacrilege set up where it ought not to be	
(let the reader understand),	(let the reader understand),	
then	then	Then
those in Judea must flee	those in Judea must flee	those in Judea must flee
to the mountains;	to the mountains;	to the mountains, and

It should be noted first of all that this saying is in the Olivet Discourse in exactly the same sequence in all three gospels. When Mark recorded these words, he was calling his readers to a thoughtful reflection as to what Jesus meant by "the desolating sacrilege set up where it ought not to be." Matthew, also inspired by the Spirit, helped his readers by making the saying a little more explicit. The "desolating sacrilege," he reminds them, was spoken about by Daniel, and what Jesus meant by "where it ought not to be" was "the holy place" (the temple in Jerusalem). Luke, equally inspired of the Spirit, simply interpreted the whole saying for the sake of his Gentile readers. He really lets them understand! What Jesus meant by all this was, "When you see Jerusalem surrounded by armies, then know that its desolation has come near."

Thus one can see how thinking horizontally and knowing that Matthew and Luke used Mark can help you to interpret any one of the gospels as you read it. Similarly, awareness of gospel parallels also helps you to see how the same materials sometimes came to be used in new contexts in the ongoing church.

Take, for another example, Jesus' lament over Jerusalem, which is one of those sayings Matthew and Luke have in common that is not found in Mark. The saying appears nearly word for word in both gospels, but in quite different settings in each. In Luke it appears (13:34–35) in a long collection of narratives and teaching as Jesus is on his way to Jerusalem (9:51–19:44; see *How to 2*, pp. 292–94). It immediately follows the warning about Herod, which Jesus has concluded with his reply, "for surely no prophet can die outside Jerusalem!" The rejection of God's messenger leads to judgment on Israel.

In Matthew it appears as a lament (23:37–39) that concludes a collection of seven woes Jesus pronounced on the Pharisees (23:13–39), the final one of which reflects the theme of the prophets being killed in Jerusalem. You should note that the saying has the same point in both gospels, even though it is placed in different settings.

The same is true of many other sayings as well. The Lord's Prayer is set in both gospels (Matt 6:7–13; Luke 11:2–4) in contexts of teaching on prayer, although the main thrust of each section is considerably different. Note also that in Matthew it serves as a model, "This, then, is how you should pray"; in Luke repetition is encouraged, "When you pray, say ..." Likewise note the Beatitudes (Matt 5:3–11; Luke 6:20–23). In Matthew "the poor" are "the poor in spirit"; in Luke they are simply "you who are poor" (6:20) in contrast to "you who are rich" (6:24). On such points most people tend to have only half a canon. Traditional evangelicals tend to read only "the poor in spirit"; social activists tend to read only "you who are poor." We insist that *both* are canonical and serve as God's word to us. In a truly profound sense the real poor are those who recognize themselves as impoverished before God. But the God of the Bible, who became incarnate in Jesus of Nazareth, is a God who pleads the cause of the oppressed and the disenfranchised. One can scarcely read Luke's gospel without recognizing his interest in this aspect of the divine revelation (see 14:12–14; cf. 12:33–34 with the Matthean parallel, 6:19–21; on this point also see *How to 2*, p. 292).

Finally, if you are interested in the serious study of the Gospels, you will need to refer to a synopsis (a presentation of the gospels in parallel columns). The very best of these is edited by Kurt Aland, titled *Synopsis of the Four Gospels* (New York: United Bible Societies, 1975).

Think Vertically

To think vertically means that when reading or studying a narrative or teaching in the Gospels, one should try to be aware of both historical contexts—that of Jesus and that of the evangelist.

Again, our first word here is one of caution. The purpose of thinking vertically is not primarily to study the life of the historical Jesus. That indeed should always be of interest to us. But the *Gospels in their present form* are the word of God to us; our own *reconstructions* of Jesus' life are not. And again, one should not overdo this kind of thinking. It is only a call for the awareness that many of the gospel materials owe their present context to the evangelists, and that good interpretation may require appreciating a given saying first in its original historical context as a proper prelude to understanding that same word in its present canonical context.

We may illustrate this from a passage like Matthew 20:1–16, Jesus' parable of the workers in the vineyard. Our concern is what does this mean in its present context in Matthew? If we first think horizontally, we will note that on either side of the parable Matthew has long sections of material in which he follows Mark very closely (Matt 19:1–30; 20:17–34 parallels Mark 10:1–52). At 10:31, Mark had the saying, "Many who are first will be last, and the last first," which Matthew kept intact at 19:30. But right at that point he then inserted this parable, which concluded with a repetition of this particular saying (20:16), only now in reverse order. Thus in Matthew's gospel the immediate context for the parable is the saying about the reversal of order between the first and the last.

When you look at the parable proper (20:1–15), you will note that it concludes with the landowner's justification of his generosity. Pay in the kingdom, Jesus says, is not predicated on what's fair, but on God's grace! In its original context this parable probably served to justify Jesus' own accepting of sinners in light of the Pharisees' finding fault with him. They think of themselves as having "borne the burden of the work" and hence worthy of more pay. But God is generous and gracious, and he freely accepts sinners just as he does the "righteous."

Given this as its most likely original setting, how does the parable now function in Matthew's gospel? The point of the parable, God's gracious generosity to the undeserving, certainly remains the same. But that point is no longer a concern to justify Jesus' own actions. Matthew's gospel does that elsewhere in other ways. Here the parable functions in a context of discipleship, where those who have forsaken all to follow Jesus are the last who have become first (perhaps indeed in contrast to the Jewish leaders, a point Matthew makes repeatedly).

Many times, of course, thinking vertically will reveal that the same point is being made at both levels. But the illustration just given shows how fruitful such thinking can be for exegesis.

Interpreting the Gospels as Wholes

An important part of the literary context is to learn to see the kinds of concerns that have gone into the composition of the Gospels that makes each one of them unique.

We have noted throughout this chapter that in reading and studying the Gospels one must take seriously not only the evangelists' interest in Jesus per se—what he did and said—but also their reasons for retelling the one story for their own readers. The evangelists, we have noted, were authors, not merely compilers. But being authors does not mean they were creators of the material; quite the opposite is true. Several factors prohibit greater creativity, including the fact that these were *the words of Jesus*, for whom they had given up everything to follow, and the somewhat fixed nature of the material in the transmission process. Thus they were authors in the sense that, with the Spirit's help, they creatively structured and rewrote the material to meet the needs of their readers. What concerns us here is to help you to be aware of each of the evangelist's compositional concerns and techniques as you read or study.

There were three principles at work in the composition of the Gospels: selectivity, arrangement, and adaptation. On the one hand, the evangelists *selected* those narratives and teachings that suited their purposes. It is true, of course, that simple concern for the preservation of what was available to them may have been one of those purposes. Nonetheless, John, who has fewer but considerably more expanded narratives and discourses, specifically tells us he has been very selective (20:30–31; 21:25). This last word, the final word in his gospel and spoken in hyperbole ("I suppose that even the whole world would not have room for the books that would be written"), probably expresses the case for the others as well. Luke, for example, chose not to include a considerable section of Mark (6:45 – 8:26).

At the same time the evangelists and their churches had special interests that also caused them to *arrange* and *adapt* what was selected. John, for example, distinctly tells us that his purpose was patently theological: "that you may believe that Jesus is the Messiah, the Son of God" (20:31). This interest in Jesus as the Jewish Messiah is probably the chief reason that the vast majority of his material has to do with Jesus' ministry in Judea and Jerusalem, over against the almost totally Galilean ministry in the Synoptics. For Jews, the Messiah's true home was Jerusalem. Thus John knows of Jesus having said that a prophet has no honor in his own home or country. This was originally said at the time of Jesus' rejection at Nazareth (Matt 13:57; Mark 6:4; Luke 4:24). In John's gospel this saying is referred to as an explanation for the Messiah's rejection in Jerusalem (4:44) — a profound theological insight into Jesus' ministry.

The principle of adaptation is also what explains most of the so-called discrepancies among the Gospels. One of the most noted of these, for example, is the cursing of the fig tree (Mark 11:12 – 14, 20 – 25; Matt 21:18 – 22). In Mark's gospel the story is told for its symbolic theological significance. Note that between the cursing and the withering, Jesus pronounces a similar judgment on Judaism by his cleansing of the temple. However, the story of the fig tree had great meaning for the early church also because of the lesson on faith that concludes it. In Matthew's gospel the lesson on faith is the sole interest of the story, so he relates the cursing and the withering together in order to emphasize this point. Remember, in each case this telling of the story is the work of the Holy Spirit, who inspired *both* evangelists.

To illustrate this process of composition on a somewhat larger scale, let us look at the opening chapters of Mark (1:14 – 3:6). These chapters are an artistic masterpiece, so well-constructed that many readers will probably get Mark's point even though not recognizing how he has done it.

There are three strands to Jesus' public ministry that are of special interest to Mark: popularity with the crowds, discipleship for the few, and opposition from the authorities. Notice how skillfully, by selecting and arranging narratives, Mark sets these before us. After the announcement of Jesus' public ministry (1:14 – 15), the first narrative records the call of the first disciples. This motif will be elaborated in the next sections (3:13–19; 4:10–12; 4:34–41; et al.); his greater concern in these first two chapters is with the other two items. Beginning with verse 21, Mark has just four periscopes: a day in Capernaum (1:21–28 and 29–34), a short preaching tour the next day (1:35–39), and the story of the healing of the leper (1:40–45). The common motif throughout is the rapid spread of Jesus' fame and popularity (see vv. 27–28, 32–33, 37, 45), which culminates with Jesus not being able to "enter a town openly.... Yet the people still came to him from everywhere." It all seems breathtaking; yet Mark has painted this picture with only four narratives, plus his repeated phrase "and immediately" (or variations [1:21, 23, 28, 29, 30, 42 NASB]) and his starting almost every sentence with "and" (note that for the purposes of good English both of these features are obscured in contemporary translations, including the NKJV!).

With this picture before us Mark next selects five different kinds of narratives that, all together, paint the picture of opposition and give the reasons for it. Notice that the common denominator of the first four pericopes is the question *why?* (2:7, 16, 18, 24). Opposition comes because Jesus forgives sin, eats with sinners, neglects the tradition of fasting, and "breaks" the Sabbath. That this last item was considered by Jesus' contemporaries to be the ultimate insult to their tradition is made clear by Mark's appending a second narrative of this kind (3:1–6).

We do not mean to suggest that in all the sections of the four gospels one will be able to trace the evangelist's compositional concerns so easily. But we do suggest that this is the kind of looking at the Gospels that is needed for a more comprehensive understanding.

SOME HERMENEUTICAL OBSERVATIONS

For the most part the hermeneutical principles for the Gospels are a combination of what has been said in previous chapters about the Epistles and historical narratives.

The Teachings and Imperatives

Given that one's exegesis has been done with care, the teachings and imperatives of Jesus in the Gospels should be brought into the twenty-first century in the same way as we do with Paul—or Peter or James—in the Epistles. Even the questions of cultural relativity need to be raised in the same way. Divorce is scarcely a valid option for couples, both of whom would be followers of Jesus—a point repeated by Paul (1 Cor 7:10–11). But in a culture such as postmodern, English-speaking North America, where one out of two adult converts will have been divorced, the question of remarriage should probably not be decided mindlessly and without redemptive concern for new converts. One's early assumptions about the meaning of the words of Jesus spoken in an entirely different cultural setting must be carefully examined. Likewise, we will scarcely have a Roman soldier forcing us to go a mile (Matt 5:41). But in this case Jesus' point, what one might call the "Christian extra," is surely applicable in any number of comparable situations.

A further important word needs to be said here. Because many of Jesus' imperatives are set in the context of expounding the Old Testament law and because to many people they seem to present an impossible ideal, a variety of hermeneutical ploys have been offered to "get around" them as normative authority for the church. We cannot take the time here to outline and refute these various attempts, but a few words are in order. (An excellent overview is given in chapter 6 of Stein's *The Method and Message of Jesus' Teachings*.)

Most of these hermeneutical ploys arose because the imperatives seem like law—and such an impossible law at that! And Christian life according to the New Testament is based on God's grace, not on obedience to law. But to see the imperatives as law is to misunderstand them. They are *not* law in the sense that one must obey them *in order to* become or remain a Christian; our salvation does not depend on perfect obedience to them. Rather, they are descriptions, by way of imperative, of what Christian life should be like *because of* God's prior acceptance of us. A no-retaliation ethic (Matt 5:38–42) is, in fact, the ethic of the kingdom—for this present age. But it is predicated on God's nonretaliatory love for us; and in the kingdom it is to be "like Father, like child" (see Matt 5:48). It is our experience of God's unconditional, unlimited forgiveness that comes first, but it is to be followed by an unconditional, unlimited forgiveness of others. Someone has said that, in Christianity, religion is grace; ethics is gratitude. Hence Jesus' imperatives are a word for us, but they are not like the Old

Testament law. They describe the lived-out love of our new life as God's loved and redeemed children—a love that is not optional, of course!

The Narratives

The narratives tend to function in more than one way in the Gospels. The miracle stories, for example, are not recorded to offer morals or to serve as precedents. Rather, they function as vital illustrations of the power of the kingdom breaking in through Jesus' own ministry. In a circuitous way they may illustrate faith, fear, or failure, but this is not their primary function. However, stories such as the wealthy man (Matt 19:16–22 // Mark 10:17–22 // Luke 18:18–23) and the request to sit at Jesus' right hand (Matt 20:20–28 // Mark 10:35–45 // Luke 22:24–27) are placed in a context of teaching, where the story itself serves as an illustration of what is being taught. It seems to us to be the proper hermeneutical practice to use these narratives in precisely the same way.

Thus the point of the wealthy man narrative is not that all Jesus' disciples must sell all their possessions to follow him. There are clear examples in the Gospels where that was not the case (cf. Luke 5:27–30; 8:3; Mark 14:3–9). The story instead illustrates the point of how difficult it is for the rich to enter the kingdom precisely because they have prior commitments to wealth as such and are trying to secure their lives thereby. But God's gracious love can perform miracles on the wealthy too, Jesus goes on to say. The Zacchaeus story (Luke 19:1–10) is an illustration of such.

Again, one can see the importance of good exegesis so that the point we make of such narratives is, in fact, the point being made in each gospel itself.

A Final, Very Important Word

Our final concern also applies to the prior discussion of the historical context of Jesus, but it is included here because it is so crucial to the hermeneutical question. The word is this: *One dare not think they can properly interpret the Gospels without a clear understanding of the concept of the kingdom of God in the ministry of Jesus.* For a brief, but good, introduction to this matter look at chapter 4 in Stein's *The Method and Message of Jesus' Teachings.* Here we will give only a brief sketch, along with some words about how this affects hermeneutics.

First of all, you should know that the basic theological framework of the entire New Testament is eschatological. Eschatology has to do with the end, when God brings this age to its close. Most Jews in Jesus' day were eschatological in their thinking. That is, they thought they lived at the very brink of time, when God would step into history and bring an end to this age and usher in the age to come. The Greek word for the "end" they were looking for is *eschatos*. Thus to be eschatological in one's thinking meant to be looking for the end.

The Jewish Eschatological Hope
The Eschaton

This Age (Satan's Time)	The Age to Come (The Time of God's Rule)
characterized by:	characterized by:
sin	the presence of the Spirit
sickness	righteousness
demon-possession	health
evil people triumph	peace

The earliest Christians, of course, well understood this eschatological way of looking at life. For them the events of Jesus' coming, his death and resurrection, and his giving of the Spirit were all related to their expectations about the coming of the end. It happened like this.

The coming of the end also meant for them a new beginning — the beginning of God's new age, the messianic age. The new age was also referred to as the kingdom of God, which meant "the time of God's rule." This new age would be a time of righteousness (e.g., Isa 11:4–5), and people would live in peace (e.g., Isa 2:2–4). It would be a time of the fullness of the Spirit (Joel 2:28–30) when the new covenant spoken of by Jeremiah would be realized (Jer 31:31–34; 32:38–40). Sin and sickness would be done away with (e.g., Zech 13:1; Isa 53:5). Even the material creation would feel the joyful effects of this new age (e.g., Isa 11:6–9).

Thus when John the Baptist announced the coming of the end to be very near and baptized God's Messiah, eschatological fervor reached fever pitch. The Messiah was at hand, the one who would usher in the new age of the Spirit (Luke 3:7–17).

Jesus came and announced with his ministry that the coming kingdom was at hand (e.g., Mark 1:14–15; Luke 17:20–21). He drove out demons, worked miracles, and freely accepted the outcasts and sinners—all signs that the end had begun (e.g., Matt 11:2–6; Luke 11:20; 14:21; 15:1–2). Everyone kept watching him to see if he really *was* the Coming One. Would he really bring in the messianic age with all of its splendor? Then suddenly he was crucified—and the lights went out.

But no! There was a glorious sequel. On the third day he was raised from the dead, and he appeared to many of his followers. Surely *now* he would "restore the kingdom to Israel" (Acts 1:6). But instead he returned to the Father and poured out the promised Spirit. Here is where problems show up for the early church and for us. Jesus announced the coming kingdom as having arrived with his own coming. The Spirit's coming in fullness and power with signs and wonders and the coming of the new covenant were signs that the new age had arrived. Yet the end of *this* age apparently had not yet taken place. How were they to understand this?

Very early, beginning with Peter's speech to the astonished onlookers in Acts 3, the early Christians came to realize that Jesus had not come to usher in the "final" end but the "beginning" of the end, as it were. Thus they came to see that with Jesus' death and resurrection, and with the coming of the Spirit, the blessings and benefits of the future had already come. In a sense, therefore, the end had already come. But in another sense the end had not yet fully come. Thus it was *already* but *not yet*.

The early believers, therefore, learned to be a truly eschatological people. They lived between the times—that is, between the *beginning* of the end and the *consummation* of the end. At the Lord's Table they celebrated their eschatological existence by proclaiming "the Lord's death until he comes" (1 Cor 11:26). *Already* they knew God's free and full forgiveness, but they had *not yet* been perfected (Phil 3:10–14). *Already* victory over death was theirs (1 Cor 3:22), *yet* they would still die (Phil 3:20–21). *Already* they lived in the Spirit, *yet* they still lived in the world where Satan could attack (e.g., Eph 6:10–17). *Already* they had been justified and faced no condemnation (Rom 8:1), *yet* there was still to be a future judgment (2 Cor 5:10). They were God's future people. They had been conditioned by the future. They knew its benefits and lived in light of its values, but they, as we, still had to live out these benefits and values in the present world. Thus the essential theological framework for understanding the New Testament looks like this:

The New Testament Eschatological View
The Eschaton

begun   consummated
THIS AGE   (Passing away)

THE AGE TO COME   (never ending)

The Cross and Resurrection	The Second Coming
Already	*Not Yet*
righteousness	completed righteousness
peace	full peace
health	no sickness or death
Spirit	in complete fullness

The hermeneutical key to much in the New Testament, and especially to the ministry and teaching of Jesus, is to be found in this kind of "tension." Precisely because the kingdom, the time of God's rule, has been inaugurated with Jesus' own coming, we are called to *life* in the kingdom, which means life under his lordship, freely accepted and forgiven but committed to the ethics of the new era and to seeing them worked out in our own lives and world in this present age.

Thus when we pray, "Your kingdom come," we pray first of all for the consummation. But because the kingdom—the time of God's rule—that we long to see consummated has already begun, the same prayer is full of implications for the present. And, of course, by implication this means that by the Spirit we are now to live out the life and values of the "age to come" that has already been set in motion through the resurrection.

CHAPTER 8

The Parables: Do You Get the Point?

It should be noted at the outset that everything said in the preceding chapter about the teaching of Jesus in the Gospels holds true for the parables. Why then should the parables need a chapter of their own in a book like this? How could these simple, direct little stories Jesus told pose problems for the reader or the interpreter? It seems that one would have to be a dullard of the first rank to miss the point of the Good Samaritan or the Prodigal Son. The very reading of these stories pricks the heart or comforts it.

Yet a special chapter is necessary because, for all their charm and simplicity, the parables have suffered a fate of misinterpretation in the church second only to the book of Revelation.

THE PARABLES IN HISTORY

The reason for the long history of the misinterpretation of the parables can be traced back to something Jesus himself said, as recorded in Mark 4:10–12 (// Matt 13:10–13 // Luke 8:9–10). When asked about the purpose of parables, he seems to have suggested that they contained mysteries for those on the inside, while they hardened those on the outside. Because he then proceeded to "interpret" the parable of the sower in a semi-allegorical way, this was seen to give license to the hardening theory and endless allegorical interpretations. The parables were considered to be simple stories for those on the outside to whom the "real meanings," the "mysteries," were hidden; these belonged only to the church and could be uncovered by means of allegory.

Thus as great and brilliant a scholar as Augustine offers the following interpretation of the parable of the good Samaritan:

A man was going down from Jerusalem to Jericho = Adam
Jerusalem = the heavenly city of peace, from which Adam fell
Jericho = the moon, and thereby signifies Adam's mortality
robbers = the devil and his angels
stripped him = of his immortality
beat him = by persuading him to sin
leaving him half dead = as a man he lives, but he died spiritually; therefore he is half dead
the priest and Levite = the priesthood and ministry of the Old Testament
the Samaritan = is said to mean Guardian; therefore Christ himself is meant
bandaged his wounds = binding the restraint of sin
oil = comfort of good hope
wine = exhortation to work with a fervent spirit
donkey ("beast") = the flesh of Christ's incarnation
inn = the church
the next day = after the resurrection
two silver coins = promise of this life and the life to come
innkeeper = Paul

As novel and interesting as all of this may be, one can be absolutely certain that it is not what Jesus intended. After all, the context clearly calls for an understanding of human relationships (Who is my neighbor?), not divine to human; and there is no reason to think that Jesus would *predict* the church and Paul in this obtuse fashion!

Indeed it is extremely doubtful whether most of the parables were intended for an inner circle at all. In at least three instances Luke specifically says that Jesus told parables *to* people (15:3; 18:9; 19:11) with the clear implication that the parables were to be understood, at least at one level. Moreover, the "expert in the law" to whom Jesus told the parable of the good Samaritan (Luke 10:25–37) clearly understood it (vv. 36–37), as did the chief priests and Pharisees the parable of the tenants (Matt 21:45). Their problem was not with understanding but with letting the parables alter their behavior!

If we have trouble at times understanding the parables, it is not because they are allegories for which we need some special interpretive keys. Rather it is related to some things we suggested in the previous chapter on the Gospels. One of the keys to understanding the parables lies in discovering the original audience to whom they were spoken; as we noted, many times they came down to the authors of the Gospels without a context.

If the parables, then, are not allegorical mysteries for the church, what did Jesus mean when responding to the disciples' inquiry about the parables (Mark 4:10–12) with language about the "mystery" of the kingdom of God? Most likely the clue to this saying lies in a play on words in Jesus' native Aramaic. The Aramaic term *methal,* which was translated *parabolē* in Greek, was used for a whole range of figures of speech in the riddle/puzzle/parable category, not just for the story variety called "parables" in English. Probably the phrase "to those on the outside everything is said in parables" (v. 11) meant that the meaning of Jesus' ministry (the secret of the kingdom) could not be perceived by those on the outside; it was like a *methal,* a riddle, to them. Hence his speaking in *mathlîn* (parables) was part of the *methal* (riddle) of his whole ministry to them. They saw, but they failed to see; they heard—and even understood—the parables, but they failed to hear in a way that led to obedience. They were looking for their idea of power and glory, not for a humble Galilean who cared for all the wrong kinds of people.

Our exegesis of the parables, therefore, must begin with the same assumptions that we have brought to every other genre so far. Jesus was not trying to be obtuse; he fully intended to be understood. Our task is first of all to try to hear what they heard. But before we can do this adequately, we must begin by looking at the question, what is a parable, since in English this word covers a variety of forms of indirect speech.

THE NATURE OF THE PARABLES
The Variety of Kinds
The first item one must note is that not all the sayings we label as parables are of the same kind. There is a basic difference, for example, between the Good Samaritan (true parable) on the one hand and the Yeast in the Dough (similitude) on the other, and both of these differ from the saying, "You are the salt of the earth" (metaphor), or "Do people pick grapes from thorn bushes, or figs

from thistles?" (epigram). Yet all of these from time to time have been brought into discussions of the parables.

The Good Samaritan is an example of a *true parable*. It is a *story*, pure and simple, with a beginning and an ending; it has something of a "plot." Other such story parables include the Lost Sheep, the Prodigal Son, the Great Banquet, the Workers in the Vineyard, the Rich Man and Lazarus, and the Ten Virgins.

The Yeast in the Dough, on the other hand, is more of a *similitude*. What is said of the yeast, or the sower, or the mustard seed was always true of yeast, sowing, or mustard seeds. Such "parables" are more like illustrations taken from everyday life, which Jesus used to make a point.

Beyond this, such sayings as "You are the salt of the earth" differ from both of these. These are sometimes called parabolic sayings, but in reality they are *metaphors* and *similes*. At times they seem to function in a way similar to the similitude, but their point—their reason for being spoken—is considerably different.

It should be noted further that in some cases, especially that of the Wicked Tenants (Matt 21:33–44 // Mark 12:1–11 // Luke 20:9–18), a parable may approach something very close to allegory, where many of the details in a story are intended to represent something else (such as in Augustine's misinterpretation of the Good Samaritan). But *the parables are not allegories*—even if at times they have what appear to us to be allegorical features. The reason we can be sure of this has to do with their differing functions.

Because the parables are not all of one kind, one cannot necessarily lay down rules that will cover them all. What we say here is intended for the parables proper, but much of what is said will cover the other types as well.

How the Parables Function

The best clues as to what the parables are is to be found in their *function*. In contrast to most of the parabolic sayings, such as not reaping figs from thorn bushes (Luke 6:43), the story parables do *not* serve to illustrate Jesus' prosaic teaching with word pictures. Nor are they told to serve as vehicles for revealing truth— although they end up clearly doing that. Rather the story parables function as a striking way of *calling forth a response* on the part of the hearer. In a sense, the parable itself *is* the message. It is told to address and capture the hearers, to bring them up short about their own actions, or to cause them to respond in some way to Jesus and his ministry. Indeed, this chapter is being rewritten shortly after watching Spielberg's marvelous film presentation of Lincoln, whose own personal wit and story-telling had a similar effect on his hearers—love or hate.

It is this "call for response" nature of the parable that causes our great dilemma in interpreting them. For in some ways to interpret a parable is to destroy what it was originally. It is like interpreting a joke. The whole point of a joke and what makes it funny is that the hearer has immediacy with it as it is being told. It is funny to the hearer precisely because they get "caught," as it were. How a joke ends is not what one instinctively expects from how it began. But it can only catch someone if they *understand the points of reference* in the joke. If you have to interpret the joke by explaining the points of reference, it no longer catches the hearer and therefore fails to capture the same quality of laughter. When the joke is interpreted, it can then be understood all right and may still be funny (at least one understands what one *should* have laughed at), but it ceases to have the same impact. Thus it no longer *functions* in the same way.

So it is with the parables. They were spoken, and we may assume that most of the hearers had an immediate identification with the points of reference that caused them to catch the point— or be caught by it. For us, however, the parables are in written form. We may or may not immediately catch the points of reference, and therefore they can never function for us in quite the same way they did for the first hearers. But by interpreting we usually are able to understand what *they* caught, or what we would have caught had we been there. And this is what we must do in our exegesis. The hermeneutical task lies beyond that: How do we recapture the punch of the parables in our own times and our own settings?

THE EXEGESIS OF THE PARABLES
Finding the Points of Reference

Let us go back to our analogy of the joke. The two items that capture the hearer of a joke and elicit a response of laughter are the same two that captured the hearers of Jesus' parables, namely, their knowledge of *the points of reference*, which in turn caused them to recognize *the unexpected turn* in the story. The keys to understanding are the points of reference—those various parts of the story with which one automatically identifies as it is being told. If one misses these in a joke, then there can be no unexpected turn, because the points of reference are what create the ordinary expectations. To put it bluntly, an explained joke is no joke at all. Similarly, if one misses the points of reference in a parable, then the force and the point of what Jesus said is likewise going to be missed.

What we mean by points of reference can best be illustrated from a parable of Jesus (Luke 7:40–42) recorded in its full original context (vv. 36–50). In the context Jesus has been invited to dinner by a Pharisee named Simon. But the invitation was not to be considered as being "in honor of a visiting famous rabbi." The failure to offer Jesus even the common hospitality of the day was surely intended as something of a put-down. When the town prostitute finds her way into the presence of the diners and makes a fool of herself over Jesus by washing his feet with her tears and wiping them with her hair, it only fortifies the Pharisees' suspicions. Jesus could not be a prophet and leave uncondemned this kind of public disgrace.

Knowing their thoughts, Jesus tells his host a simple story. Two men owed money to a moneylender. One owed five hundred denarii (a denarius was a day's wage); the other owed fifty. Neither could pay, so he canceled the debts of both. The point: Who, do you think, would have responded to the moneylender with the greater display of love?

This story needed no interpretation, although Jesus proceeded to drive the point home with full force. There are three points of reference: the moneylender and the two debtors. And the identifications are immediate. God is like the moneylender; the town harlot and Simon are like the two debtors. The parable is a word of judgment calling for response from Simon. He could scarcely have missed the point. When it is over, he has egg all over his face. Such is the force of a parable.

We should note further that the woman heard the parable as well. She, too, will identify with the story as it is being told. But what she will hear is not judgment, but Jesus'—and therefore God's—acceptance of her.

Note well: This is *not* an allegory; it is a parable. A true allegory is a story where each element in the story means something quite foreign to the story itself. Allegory would give meaning to the five hundred denarii and the fifty denarii, as well as to any other details one might find. Furthermore, and this is especially important, the point of the parable is *not* in the points of reference, as it would be in a true allegory. The points of reference are only those parts of the story that draw the hearer into it, parts with which one is to identify in some way as the story proceeds. The point of the story is to be found in the *intended response*. In this parable it is a word of judgment on Simon and his friends or a word of acceptance and forgiveness to the woman.

Identifying the Audience

In the above illustration we also pointed out the significance of identifying the audience, because the meaning of the parable has to do with how it was originally heard. For many of the parables, of course, the audience is given in the Gospels. In such cases the task of interpretation is a combination of three things: (1) sit and listen to the parable again and again, (2) identify the points of reference intended by Jesus that would have been picked up by the original hearers, and (3) try to determine how the original hearers would have identified with the story, and therefore what they would have heard.

Let us try this on two well-known parables: the Good Samaritan (Luke 10:25–37) and the Prodigal Son (Luke 15:11–32). In the case of the Good Samaritan, the story is told to an expert in the law who, wanting to justify himself, Luke says, had asked, "And who is my neighbor?" As you read the parable again and again, you will notice that it does not answer the question the way it was asked. But in a more telling way it exposes the smug self-righteousness of the questioner. He knows what the law says about loving one's neighbor as oneself, and he is ready to define "neighbor" in terms that will demonstrate that he piously obeys the law.

There are really only two points of reference in the story—the man in the ditch and the Samaritan—although other details in the parable help to build the effect. Two items in particular need to be noted: (1) The two who pass by on the other side are priestly types—the religious order that stands over against the rabbis and the Pharisees, who are the experts in the law. (2) Almsgiving to the poor was the Pharisees' big thing. This was how they loved their neighbors as themselves.

Notice, then, how the teacher of the law is going to get caught by the parable. A man falls into the hands of robbers on the road from Jerusalem to Jericho, a common enough event. Two priestly types next go down the road and pass by on the other side. The story is being told from the point of view of the man in the ditch, and the teacher of the law has now been "set up." *Of course,* he would think to himself, *who could expect anything else from priests? The next person down will be a Pharisee, and he will show himself neighborly by helping the poor chap.* But no, it turns out to be a Samaritan! You will have to appreciate how contemptuously the Pharisees held the Samaritans if you are going to hear what he heard. Notice that he is not able even to bring himself to use the word "Samaritan" at the end. This outsider is merely "the one who"!

Do you see what Jesus has done to this man? The second Great Commandment is to love one's neighbor as oneself. The expert in the law had neat little systems that allowed him to love within limits. What Jesus does is to expose the prejudice and hatred of his heart, and therefore his real lack of obedience to this commandment. "Neighbor" can no longer be defined in limiting terms. His lack of love is not that he will not have helped the man in the ditch but that he hates Samaritans (and looks down on priests). In effect, the parable destroys the question rather than answering it.

Similarly, we may consider the Prodigal Son. The context is the Pharisees' murmuring over Jesus' acceptance of and eating with the wrong kind of people (Luke 15:1–2). The three parables of lost things that follow are Jesus' justification of his actions. In the parable of the lost son there are just three points of reference—the father and his two sons. Here again, where one sat determined how one heard, but in either case the point is the same: God not only freely forgives the lost but accepts them with great joy. Those who consider themselves righteous reveal themselves to be unrighteous if they do not share the father's and the lost son's joy.

Jesus' table companions, of course, will identify with the lost son, as all of us well should. But this is not the real force of the parable, which is to be found in the attitude of the second son. He was "always with" the father, yet he had put himself on the outside. He failed to share the father's heart with its love for a lost son. As a friend recently put it, "Can you imagine anything worse than coming home and falling into the hands of the older brother?" Ouch!

In each of these cases, and others, the exegetical difficulties you will encounter will stem mostly from the cultural gap between you and Jesus' original audience, which may cause you to miss some of the finer points that go into the makeup of the whole story. Here is where you will probably need outside help. But do not neglect these matters, for the cultural customs are what help to give the original stories their life.

The "Contextless" Parables

But what of those parables that are found in the Gospels without their original historical context? Since we have already illustrated this concern in the previous chapter, from the parable of the workers in the vineyard (Matt 20:1–16), we will only briefly review here. Again, it is a matter of trying to determine the points of reference and the original audience. The key is in the repeated rereading of the parable until its points of reference clearly emerge. Usually this will also give one an instant clue to its original audience.

Thus in the Workers in the Vineyard, there are only three points of reference: the landowner, the full-day workers, and the one-hour workers. This is easily determined because these are the only people brought into focus as the story wraps up. The original audience is also easily determined. Who would have been "caught" by a story like this? Obviously the hearers who identify with the full-day laborers, since they alone are in focus at the end.

The point is similar to that of the Prodigal Son. God is gracious, and the righteous should not begrudge God's generosity. What has happened in its present Matthean context in this instance, however, is that the same point is now being made to a new audience. In the context of discipleship it serves as an assurance of God's generosity, despite the condemnation or hatred of others.

One can see this same scenario happening in Matthew's version of the parable of the lost sheep (18:12–14). In Luke's gospel this parable functions along with the Lost Coin and Prodigal Son as a word to the Pharisees. The lost sheep is clearly a sinner, whose finding brings joy in heaven. Again, as a word to the Pharisees, it justifies Jesus' acceptance of the outcasts; but when heard by the outcasts it assures them that they are the objects of the loving shepherd's search. In Matthew, the parable is a part of the collection of sayings on relationships within the kingdom. In this new context the same point is being made: God's care for the lost. But here the "lost" are sheep who have "wandered off." In Matthew's context it speaks to the question of what we are to do for those "little ones" who are of weak faith and who tend to go astray. Just before the parable (vv. 6–9) Matthew's community is told that no one of them had better be responsible for causing a "little one" to go astray. The parable of the lost sheep (vv. 10–14), on the other hand, tells them they should seek out the wandering one and love them back into the fold. Same parable, same point, but to a brand-new audience.

The Parables of the Kingdom

So far our illustrations have all been taken from parables of conflict between Jesus and the Pharisees. But there is a much larger group of parables—the parables of the kingdom—that need special mention. It is true that all of the parables we have already looked at are also parables of the kingdom. They express the dawning of the time of salvation with the coming of Jesus. But the parables we have in mind here are those that expressly say, "The kingdom of God is like...."

First, it must be noted that the introduction, "The kingdom of God is like ...," is *not* to be taken with the first element mentioned in the parable. That is, the kingdom of God is *not* like a mustard seed, or treasure hidden in a field, or a merchant. The expression literally means, "It is like this with the kingdom of God...." Thus the whole parable tells us something about the nature of the kingdom, not just one of the points of reference or one of the details.

Second, it is tempting to treat these parables differently from those we have just looked at, as though they actually were teaching vehicles rather than stories calling for response. But that would be to abuse them. Granted, the divinely inspired collections in Mark 4 and Matthew 13 in their present arrangement are intended to teach *us* about the kingdom. But originally these parables were a part of Jesus' actual proclamation of the kingdom as dawning with his own coming. They are themselves vehicles of the message, calling for response to Jesus' invitation and call to discipleship.

Take, for example, the interpreted parable of the sower (Mark 4:3–20; Matt 13:3–23; Luke 8:5–15), which is rightfully seen by Mark as the key to the rest. You will notice that what Jesus has interpreted are the points of reference: The four kinds of soil are like four kinds of responses to the proclamation of the kingdom.

But the *point* of the parable is the urgency of the hour: "Take heed how you hear. The word is being sown — the message of the good news of the kingdom, the joy of forgiveness, the demand and gift of discipleship. It is before all, so listen, take heed; be fruitful soil." It will be noted, therefore, that most of these parables are addressed to the multitudes as potential disciples.

Since these parables are indeed parables of the *kingdom*, we find them proclaiming the kingdom as "already/not yet." But their main thrust is the "already." The kingdom has already come; God's hour is at hand. Therefore, the present moment is one of great urgency. Such urgency in Jesus' proclamation has a twofold thrust: (1) Judgment is impending; disaster and catastrophe are at the door. (2) But there is good news: salvation is freely offered to all.

Let us look at a couple of parables that illustrate these two aspects of the message.

1. We begin with the parable of the rich fool (Luke 12:16–20), which Luke has set in a context of attitudes toward possessions in light of the presence of the kingdom. The parable is easy enough. A rich man, because of his hard work, thinks he has secured his life and is resting complacently. But as Jesus says elsewhere, "Whoever wants to save their life will lose it" (Matt 16:25 // Mark 8:35 // Luke 9:24). Thus the man is a fool in the biblical sense — he tries to live without taking God into account. But sudden disaster is about to overtake him.

The point of the parable, you will note, is *not* the unexpectedness of death. It is the urgency of the hour. The kingdom is *at hand*. One is a fool to live for possessions, for self-security, when the end is right at the door. Note how this is supported by the context. A man wants his brother to divide the inheritance. But Jesus refuses to become involved in their arbitration. His point is that desire for possession of property is irrelevant in light of the present moment.

This is also how we should understand that most difficult of parables — the Shrewd Manager (Luke 16:1–8). Again, the story is simple enough. A property manager was embezzling, or otherwise squandering, his master's money. He was called to produce accounts and knew his number was up, so he pulled off one more enormous rip-off. He let all those owing money adjust their accounts themselves, probably hoping to secure friends on the outside. The punch of this parable, and the part most of us have difficulty handling as well, is that the original hearers expect disapproval. Instead this monkey business is *praised*!

What could possibly be Jesus' point in telling a story like that? Most likely he is challenging his hearers with the urgency of the hour. If they are properly indignant over such a story, how much more should they apply the lessons to themselves. They are in the same position as the manager who saw imminent disaster, but the crisis that threatens them is incomparably more terrible. That man acted (note that Jesus does not excuse his action); he did something about his situation. For you, too, Jesus seems to be saying, the urgency of the hour demands action; everything is at stake.

2. The urgent hour that calls for action, repentance, is also the time of salvation. Thus the kingdom as present is also Good News. In the twin parables of the hidden treasure and the pearl of great value (Matt 13:44–46), the emphasis is on the joy of discovery. The kingdom overtakes the one; it is sought by the other. In joy they liquidate their holdings for the treasure and the pearl. The kingdom is not the treasure; and it is not the pearl. The kingdom is God's gift. The "discovery" of the kingdom brings unutterable joy. You will notice how this same motif is thoroughgoing also in the three parables of the lost things in Luke 15.

This, then, is how one needs to learn to read and study the parables. They are not to be allegorized. They are to be heard— heard as calls to respond to Jesus and his mission.

THE HERMENEUTICAL QUESTION

The hermeneutical task posed by the parables is unique. It has to do with the fact that when they were originally spoken, they seldom needed interpretation. They had immediacy for the hearers, inasmuch as part of the effect of many of them was their ability to "catch" the hearer. Yet they come to us in written form and in need of interpretation precisely because we lack the immediate understanding of the points of reference the original hearers had. What, then, do we do? We suggest two things.

1. As always, we concern ourselves basically with the parables in their present biblical contexts. The parables are in a written context, and through the exegetical process just described we can discover their meaning, their *point,* with a high degree of accuracy.

What we need to do then is what Matthew did (e.g., 18:10–14; 20:1–16): *translate that same point into our own context.*

With the story parables one might even try retelling the story in such a way that, with new points of reference, one's own hearers might feel the anger, or joy, the original hearers experienced. The following version of the Good Samaritan is not defended as inspired! Hopefully it will illustrate a hermeneutical possibility. As an audience it assumes a typical, well-dressed, middle-American Protestant congregation.

> A family of disheveled, unkempt individuals was stranded by the side of a major road on a Sunday morning. They were in obvious distress. The mother was sitting on a tattered suitcase, hair uncombed, clothes in disarray, with a glazed look to her eyes, holding a smelly, poorly clad, crying baby. The father was unshaved, dressed in coveralls, a look of despair on his face as he tried to corral two other youngsters. Beside them was a run-down old car that had obviously just given up the ghost.
>
> Down the road came a car driven by the local bishop; he was on his way to church. And though the father of the family waved frantically, the bishop could not hold up his parishioners, so he acted as though he didn't see them.
>
> Soon came another car and again the father waved furiously. But the car was driven by the president of the Kiwanis Club, and he was late for a statewide meeting of Kiwanis presidents in a nearby city. He, too, acted as though he did not see them and kept his eyes straight on the road ahead of him.
>
> The next car that came by was driven by an outspoken local atheist, who had never been to church in his life. When he saw the family's distress, he took them into his own car. After inquiring as to their need, he took them to a local motel, where he paid for a week's lodging while the father found work. He also paid for the father to rent a car so he could look for work and gave the mother cash for food and new clothes.

One of the authors presented this story once. The startled and angry response made it clear that his hearers had really "heard" the parable for the first time in their lives. You will notice how true to the original context this is. The evangelical Protestant was thinking, *of course,* about the bishop and the Kiwanis president. *Then, surely one of my own will be next.* After all, we have always talked about the *Good* Samaritan as though Samaritans were the most respected of people. But nothing would be more offensive to the good churchgoer than to praise the actions of an atheist, which, of course, is precisely where the expert in the law was at the original telling.

This may be a bit strong for some, and we insist that you make sure you have done your exegesis with great care before you try it. But our experience is that most of us are a bit high on ourselves, and the retelling of some of Jesus' parables would help to get at our own lack of forgiveness (Matt 18:23–35), or our own anger at grace when we want God to be "fair" (Matt 20:1–6), or our pride in our own position in Christ as compared to the "bad guys" (Luke 18:9–14). We did not know whether to laugh or cry when we were told of a Sunday school teacher who, after an hour of excellent instruction on this latter parable in which he had thoroughly explained the abuses of Pharisaism, concluded in prayer—in all seriousness: "Thank you, Lord, that we are not like the Pharisee in this story"! And we had to remind each other not to laugh too hard, lest our laughter be saying, "Thank you, Lord, that we are not like that Sunday school teacher."

2. Our other hermeneutical suggestion is related to the fact that all of Jesus' parables are in some way vehicles that proclaim the kingdom. Hence it is necessary for you to immerse yourself in the meaning of the kingdom in the ministry of Jesus. In this regard we highly recommend that you read George E. Ladd's *The Presence of the Future* (Grand Rapids: Eerdmans, 1974).

The urgent message of the kingdom as present and soon to be consummated is still needed in our own day. Those who are trying to secure their lives by possessions urgently need to hear the word of impending judgment, and the lost desperately need to hear the Good News. Joachim Jeremias eloquently put it this way (*Rediscovering the Parables* [New York: Scribner, 1966], p. 181):

> The hour of fulfillment has come; that is the keynote of them all. The strong man is disarmed, the powers of evil have to yield, the physician has come to the sick, the lepers are cleansed, the heavy burden of guilt is removed, the lost sheep is brought home, the door of the Father's house is opened, the poor and the beggars are summoned to the banquet, a master whose kindness is undeserved pays wages in full, a great joy fills all hearts. God's acceptable year has come. For there has appeared the one whose veiled majesty shines through every word and every parable—the Saviour.

CHAPTER 9

The Law(s): Covenant Stipulations for Israel

Along with the patriarchal narratives found in Genesis, the three defining narratives for Israel as a people are found in the book of Exodus (see *How to 2,* pp. 35–38). First, their miraculous deliverance (the "exodus") from slavery in Egypt, the most powerful empire in the ancient world at that time (Exod 1–18); second, the return of the presence of God as distinguishing his people from all other peoples on earth (Exod 33; 40); and third, God's reconstituting them as a people for his name at the foot of Mount Sinai (Exod 19–Num 10:10). It is hard for us even to imagine the enormity of difficulty involved in this third matter.

Here were people who for hundreds of years had known only slavery and Egyptian culture. And now God was about to reconstitute them into a totally new people on the face of the earth. Not only must they be formed into an army of warriors in order to conquer the land promised to their ancestors, but they must also be formed into a community that would be able to live together both during their time in the wilderness and eventually in the land itself. At the same time they needed direction as to how they were to be *God's* people—both in their relationships with each other and in their relationship with God—so that they would shed the ways and culture of Egypt and not adopt the ways and culture of the Canaanites whose land they were to possess. A further challenge was the rapid assimilation of large numbers of non-Israelites into the people of Israel, not just ethnically, but, far more importantly, religiously (Exod 12:38).

And this is the role of the law in Israel's history. It was God's *gift* to his people to establish the ways they were to live in community with one another and to provide for their relationship with and worship of Yahweh, their God. At the same time the law set boundaries with regard to their relationships with the cultures around them. A formidable task indeed!

If we are going to read and understand the law well, we must begin with this understanding of its role in Israel's own history. At the same time we must be aware of its covenantal nature—because our understanding not only of the law, but of the prophetic texts and of the New Testament story itself as a new covenant, depends on it. So the first purpose of this chapter is to guide you into a good understanding of the nature and role of the law(s) in Israel. But we also care about its second purpose. What role do these laws have for those of us who live under God's new covenant with his people?

WHAT IS THE LAW?

In order to appreciate the role of the Old Testament law in Scripture, we need to face three matters at the outset, matters brought about by "law" language in the Bible itself. First, the word "law" itself has more than one connotation when it is used throughout Scripture: It is used (1) in the plural to refer to the "laws"—those 600-plus specific commandments that the Israelites were expected to keep as evidence of their loyalty to God (e.g., Exod 18:20); (2) in the singular to refer to all of these laws collectively (e.g., Matt 5:18); (3) in the singular to refer to the Pentateuch (Genesis to Deuteronomy) as the "Book of the Law" (e.g., Josh 1:8); (4) in the singular by some writers in the New Testament to refer theologically to the entire Old Testament religious system (e.g., 1 Cor 9:20); (5) in the singular by some New Testament personages to refer to the Old Testament law (in sense 2 above) as it was interpreted by the rabbis (e.g., Peter in Acts 10:28). Our interest in this chapter is primarily with helping Christians to read and understand uses 1 and 2 in order to come to appreciate what the many stipulations God gave Israel meant for them and how we may best read them in our own day.

The second matter has to do with use 3 above, the fact that the Pentateuch itself is by New Testament writers frequently referred to as "the Law" (e.g., "the Law and the Prophets" in Matt 5:17; Luke 16:16). Two things need to be pointed out: (1) The commandments themselves are found almost exclusively in only four of the five books called "the Law": Exodus, Leviticus, Numbers, and Deuteronomy. (2) These books also contain much other material besides lists of laws, and this material is primarily narrative (see ch. 5). The reason for this is that the covenantal law between Yahweh and Israel, which begins in Exodus 20, cannot be understood apart from the narrative in which it is embedded—including (especially) Genesis, which, in fact, contains only a handful of "basic" commandments, such as "Be fruitful and increase in number; fill the earth and subdue it" (Gen 1:28); "Whoever sheds human blood, by humans shall their blood be shed" (Gen 9:6); and "You must keep my covenant" (Gen 17:9), laws that are not specifically limited to Israel and its special covenant with Yahweh. And this is why there is not an exact correspondence between what we would call "laws" and what are called "books of the Law" in the Old Testament.

Third, the most difficult problem for most Christians with regard to these commandments is the hermeneutical one. How do any of these specific legal formulations apply to us, or do they? Because this is the crucial matter, we turn next to some observations about Christians and the law, which in turn will aid in the exegetical discussion that follows.

CHRISTIANS AND THE OLD TESTAMENT LAW

We begin by noting that contemporary believers are not expected to express their loyalty to God by keeping the Old Testament law(s), since we are related to God under a new covenant. And in any case, how could anyone possibly do so, since there is no longer any temple or central sanctuary on whose altar you can offer such things as the meat of animals (Lev 1–5)? In fact, if you killed and burned animals as described in the Old Testament, you would probably be arrested for cruelty to animals! But if we are *not* supposed to observe the Old Testament law(s), then what did Jesus mean when he said, "Truly I tell you, until heaven and earth disappear, not the smallest letter, not the least stroke of a pen, will by any means disappear from the Law until everything is accomplished" (Matt 5:18)? This question needs an answer as to *how* the Old Testament law still functions for Christians.

We suggest six initial guidelines for understanding the relationship of the contemporary believer to the Old Testament law. These guidelines will require explanation, some of which we include immediately and some of which will appear more fully later in this chapter.

1. *The Old Testament law is a covenant.* A covenant is a binding contract between two parties, both of whom have obligations specified in the covenant. In Old Testament times, covenants were often given by an all-powerful suzerain (overlord) to a weaker, dependent vassal (servant). On the one hand, the suzerain guaranteed the vassal benefits and protection. But in turn, the vassal was obligated to be loyal solely to the suzerain, with the warning that any disloyalty would bring punishments as specified in the covenant. How was the vassal to show loyalty? By keeping the stipulations (rules of behavior) also specified in the covenant. A covenant put in place a relationship—in Israel's case, a relationship with the one true God, who alone could save and sustain them. So the rules were very important. No rules? No relationship! As long as the vassal kept the stipulations, the suzerain knew that the vassal was loyal. But when the stipulations were violated, the suzerain was required by the covenant to take action to punish the vassal. In an extreme case, the relationship could even be altered or suspended by the suzerain (Deut 4:25–27; 28:20).

What is important for your understanding is that in making a covenant with Israel on Sinai, God used this well-known covenant form when he constituted the binding contract between himself (Yahweh = "the LORD") and his vassal, Israel. In return for benefits and protection, Israel was expected to keep the many stipulations (i.e., commandments) contained in the covenantal law such as we find it in Exodus 20–Deuteronomy 33.

The covenant format had six parts to it: preamble, prologue, stipulations, witnesses, sanctions, and document clause. The *preamble* identified the parties to the agreement ("I am the LORD your God" [Exod 20:2]), while the *prologue* gave a brief history of how the parties became connected to one another ("[I] brought you out of Egypt" [Exod 20:2]). The *stipulations,* as we have noted, are the individual laws themselves. The *witnesses* are those who will enforce the covenant (the Lord himself, or sometimes "heaven and earth," a meristic way of saying that all of God's creation is concerned with the covenant being kept—e.g., Deut

4:26; 30:19). The *sanctions* are the blessings and curses that function as incentives for keeping the covenant (e.g., Lev 26 and Deut 28 – 33). The *document clause* is the provision for regular review of the covenant so that it will not be forgotten (e.g., Deut 17:18 – 19; 31:9 – 13). Both the first statement of the law (at Sinai, Exod 20 – Lev 27, with supplementation in Numbers) and the second statement (just prior to the conquest, as found in Deuteronomy) reflect this six-part format.

The importance of this first observation can hardly be overemphasized. It is its covenant nature that makes "the law" so important to one's understanding the Old Testament as a whole. As such, it is an essential part of Israel's *story* (see ch. 5, pp. 93 – 111), which also explains in part why the laws themselves may seem in general to be so oddly organized. Furthermore, apart from the covenantal nature of the law, you will not be able to understand the role of the prophets in Israel (see ch. 10). So even though we are not expected to "keep" these laws, they are essential for us to read and know if we are going to appreciate the biblical story — God's story — and our own place in the story.

2. *The Old Testament is not our Testament.* Testament is another word for covenant. The Old Testament represents God's previous covenant with Israel made on Mount Sinai, which is one we are no longer obligated to keep. Therefore we can hardly begin by assuming that the old covenant should automatically be binding on us. We should assume, in fact, that *none* of its stipulations (laws) are binding on us unless they are *renewed* in the new covenant. That is, unless an Old Testament law is somehow restated or reinforced in the New Testament, it is no longer directly binding on God's people (cf. Rom 6:14 – 15). There have been changes from the old covenant to the new covenant. The rules have changed because, in Christ, the relationship has changed. God expects of his people — us — somewhat different evidences of obedience and loyalty from those he expected from the Old Testament Israelites. The *loyalty* itself is still expected. It is *how* one shows this loyalty that has been changed in certain ways.

3. *Two kinds of old-covenant stipulations have clearly not been renewed in the new covenant.* While a complete coverage of the categories of Old Testament law would take a book of its own, the portion of laws from the Pentateuch that no longer apply to Christians can be grouped conveniently into two categories: (1)

the Israelite civil laws and (2) the Israelite ritual laws. While some Old Testament laws do still apply to us (see #4 below), these do not, just as laws in Canada do not apply to people in the United States.

The *civil laws* are those that specify penalties for various crimes (major and minor) for which one might be arrested and tried in Israel. These are the laws that shaped the daily life of Israel as God's people in their relationships with one another and toward their culture. So when you read them, think in terms of their role in ancient Israelite society; and think also in terms of how they reveal something about God's own character. On the other hand, such laws in the end apply only to citizens of ancient Israel, and no one living today is a citizen of ancient Israel.

The *ritual laws* constitute the largest single block of Old Testament laws and are found throughout Leviticus, as well as in many parts of Exodus, Numbers, and Deuteronomy. These told the people of Israel how to carry out the practices of old-covenant worship, detailing everything from the design of the implements of worship, to the priests' responsibilities, to what sorts of animals should be sacrificed and how. The sacrificing (ceremonial killing, cooking, and eating) of animals was central to the Old Testament way of worshiping God. Without the shedding of blood, no forgiveness of sins was possible (see Heb 9:22). When Jesus' once-for-all sacrifice was accomplished, however, this old-covenant approach was immediately made obsolete. It no longer figures in Christian practice, although worship—in the *new*-covenant manner—continues.

But some will ask, "Didn't Jesus say that we are still under the Law, since not a jot or tittle, not the least stroke of a pen, would ever drop out of the Law?" The answer is, no, he did not say that. What he said (see Luke 16:16–17) was that the Law cannot be changed. Jesus came to establish a new covenant (see Luke 22:20; cf. Heb 8–10), and in so doing "fulfilled" the purpose of the old, thus bringing its time to an end. The fulfillment itself Jesus called a "new command"—the law of love (John 13:34–35).

There are many modern analogies to this sort of change of stipulations from covenant to covenant. In the case of labor contracts, for example, a new contract may specify changes in working conditions, different staffing structures, different pay scales, etc. Yet it may also retain certain features of the old contract—seniority, work breaks, provisions against arbitrary firing, etc. To be sure, a labor contract is hardly on the level of the covenant between God and Israel, but it is a type of covenant and therefore helps illustrate in a familiar way the fact that a new covenant can be quite different from an old covenant, *yet not necessarily totally different*. This is also the case with the biblical covenants.

4. Part of the old covenant is renewed in the new covenant. Which part do we refer to? The answer is that some aspects of the Old Testament ethical law are actually restated in the New Testament as applicable to Christians. But such laws derive their continued applicability from the fact that they serve to support the two basic laws of the new covenant, on which depend all the Law and the Prophets (Matt 22:40): "Love the Lord your God with all your heart and with all your soul and with all your mind" (see Deut 6:5) and "Love your neighbor as yourself" (see Lev 19:18). Jesus thus excerpts some Old Testament laws, giving them new applicability (read Matt 5:21–48), redefining them in terms of love for neighbor rather than simply as prohibitions to be "kept," and in so doing broadens the perspective considerably! Thus we say that aspects rather than simply the laws themselves are renewed from the old covenant to the new.

5. All of the Old Testament law is still the word of God for us even though it is not still the command of God to us. The Bible contains all sorts of commands that God wants us to know about, which are not directed toward us personally. If we are not concerned about building parapets around the roof of our houses (Deut 22:8), we should nonetheless delight in a God who cared that houseguests not fall off a (usually flat) roof with which they were unfamiliar; and therefore God's people were taught to build their houses with that sort of love for neighbor in mind. This fits into our understanding of the law as part of Israel's story, since we cannot know the significance of our story, the story of the new covenant, without knowing well how the law functioned in Israel's story, the story of the former covenant.

6. Only that which is explicitly renewed from the Old Testament law can be considered part of the New Testament "law of Christ" (cf. Gal 6:2). Included in such a category would be the Ten Commandments, since they are cited in various ways in the New Testament as still binding on Christians (see Matt 5:21–37; John 7:23), and the two great commandments carried over into

the New Testament—"Love the LORD your God with all your heart and with all your soul and with all your strength" (Deut 6:5) and "Love your neighbor as yourself" (Lev 19:18). And in this case these two "laws" perfectly display God's character, which is to be reproduced in God's children. No other specific Old Testament laws can be demonstrated to be binding on Christians, valuable as it is for Christians to know all of the laws.

THE ROLE OF THE LAW IN ISRAEL AND IN THE BIBLE

Even though the Old Testament laws are not our laws, it would be a mistake to conclude that the law is no longer a valuable part of the Bible. To the contrary, not only did it function in the history of salvation to lead us to Christ, as Paul says (Gal 3:24), but without it we would not be able to understand what it meant for Israel to be God's people. Note well that nowhere in the Old Testament is it suggested that anyone was saved by keeping the law. Rather the law was God's gift to Israel—his way of setting them apart from their pagan neighbors, of setting stipulations and boundaries for their conduct so that they might know how they were to love the Lord their God and to love each other. In other words, the rules of his law gave them an understanding of their relationship both to God and to each other. This is why in the Old Testament the righteous regularly express delight in God's law (e.g., Pss 19 and 119). And when people did not keep the law perfectly, God also provided for them the means of forgiveness and atonement.

Israel's problem in the Old Testament was not with their *inability* to keep the law; it was with their *choosing* not to do so. The story of Israel as recorded in most of the Old Testament is a long and sad story of disobedience, of constant flirtation with and attraction to the gods of their neighbors. Isaiah saw clearly that people become like the gods they worship; hence Israel is described as having eyes but not seeing, and having ears but not hearing (Isa 6:9–10)—just like the idols they were attracted to and finally worshiped. Hence, instead of being Yahweh's people— a people who exemplified his character of justice and mercy, caring for the needy in the land, etc.—they were full of greed, capriciousness, and sexual immorality, like the baals of the Canaanites.

So the *role* of the law in Israel is especially important for us to know well, because here we see examples of God's own character being expressed in the laws he gave to Israel as they worshiped him and lived in loving relationship with one another. And here we understand why there had to be a new covenant accompanied by the gift of the Spirit (Ezek 36:25–27; 2 Cor 3:6), so that God's people would bear his likeness by being conformed to the image of his Son (Rom 8:29).

All of this is to say again that the law was not thought of in Israel as a "means of salvation." It was neither given for that reason nor could it possibly function in that way. Rather, it functioned as a way of setting out parameters of relationships and of establishing loyalty between God and his people. The law simply represented the terms of the agreement of loyalty that Israel had with God.

The law in this sense thus stands as a paradigm (model). It is hardly a complete list of all the things one could or should do to please God in ancient Israel. The law presents, rather, examples or samples of what it means to be loyal to God. In order to help with your reading of the laws, it should prove useful for you to understand the two basic forms in which they are given.

Apodictic Law

In light of what has just been said, consider the following passage:

> When you reap the harvest of your land, do not reap to the very edges of your field or gather the gleanings of your harvest. Do not go over your vineyard a second time or pick up the grapes that have fallen. Leave them for the poor and the foreigner. I am the LORD your God.
> Do not steal.
> Do not lie.
> Do not deceive one another.
> Do not swear falsely by my name and so profane the name of your God. I am the LORD.
> Do not defraud or rob your neighbor.
> Do not hold back the wages of a hired worker overnight.
> Do not curse the deaf or put a stumbling block in front of the blind, but fear your God. I am the LORD.
>
> *Leviticus 19:9–14*

Notice first, by the thrice-repeated "I am the LORD," how clearly tied to Yahweh's own character these laws are. The Israelites as God's people were to worship, and thus be like, their God. Such commandments as these, therefore, were binding on all Israelites at all times. Commands like these that begin with "do" or "do not" are what we call apodictic laws. They are direct commands, usually in the second person imperative, generally applicable, telling the Israelites the sorts of things they are supposed to do to fulfill their part of the covenant with God. It is fairly obvious, however, that such laws are not exhaustive. Look closely, for example, at the harvesting welfare laws with which the series begins (vv. 9 and 10). Note that only field crops (wheat, barley, etc.) and grapes are actually mentioned. Does this mean that if you raised sheep or harvested figs or olives, you were under no obligation to share your abundance with the poor and resident foreigner? Would others bear the burden of making the Old Testament divinely commanded welfare system work while you got off scot-free? Of course not. The law is paradigmatic—it sets *a standard by an example* rather than by mentioning every possible circumstance. But at the same time it is also universally applicable to all who own land and raise cattle or crops.

Again, consider the final two commands (vv. 13b and 14). The point of these statements is to prohibit holding up payment to day workers, and abusing people with disabilities. What if you withheld payment to a worker almost all night but then gave it to him just before dawn? The teachers of the law and the Pharisees of Jesus' day might have argued that your actions were justified since the law plainly says "overnight." But narrow, selfish legalism of this sort is, in fact, a distortion of the law. The statements in the law were intended as a reliable *guide* with general applicability—not a technical description of all possible conditions one could imagine. Likewise, if you harmed a person who is mute, or one who is lame or has mental disabilities, would you still have kept the final command in the list? Certainly not. The "deaf" and the "blind" are merely selected examples (= ear and eye; thus sight and sound) of all persons whose physical weaknesses demand that they be respected and aided rather than disregarded or despised.

Modern societies often have relatively exhaustive legal codes. The federal and state legal codes in the United States, for example, contain thousands of specific laws against all sorts of violations. Even so, it always requires a judge (and often a jury) to determine whether a law has been transgressed by an accused individual because it is impossible to write laws so comprehensive in wording that they specify every possible way of violating the intended rule.

Accordingly, the Old Testament law is much closer to the United States Constitution — setting out in broad sweep and outline the characteristics of justice and freedom in the land — than it is to the federal and state codes.

Note that our explanation that the Old Testament apodictic (general, unqualified) laws are paradigmatic (examples rather than exhaustive) is no help to the person who wishes to make obedience to those laws easy. Rather, we have pointed out that these laws, though limited *in wording*, are actually very comprehensive *in spirit*. If one therefore were to set out to keep the spirit of the Old Testament law, he or she would surely fail eventually. No human being can please God consistently in light of such high, comprehensive standards (cf. Rom 8:1–11). Only the pharisaical approach — obeying the letter rather than the spirit of the law — has much possibility of success. But it is a worldly success only, not one that results in actually keeping the law as God intended it to be kept (Matt 23:23).

Thus we make here a preliminary hermeneutical observation: Although not its primary intent, the law shows us *how impossible it is to please God on our own*. This, of course, is not a new observation. Paul said the same thing in his letter to the believers in Rome (Rom 3:20). But the point is applicable for *readers* of the law, not just as a theological truth. When we read the Old Testament law, we ought to be humbled to appreciate how unworthy we are to belong to God. We ought to be moved to praise and thanksgiving that he provided for us a way to be accepted in his sight apart from humanly fulfilling the Old Testament law! For otherwise we would have no hope at all of pleasing God.

Casuistic Law

Apodictic law has a counterpart in another sort of law, which we call casuistic (case-by-case) law. Consider the following passage from Deuteronomy:

> If any of your people — Hebrew men or women — sell themselves to you and serve you six years, in the seventh year you must let them go free. And when you release them, do not send them away empty-handed. Supply them liberally from your flock, your threshing floor and your winepress. Give to them as the LORD your God has blessed you. Remember that you were slaves in Egypt and the LORD your God redeemed you. That is why I give you this command today.

But if your servant says to you, "I do not want to leave you," because he loves you and your family and is well off with you, then take an awl and push it through his earlobe into the door, and he will become your servant for life. Do the same for your female servant.

Deuteronomy 15:12–17

The elements in a law like this are conditional—they describe certain conditions that may prevail in certain types of situations involving certain types of people, but not necessarily in every situation involving every person. Casuistic laws, usually involving third-person descriptions, give examples of what may be the case or what may happen, and what ought to be done if it does. In contrast to apodictic laws, which prescribe what must always be done by everyone in all situations, casuistic laws single out particular cases that apply only to some people in some situations, not to everyone in all situations. The recipients of the law were expected to understand that they had broader implications.

Thus the law just cited applies only in the case that (1) you, an Israelite, have at least one servant, or (2) you, an Israelite, have a servant who does or does not wish to remain as your servant voluntarily after the mandatory minimum term of service has passed. If you are not an Israelite or do not have servants, the law does not apply to you. If you yourself are a servant, this law, because it is directed to your boss, applies only *indirectly* to you in that it protects your rights. But the law does not pertain to everyone. It is conditional—based on a long-term special labor contract (somewhat like a multiyear military enlistment in modern times), a *possible* condition that may or may not apply to a given person at a given time.

Such casuistic or case-by-case laws constitute a large portion of the 600-plus commandments found in the Old Testament Pentateuchal law. Interestingly, none of them is explicitly renewed in the new covenant. Because such laws apply specifically to Israel's civil, religious, and ethical life, they are by their very nature limited in their applicability and therefore unlikely to apply to the Christian. What hermeneutical principles then can a Christian learn from the casuistic laws? Looking at the Deuteronomy passage cited above we may note several items.

First, although we personally might not have servants, we can see that God's provision for long-term service under the old covenant was hardly a brutal, harsh regulation. We could scarcely justify the sort of slavery practiced in most of the world's history—including American history, for example—from such a law. Letting servants go free after only six years of service, and with enough resources to start a new life, provided a major limitation on the practice of contractual servitude, so that the practice could not be abused beyond reasonable limits. Note especially how this law is related to Israel's own story. As redeemed slaves, who once had no hope of ever earning their freedom, they are to show mercy to those who find it necessary to become servants amongst their own people.

Second, we learn that God loves both servants and slaves. His love is seen in the stringent safeguards built into the law, as well as in the final set (vv. 14 and 15), which demand generosity toward the servants, inasmuch as their God had shown such generosity toward Israel, God's own people, a group of former slaves.

Third, we learn that long-term service could be practiced in such a benign fashion that servants were actually better off being in service than being free. That is, the servant's boss, by assuming the obligation to provide food, clothing, and housing for one's servants, was in many cases keeping them alive and well. On their own, they could die of starvation, or perhaps exposure, if they lacked the resources to survive in the harsh economic conditions that prevailed in ancient Palestine.

Fourth, the servant's boss did not really own the servant in a total sense. He owned the servant *contractually*, subject to a host of restrictions spelled out or alluded to in a number of other laws on service. His power over the servant was not absolute under the law. God was the owner of both the boss and the servant. God had redeemed (bought back) all the Hebrews, as the gentle reminder at the end of the first set (v. 15) states, and had owner's claim on all of them—servant or free.

These four observations are valuable lessons for us. It does not matter that the law code of this set (Deut 15:12–17) is not a command directly to us or about us. What matters is how much we can learn from this law about God, his demands of fairness, his ideals for the Israelite society, and his relationship to his people, especially as regards the meaning of "redemption." This law, then, provides us with (1) an important part of the background for the New Testament teaching on redemption, (2) a clearer picture of how Old Testament servitude was quite different from what most modern people usually think of as slavery, and (3) a perspective on the love of God that we may not otherwise have had. This legal passage, in other words, is still the word of God for us, though it is obviously not a command from God to us.

Not everything, however, about servants in ancient Israel can be learned from this law. For example, certain rules for servants of foreign origin are different in scope. Indeed, all the laws on servitude and/or slavery in the Pentateuch put together still only touch the surface. It should be obvious that a few hundred laws can function only in a paradigmatic way, that is, as examples of how people should behave, rather than exhaustively. If even the modern criminal and civil codes with their thousands of individual statutes cannot exhaustively give guidance to a society, then the Old Testament law should not be understood as all-encompassing. Nevertheless, because it does contain the *sorts* of standards God set for his old-covenant people, it should be particularly instructive to us as we of the new covenant seek to do his will.

THE OLD TESTAMENT LAW AND OTHER ANCIENT LAW CODES

The Israelites were not the first people to live by laws. Several other law codes from ancient nations have survived from times even earlier than the time the law was given to Israel through Moses (1440 BC or later, depending on the date of the exodus from Egypt). When these earlier laws are compared to the Old Testament law, it becomes evident that the law given to Israel represents a definite ethical advancement over its predecessors. Consider, for example, the following two sets of laws. The first is from the *Laws of Eshnunna*, an Akkadian law code dated about 1800 BC:

> If a free man has no claim against another free man, but seizes the other free man's servant girl, detains the one seized in his house, and causes her death, he must give two servant girls to the owner of the servant girl as compensation. If he has no claim against him but seizes the wife or child of an upper-class person and causes their death, it is a capital crime. The one who did the seizing must die (Eshnunna, laws 23, 24, author's translation; cf. J. B. Pritchard, ed., *The Ancient Near East*. [Princeton and Oxford: Princeton University Press, 2011], p. 152).

The second is from the famous *Law Code of Hammurabi*, a Babylonian king who "enacted the law of the land" in 1726 BC:

> If a free nobleman hit another free nobleman's daughter and caused her to have a miscarriage, he must pay ten shekels of silver for her fetus. If that woman died, they must put his daughter to death. If by a violent blow he caused a commoner's daughter to have a miscarriage, he must pay five shekels of silver. If that woman died, he must pay 1/2 mina of silver. If he hit a free nobleman's female servant and caused her to have a miscarriage, he must pay two shekels of silver. If that female servant died, he must pay 1/3 mina of silver (Hammurabi, laws 209–14, author's translation; cf. J. B. Pritchard, ed., *The Ancient Near East*. [Princeton and Oxford: Princeton University Press, 2011], p. 175).

There are several issues in these laws that may bear looking at, but we wish to draw attention to one in particular—the class distinctions built into them. Note that the laws provide only for fines as punishment for causing the death of a servant or a commoner, whereas the penalty for causing the death of a member of the nobility is death. Note also that male members of the nobility were practically immune from personal punishment so long as the harm they brought was to a woman. Thus in the second group of laws (Hammurabi, laws 209–14), even when the nobleman causes the death of another nobleman's daughter, he himself does not suffer. Rather, his daughter is put to death. In the first set of laws (Eshnunna, laws 23, 24), likewise, the death of a servant is simply compensated for by the payment of two servants. The killer goes free.

In such laws, then, women and servants are treated like property. Harm to either of them is handled in the same way that harm to an animal or a material possession is handled in other laws in these law codes.

Ethically, the Old Testament law represents a quantum leap ahead over such codes. The prohibition against murder is absolutely unqualified by sex or social status: "You shall not murder" (Exod 20:13). "Anyone who strikes a person with a fatal blow is to be put to death" (Exod 21:12). As regards compensation for injury to servants, there has been an advance as well: "An owner who knocks out the tooth of a male or female slave must let the slave go free to compensate for the tooth" (Exod 21:27). Servants, in general, had a very different status in the Old Testament law from their status under the earlier laws. "If a slave has taken refuge with you, do not hand them over to their master. Let them live among you wherever they like and in whatever town they choose" (Deut 23:15–16). And in contrast to the provision in the laws of Hammurabi that allowed a nobleman to force his daughter to be put to death for a death he had caused, the Old Testament law is explicit that "parents are not to be put to death for their children, nor children put to death for their parents; each will die for their own sin" (Deut 24:16).

THE OLD TESTAMENT LAW AS BENEFIT TO ISRAEL

In terms of its ability to provide eternal life and true righteousness before God, the law itself was quite inadequate. But, then, it was not designed for such purposes. Yet when its own purposes are properly understood, the law should be recognized as beneficial to the Israelites, a marvelous example of God's mercy and grace to his people. We conclude with a few examples to help you read it in the way it was intended. So, read it in that light when you come across the kinds of laws we have sampled here.

The Food Laws

Example: "And the pig, though it has a divided hoof, does not chew the cud; it is unclean for you" (Lev 11:7).

The food laws, such as this prohibition against pork, are not intended by God to represent arbitrary and capricious restrictions on Israelite tastes. Rather, they have a serious protective purpose. The vast majority of the foods prohibited are those that (1) are more likely to carry disease in the arid climate of the Sinai desert and/or the land of Canaan; or (2) are foolishly uneconomical to raise as food in the particular agrarian context of the Sinai desert and/or the land of Canaan; or (3) are foods favored for religious sacrifice by groups whose practices the Israelites were not to copy. Moreover, in light of modern medical research indicating that food allergies vary according to ethnic populations, the food laws undoubtedly kept Israel away from certain allergies. The desert did not contain many pollens to bother the Israelite pulmonary tract, but it did contain some animals whose meat could irritate their digestive or nervous systems. It is especially interesting to note that the main source of Israel's meat—lamb—is the least allergenic of all popular meats, according to specialists in food allergies.

Laws about the Shedding of Blood

Example: "Bring the bull to the front of the tent of meeting, and Aaron and his sons shall lay their hands on its head. Slaughter it in the LORD's presence at the entrance to the tent of meeting. Take some of the bull's blood and put it on the horns of the altar with your finger, and pour out the rest of it at the base of the altar" (Exod 29:10–12).

Such laws as this set an important standard for Israel. Sin deserves punishment. God revealed to his people through the law that the one who sins against God does not deserve to live. But God also provided a procedure by which the sinner might escape death: a substitute's blood could be shed. Thus God offered to accept the death of another living thing—an animal—in place of the death of the sinner among his people. The sacrificial system of the law incorporated this procedure into the life of Israel. It was a necessary part of the survival of the people, picked up and cited in the New Testament. "Without the shedding of blood there is no forgiveness" (Heb 9:22). Most important, the laws that required a substitutionary sacrifice set a precedent for the work of Christ's substitutionary atonement. The principle stated in Hebrews is a thoroughly biblical one. Christ's death provides a fulfillment of the law's demand and is the basis for our acceptance with God. The Old Testament law serves as a vivid background for that greatest of events in history.

Unusual Prohibitions

Example: "Do not cook a young goat in its mother's milk" (Deut 14:21).

"What's wrong with that?" you may ask. And why are this and other laws like "Do not mate different kinds of animals," or, "Do not plant your field with two kinds of seed," or, "Do not wear clothing woven of two kinds of material" (Lev 19:19) in the Old Testament?

The answer is that these and other prohibitions were designed to forbid the Israelites to engage in the fertility cult practices of the

Canaanites. The Canaanites believed in what is called sympathetic magic, the idea that symbolic actions can influence the gods and nature. They thought that boiling a goat kid in its mother's milk would magically ensure the continuing fertility of the flock. Mixing animal breeds, seeds, or materials was thought to "marry" them so as magically to produce "offspring," that is, agricultural bounty in the future. God could not and would not bless his people if they practiced such nonsense. Knowing the intention of such laws—to keep the Israelites from being led into the Canaanite religion that stood so utterly over against God and his character—helps you see that they are not arbitrary but crucial, and to the original recipients, graciously beneficial.

Laws Giving Blessings to Those Who Keep Them

Example: "At the end of every three years, bring all the tithes of that year's produce and store it in your towns, so that the Levites (who have no allotment or inheritance of their own) and the foreigners, the fatherless and the widows who live in your towns may come and eat and be satisfied, and so that the LORD your God may bless you in all the work of your hands" (Deut 14:28–29).

Of course, all of Israel's laws were designed to be a means of blessing for the people of God (Lev 26:3–13). Some of them, however, specifically mention that obedience will provide a blessing. Thus this third-year tithe law predicates blessing upon obedience. If the people do not care for the needy among them—those without "land" such as the Levites, orphans, and widows—God will withhold prosperity. The tithe belongs to God, who has thus delegated how it is to be used. If this command is violated, it is a theft of God's money. This law provides benefit for the needy, and benefit for those who benefit the needy. Such a law is neither restrictive nor punitive. It is instead a vehicle for good practice, and as such it is instructive to us as well as to ancient Israelites.

IN SUMMARY: SOME DOS AND DON'TS

As a distillation of some of the things we have talked about in this chapter, we present here a brief list of hermeneutical guidelines that we hope will serve you well whenever you read the Old Testament Pentateuchal law. Keeping these principles in mind may help you to avoid mistaken applications of the law while seeing its instructive and faith-building character.

1. Do see the Old Testament law as God's fully inspired word *for* you.
2. Don't see the Old Testament law as God's direct command *to* you.
3. Do see the Old Testament law as the basis for the old covenant, and therefore for Israel's history.
4. Don't see the Old Testament law as binding on Christians in the new covenant except where specifically renewed.
5. Do see God's justice, love, and high standards revealed in the Old Testament law.
6. Don't forget to see that God's mercy is made equal to the severity of the standards.
7. Do see the Old Testament law as a paradigm—providing examples for the full range of expected behavior.
8. Don't see the Old Testament law as complete. It is not technically comprehensive.
9. Do remember that the *essence* of the law (the Ten Commandments and the two chief laws) is repeated in the Prophets and renewed in the New Testament.
10. Don't expect the Old Testament law to be cited frequently by the Prophets or the New Testament. Legal citation was first introduced only in the Roman era, long after the Old Testament was complete.
11. Do see the Old Testament law as a generous gift to Israel, bringing much blessing when obeyed.
12. Don't see the Old Testament law as a grouping of arbitrary, annoying regulations limiting people's freedom.

CHAPTER 10

The Prophets: Enforcing the Covenant in Israel

More individual books of the Bible come under the heading of prophecy than under any other heading. Four "Major" Prophets (Isaiah, Jeremiah, Ezekiel, Daniel) and twelve "Minor" Prophets (the final twelve books of the Old Testament), written in ancient Israel between about 760 and 460 BC, contain a vast array of messages from God.

The Minor Prophets are so-called only because the books are relatively short in length; the term "minor" comes from centuries past, when in Latin these books were called *prophetes minores* (where "minor" meant "shorter," not "less important"). The Major Prophets, on the other hand, are relatively long books (the term "major" in Latin means "larger" = "longer"). The terms themselves, therefore, convey absolutely nothing about the importance of what is in the various shorter or longer Prophetic Books. Indeed, many of the greatest statements from the Old Testament are found in the Minor Prophets, such as "the righteous person will live by his faithfulness" (Hab 2:4; cf. Rom 1:17; Gal 3:11), or "In the place where it was said to them, 'You are not my people,' they will be called 'children of the living God'" (Hos 1:10; cf. Rom 9:26).

One should also be aware that ancient Judaism actually grouped the twelve shorter prophetic books into one large book, called "The Book of the Twelve," or simply "The Twelve." This grouping, long ignored but now increasingly appreciated and influential, produced a book whose length falls right in the middle of the length of the Major Prophets—longer than two of them

(Ezekiel and Daniel) and shorter than the other two (Isaiah and Jeremiah). Thus historically they were never considered "minor" in any way whatsoever.

THE NATURE OF PROPHECY

We should note at the outset that the Prophetic Books are among the most difficult parts of the Bible for people of later times to interpret or read with understanding. The reasons for this are primarily related to misunderstandings as to their *function* and *form*. But before we discuss these two matters, some preliminary comments are in order.

The Meaning of Prophecy

The primary difficulty for most modern readers of the Prophets stems from an inaccurate prior understanding of the word "prophecy." For most people this word means what appears as the first definition in most dictionaries: "foretelling or prediction of what is to come." It often happens, therefore, that many Christians refer to the Prophetic Books *only* for predictions about the coming of Jesus and/or certain features of the new-covenant age—as though prediction of events far distant from their own day was the main concern of the prophets. In fact, using the Prophetic Books in this way is highly selective. Consider in this connection the following statistics: Less than 2 percent of Old Testament prophecy is messianic. Less than 5 percent specifically describes the new-covenant age. Less than 1 percent concerns events yet to come in our time.

The prophets *did* indeed announce the future. But it was usually the more immediate future of Israel, Judah, and other nations surrounding them that they announced rather than *our* future. One of the keys to understanding the Prophetic Books, therefore, is that for us to see their prophecies fulfilled, we must look back on times that for them were still future but for us are past.

The Prophets as Spokespersons

To see the prophets as primarily predictors of future events is to miss their primary function, which was to *speak for God* to their own contemporaries. It is the "spoken" nature of their prophecies that causes many of our difficulties in understanding.

For example, of the hundreds of prophets in ancient Israel in Old Testament times, only sixteen would speak oracles (messages from God) that were to be collected and written up into books. We know that other prophets, such as Elijah and Elisha, played a very influential role in delivering God's word to his people, and to nations other than Israel as well. But we know more about the actions of these prophets than we do of their words. What they *did* was described in far greater length than what they *said*—and what they said was placed specifically and clearly in the context of their times by the writers of the Old Testament narratives in which they appear. Of a few prophets, such as Gad (1 Sam 22; 2 Sam 24; et al.), Nathan (2 Sam 7; 12; 1 Kgs 1; et al.), or Huldah (2 Kgs 22), we have a combination of prophecy and biography—a situation paralleled in the case of Jonah and, to a lesser extent, Jeremiah and Daniel. But generally in the narrative books of the Old Testament we hear *about* prophets and very little *from* prophets. In the Prophetic Books, however, we hear *from* God *via* the prophets and very little about the prophets themselves. This single difference accounts for most of the problems people have in making sense of the Prophetic Books in the Old Testament.

Furthermore, have you ever noticed how difficult it is to read any of the longer Prophetic Books through in one sitting? Why do you suppose this is? Primarily, we think, because they were probably not intended to be read that way. For the most part these longer books are *collections of spoken oracles* not always presented in their original chronological sequence, often without hints as to where one oracle ends and another begins, and often without hints as to their historical setting. And most of the oracles were spoken in poetry! We will say more about this below.

The Problem of History

Another matter complicates our understanding of the Prophetic Books—the problem of historical distance. Indeed, by the very nature of things, we modern readers will find it much harder to understand in our own time the word of God as it was spoken by the prophets than did the Israelites who heard those same words in person. Things clear to them tend to be opaque to us. Why? Partly because those in a speaker's audience have certain obvious advantages over those who read a speaker's words much later, and, to boot, secondhand (cf. what was said about the parables in ch. 8), not to mention that so much of it comes to us by way of Hebrew *poetry*, which itself took a quite different form from what most modern readers expect regarding "poetry." But this is not where the difficulties really lie for the most part. Rather, as people far removed from the religious, historical, and cultural life of ancient Israel, we simply have great trouble putting the words spoken by the prophets in their original historical context. It is often hard for us to see what they are referring to and why—which is also why a contemporary reader often needs some outside help in order to understand them better.

THE FUNCTION OF PROPHECY IN ISRAEL

To understand what God would say to us through these inspired books, we must first have a clear understanding as to the role and function of the prophet in Israel. Four items must be emphasized:

1. *The prophets were covenant enforcement mediators.* We explained in the preceding chapter how Israel's law constituted a covenant between God and his people, modeled after the ancient suzerainty treaties and thus containing both stipulations and sanctions. God's covenant with Israel, therefore, contains not only regulations and statutes for them to keep but describes the sorts of sanctions that accompany the law: the sorts of blessings his people will receive if they keep the law, and the sorts of punishments ("curses") that God will necessarily mete out if they do not. Thus God does not merely give Israel his law, but he enforces it.

This is where the prophets come in. God announced the enforcement (positive or negative) of his law through them, so that the events of blessing or cursing would be clearly understood by his people. Moses was the mediator for God's law when God first announced it and thus is a paradigm (model) for the prophets. They are God's mediators, or spokespersons, for the covenant. Through them God reminds people in the generations after Moses that if his law is kept, blessing will result; but if not, punishment will ensue.

The kinds of blessings that will come to Israel for faithfulness to the covenant are found in three Old Testament passages (Lev 26:14–38; Deut 4:32–40; and 28:1–14). But these blessings are announced with a warning: If Israel does *not* obey God's law, the blessings will cease. The sorts of curses (punishments) that Israel could expect if they violated the law are found especially in three places (Lev 26:14–39; Deut 4:15–28; and throughout Deut 28:15–32:42).

Therefore, one must always bear in mind that the prophets did not invent the blessings or curses they announced. They may have worded these blessings and curses in novel, captivating ways, as they were inspired to do so. But they pronounced *God's* word, not their own. Through them God announced his intention to enforce the covenant, for benefit or for harm—depending on the faithfulness of Israel—but always on the basis of and in accordance with the categories of blessing and cursing already contained in the Leviticus and Deuteronomy passages noted above. If you will take the trouble to read these chapters from the Pentateuch with care, you will be rewarded with a much better understanding of why the prophets said the things that they did.

Briefly, what one finds is this. The law contains certain categories of corporate blessings for covenant faithfulness: life, health, prosperity, agricultural abundance, respect, and safety. Most of the specific blessings mentioned will fall under one of these six general groupings. As regards curses, the law describes corporate punishments, which we happen to find convenient (and memorizable) to group under ten headings that begin with the letter *d*: death, disease, drought, dearth, danger, destruction, defeat, deportation, destitution, and disgrace. Most of the curses will fit under one of these categories.

These same categories apply in what God communicates through the prophets. For example, when God wishes to predict future blessing for the nation (not any given individual) through the prophet Amos, this is done in terms of metaphors of agricultural abundance, life, health, prosperity, respect, and safety (Amos 9:11–15). When announcing doom for the disobedient nation of Hosea's day, God does so according to one or more of the ten *d*'s listed above (e.g., destruction in Hos 8:14, or deportation in Hos 9:3). These curses are often metaphorical, though they can be literal as well. They are always corporate, referring to the nation as a whole.

Blessings or curses, it should be noted, do not guarantee prosperity or dearth to any specific individual. Statistically, a majority of what the prophets announce in the eighth, seventh, and early sixth centuries BC is curse, because the major defeat and destruction of the northern kingdom did not occur until 722 BC and that of the southern kingdom (Judah), 586 BC. The Israelites, north and south, were heading for punishment during that era, so naturally warnings of curse rather than blessing predominated as God sought to get his people to repent. After the destruction of both north and south, that is, after 586 BC, the prophets were moved more often to speak blessings rather than curses. This is because once the punishment of the nation was complete, God's basic plan resumed, to show mercy (see Deut 4:25 – 31 for a condensed description of this sequence).

As you read the Prophetic Books, look for this simple pattern: (1) an identification of Israel's sin *or* of God's love for his people; (2) a prediction of curse or blessing, depending on the circumstance. Most of the time, this is what the prophets are conveying, according to God's inspiration of them.

2. *The prophets' message was not their own, but God's.* As you read the Prophetic Books with some care, you will easily pick up that each prophet has his own unique style, vocabulary, emphases, idioms, and concerns. The unique features of each of their books is highlighted in *How to 2,* pages 171–265. Here we want to emphasize, in keeping with what has just been said, that God is the one who raised up the prophets to speak his word to Israel (cf. Exod 3 – 4; Isa 6; Jer 1; Ezek 1 – 3; Hos 1:2; Amos 7:14 – 15; Jonah 1:1; et al.). If a prophet presumed to take the office of prophet upon himself or herself, this would be good cause to consider such a person a false prophet (cf. Jer 14:14; 23:21). The prophets responded to a divine call. The Hebrew word for prophet (*nābî'*) comes in fact from the Semitic verb "to call" (*nabû*). You will note as you read the Prophetic Books that they preface, or conclude, or regularly punctuate their oracles with reminders like "This is what the LORD says" or "declares the LORD." A majority of the time, in fact, the prophetic message is relayed directly as received from the Lord, in the first person, so that God speaks personally, in terms of "I" or "me."

Read, for example, the two companion narratives in Jeremiah 27 and 28. Consider Jeremiah's difficult task in relaying to the people of Judah that it would be necessary for them to submit to the imperial armies of their enemy, Babylon, if they wished to please God. His hearers (most of them, at least) considered this message to be the equivalent of treason. Indeed, Jeremiah had already been put on trial for sedition (26:7–24). When the prophet delivers the message, however, he makes it abundantly clear that they are not hearing his views on the matter, but God's. He begins by reminding them, "This is what the LORD said to me ..." (27:2), and then quotes God's command, "Then send word ..." (27:3); "Give them a message ..." (27:4), and adds "declares the LORD" (27:11). The prophet's word is God's word. It is delivered on God's authority (28:15–16), not his own.

3. *The prophets were God's direct representatives.* As vehicles through whom God's word was delivered both to Israel and other nations, the prophets held a kind of societal office. They were like ambassadors from the heavenly court who relayed the divine sovereign's will to the people. The prophets were, on their own, neither radical social reformers nor innovative religious thinkers. The social reforms and the religious thought that God wished to impart to the people had already been revealed in the covenantal law. No matter which group broke those laws, God's word through the prophet held punishment. Whether the guilt for covenant violations lay with the royalty (e.g., 2 Sam 12:1–14; 24:11–17; Hos 1:4) or with the clergy (Hos 4:4–11; Amos 7:17; Mal 2:1–9), or any other group, the prophet conveyed God's message of national curse faithfully. Indeed, at God's bidding, prophets even installed or deposed kings (1 Kgs 19:16; 21:17–22) and declared war (2 Kgs 3:18–19; 2 Chr 20:14–17; Hos 5:5–8) or spoke against war (Jer 27:8–22).

What we read in the Prophetic Books, then, is not merely God's word as the prophet saw it but God's word as God wished the prophet to present it. The prophet does not act or speak independently of God. In fact, the introductory wording in many prophetical books that is usually translated "the word of the LORD came to [name of prophet]" is probably better translated "the word of the LORD was entrusted to [name of prophet]." Prophets held a deep responsibility to preserve and convey that word widely and repeatedly, no matter the difficulty or opposition.

4. *The prophets' message is not original.* The prophets were inspired by God to present to their generation the essential content of the original Mosaic covenant's warnings and promises (curses and blessings). Therefore, when we read the prophets' words, what we read is not new in concept but new in wording—in each prophet's own style and vocabulary—of the same message

in essence delivered by God originally through Moses. As one should expect, the exact wording may be unique, and in that sense "novel," but the concepts expressed restate faithfully what God had already expressed to his people in Exodus, Leviticus, Numbers, and Deuteronomy.

The form in which that message is conveyed can, of course, vary substantially. God raised up the prophets to gain the attention of the people to whom they were sent. Gaining people's attention may involve rephrasing and restructuring something they have already heard many times so that it has a certain kind of newness. But this is not at all the same as actually initiating a new message or altering the old message. The prophets are not inspired to make any points or announce any doctrines that are not already contained in the Pentateuchal covenant.

As one example of this keeping faith with the message, consider how Hosea begins his description of Israel's unfaithfulness to Yahweh: "There is only cursing, lying and murder, stealing and adultery" (4:2). In this declaration, which is part of a long description of Israel's unfaithfulness in Hosea's day (750–722 BC), five of the Ten Commandments are summarized, each by a single term. He begins with "cursing," the third commandment—"You shall not misuse the name of the LORD your God" (Exod 20:7; Deut 5:11); then "lying," the ninth commandment—"You shall not give false testimony" (Exod 20:16; Deut 5:20); then "murder," the sixth commandment—"You shall not murder" (Exod 20:13; Deut 5:17); then "stealing," the eighth commandment—"You shall not steal" (Exod 20:15; Deut 5:19); and finally "adultery," the seventh commandment—"You shall not commit adultery" (Exod 20:14; Deut 5:18).

It is as interesting to note what the inspired prophet does *not* do as what he does do. That is, Hosea does not cite the Ten Commandments verbatim. He mentions five of them in a one-word summary fashion much as Jesus does much later in his own recalling of the commandments (Mark 10:19; cf. Matt 18:18–19; Luke 18:20). But mentioning five, even out of their usual order, is a very effective way of communicating to the Israelites that they have broken the Ten Commandments. For upon hearing five of the commandments, the hearer would think, *And what of the others? What of the usual order? The original wording is ...* The audience would begin thinking of all ten, reminding themselves of what the covenant law calls for in terms of basic righteousness. In citing five of the commandments for a similar effect, Hosea did not change anything in the law, any more than Jesus did. But he did impress the law upon his hearers in a way that simply repeating it word for word might never have done.

A second example concerns the messianic prophecies. Are these new? Not at all. Certainly, the kind of *detail* about the life and role of the Messiah that we find in the four Servant Songs of Isaiah (chs. 42; 49; 50; 53) may be considered new. But God did not bring the notion of a Messiah to the people for the first time through the prophets. It had in fact originated with the law. Otherwise how could Jesus have described his life as fulfilling what was written "in the Law of Moses, the Prophets and the Psalms" (Luke 24:44)? Among other portions of the Mosaic law that foretell the Messiah's ministry, a key moment in Deuteronomy is prominent: "I will raise up for them a prophet like you from among their fellow Israelites, and I will put my words in his mouth. He will tell them everything I command him" (18:18).

As John also reminds us in his gospel (1:45), the law already spoke of Christ. It was hardly a new thing for the prophets to speak of him. The mode, the style, and the specificity with which they made their inspired predictions did not need to be restricted to what the Pentateuch already contained. But the essential fact that there would be a new covenant ushered in by a new "Prophet" (using the language of Deut 18) was, in fact, an old story.

THE EXEGETICAL TASK
The Need for Outside Help
We noted in chapter 1 that there is a popular notion that everything in the Bible ought to be clear to everyone who reads it, since the Holy Spirit dwells in us. The reasoning is that if God wrote the Bible for *us* (for all believers), we should be able to understand it completely the first time we read it, since we have the Holy Spirit in us. But such a notion lacks proper perspective. Parts of the Bible are obvious on the surface, but other parts are not. In accordance with the fact that God's thoughts are profound compared with human thoughts (Ps 92:5; Isa 55:8) it should not be surprising that some parts of the Bible will require time and patient study in order to understand.

The Prophetic Books require just such time and study. People often approach these books casually, as if a surface reading through the writings of the Prophets will yield a high level of understanding. This cannot be done with school textbooks and it does not work with the Prophets either—in part because so many of these oracles are in poetry, but mostly because they spoke into historical, cultural, and political settings that are so different from ours.

Besides the "Overview" and "Specific Advice" sections found in *How to 2,* we repeat here, specifically for the interpretation of the Prophetic Books, the three other kinds of helps that are available to you. The first source would be *Bible dictionaries,* which provide articles on the historical setting of each book, its basic outline, the special features it contains, and issues of interpretation of which the reader must be aware. We recommend that you make it a practice to read a Bible dictionary article on a given prophetic book before you start to study that book. You need to know the background information in order to be able to catch the point of much of what a prophet conveys. God's word came through the prophets to people in *particular situations.* Its value to us depends partly on our ability to appreciate those situations so that we can in turn apply the word wisely to our own.

A second source of help would be *commentaries* (see appendix). These provide lengthy introductions to each book, somewhat in the manner of the Bible dictionaries, though often less usefully organized. But more important, they provide explanations of the meaning of the individual verses. Commentaries may become essential if you are studying carefully a relatively small portion of a prophetic book, that is, less than a chapter at a time.

A third source of help would be *Bible handbooks.* The best of these combine features of both Bible dictionaries and commentaries, though they do not go into as great detail on either the introductory materials or the verse-by-verse explanations. When one is reading through several chapters at a time of a prophetic book, however, a Bible handbook can yield a lot of helpful guidance in a minimal amount of time.

Finally, you may also want to consult the individual chapters in *How to 2* (pp. 174–265) to see how the various Prophetic Books "work" as individual books within the larger biblical story.

The Historical Context

In chapter 7, regarding the study of Jesus, the term "historical context" referred both to the larger arena into which Jesus came and to the specific context of any one of his deeds and sayings. In studying the writings of the prophets, the historical context can likewise be large (their era) or specific (the context of a single oracle). To do good exegesis you need to understand both kinds of historical context for all the Prophetic Books.

The Larger Context

It is interesting to note that the sixteen Prophetic Books of the Old Testament come from a rather narrow band in the whole panorama of Israelite history (i.e., about 760–460 BC). Why do we have no books of prophecy from Abraham's day (about 1800 BC) or Joshua's day (about 1400 BC) or David's day (about 1000 BC)? Didn't God speak to his people and their world before 760 BC? The answer is, of course he did, and we have much material in the Bible about those ages, including some that deals with prophets (e.g., 1 Kgs 17–2 Kgs 13). Moreover, remember that God spoke especially to Israel in the law, which was intended to stand for the entire remaining history of the nation until it would be superseded by the new covenant (Jer 31:31–34).

Why, then, is there such a concentrated writing down of prophetic words during the three centuries between Amos (ca. 760 BC, the earliest of the "writing prophets") and Malachi (ca. 460 BC, the latest)? The answer is that this period in Israel's history called especially for *covenant enforcement mediation*—the task of the prophets. A second factor was the evident desire of God to record for all subsequent history the warnings and blessings that those prophets announced on his behalf during those pivotal years.

Those years were characterized by three things: (1) unprecedented political, military, economic, and social upheaval; (2) an enormous level of religious unfaithfulness and disregard for the original Mosaic covenant; and (3) shifts in populations and national boundaries, including enormous shifts in the balance of power on the international scene. In these circumstances God's word was needed anew. God raised up prophets and announced his word accordingly.

As you make use of dictionaries, commentaries, and handbooks, you will note that by 760 BC Israel was a nation divided permanently by a long, ongoing civil war. The northern tribes, called "Israel," or sometimes "Ephraim," were separated from the southern tribe of Judah. The north, where disobedience to the covenant far outstripped anything yet known in Judah, was slated for destruction by God because of its sin. Amos, beginning around 760, and Hosea, beginning around 755, announced the impending destruction. In 722 BC the north fell to Assyria, the superpower in the Middle East at that time. Thereafter, the mounting sinfulness of Judah and the rise of another superpower, Babylon, constituted the subject matter of many prophets, including Isaiah, Jeremiah, Joel, Micah, Nahum, Habakkuk, Zephaniah, and Ezekiel (chs. 1–24). In 587 BC Judah, too, was destroyed for its disobedience. Afterward, Ezekiel (chs. 33–48), Daniel, Haggai, Zechariah, and Malachi announced God's will for the restoration of his people (beginning with a return from exile in 538 BC), the rebuilding of the nation, and the reinstitution of orthodoxy. All of this follows the basic pattern laid out in Deuteronomy 4:25–31.

The prophets speak in large measure directly to *these* events. Unless you know these events, and others within this era too numerous to mention here, you probably will not be able to follow very well what the prophets are saying. God spoke in history and about history. To understand God's Word we must know something of that history.

The Specific Context

Each prophetic oracle was delivered in a specific historical setting. God spoke through his prophets to people in a given time and place and under given circumstances. Therefore, a knowledge of the date, audience, and situation, when these are known, contributes substantially to your ability to comprehend an oracle. In order to help you with this task, we offer the following example.

Read Hosea 5:8–12, a brief, self-contained oracle grouped with several other oracles in the chapter. A good commentary will identify for you the fact that this oracle is in the form of a war oracle, one of a type (form) that announces the judgment of God as carried out through battle. The usual elements of such a form are these: the call to alarm, the description of attack, and the prediction of defeat. Just as it is helpful for you to recognize the form, it is also helpful to recognize the specific content.

The *date* is 734 BC. The *audience* is the northern Israelites (called here "Ephraim") to whom Hosea preached. Specifically the message was to certain cities that lay on the road that ran from the Judean capital, Jerusalem, to the center of Israelite false worship, Bethel. The *situation* is war. Judah counterattacked Israel after Israel and Syria had invaded Judah (see 2 Kgs 16:5). The invasion had been beaten back with the help of the superpower Assyria (2 Kgs 16:7–9). God through Hosea sounds the alarm metaphorically in cities located in the territory of Benjamin (Hos 5:8), which is part of the northern kingdom. Destruction is sure (v. 9) because Judah will capture the territory it invades ("moving the boundary stones" as it were). But Judah, too, will get its due. God's wrath will fall on them both for this act of war and for their idolatry (cf. 2 Kgs 16:2–4). Judah and Israel were under obligation to the divine covenant, which forbade such internecine war. So God would punish this violation of his covenant.

Knowing these few facts makes a great deal of difference in one's ability to appreciate the oracle in Hosea 5:8–12. Refer to the commentaries or handbooks as you read the Prophetic Books, and, as always, try to be aware of the date, audience, and situation of the oracles you read.

The Isolation of Individual Oracles

When one comes to the actual study or exegetically informed reading of the Prophetic Books, the first thing one must learn to do is to THINK ORACLES (as one must learn to "think paragraphs" in the Epistles). This is not always an easy task, but to know that even though it is difficult but necessary to do this can be the beginning of some exciting discoveries.

Most of the time what the prophets said is presented in their books in run-on fashion. That is, the words they spoke at various times and places over the years of their ministry have been collected and written down without any divisions to indicate where one oracle ends and another begins. Moreover, even when one can assume by a major change of subject that a new oracle has probably begun, the lack of explanation (i.e., editorial remarks or transitions) still leaves one asking whether this was said on the same day to the same audience, or was it said years later—or earlier—to a different group under different circumstances? The answer can make a big difference for one's understanding.

Some parts of the Prophetic Books provide exceptions. In Haggai and the early chapters of Zechariah, for example, each prophecy is dated. With the help of your Bible dictionary, handbook, or commentary, you can follow the progression of these prophecies in their historical context rather easily. And some of the prophecies in other books, notably Jeremiah and Ezekiel, are likewise dated and placed in a setting by the prophet (or inspired collector).

But it simply does not work this way most of the time. For example, read Amos 5 in a version of the Bible that does not insert explanatory titles (these headings are only scholarly opinion), and ask yourself whether the chapter is all one prophecy (oracle) or not. If it *is* a single oracle, why does it have so many changes of subject: lament over Israel's destruction (vv. 1–3); invitation to seek God and live (vv. 5–6, 14); attacks on social injustice (vv. 7–13); prediction of miseries (vv. 16–17); description of the Day of the Lord (vv. 18–20); criticism of hypocritical worship (vv. 21–24); and a brief overview of Israel's sinful history that culminates in a prediction of exile (vv. 25–27)? If it is *not* a single oracle, how are its component parts to be understood? Are they all independent of one another? Are some to be grouped together? If so, in what ways?

In fact it is now generally agreed that our chapter 5 contains three oracles. The first (vv. 1–3) forms a single short lament oracle announcing punishment; the second (vv. 4–17) forms a single (though complex) oracle of invitation to blessing and warning of punishment; and the third (vv. 18–27) forms a single (though complex) oracle warning of punishment. The smaller changes of subject, then, do not each indicate the beginning of a new oracle.

Likewise, the chapter divisions do not correspond with individual oracles either. Oracles are isolated by attention to their known forms (see below). All three of the oracles in chapter 5 were given late in the reign of King Jeroboam of Israel (793–753 BC) to a people whose relative prosperity caused them to consider it unthinkable that their nation would be so devastated as to cease to exist in just a generation. A good commentary or Bible handbook will explain such things to you as you read. Do not handicap yourself needlessly by trying to read these great moments without some helps, since they will greatly multiply your understanding as you read.

The Forms of Prophetic Utterance

Since the isolation of individual oracles is one key to help your understanding of the Prophetic Books, it is helpful, indeed important, for you to know something about the different *forms* the prophets used to compose their oracles. Just as the whole Bible is composed of many different kinds of literature and literary forms, so also the prophets employed a variety of literary forms in the service of their divinely inspired messages. The commentaries can identify and explain these forms. We have selected five of the most common forms to help alert you to the importance of recognizing and rightly interpreting the literary techniques involved. And here again we urge you to get into the habit of reading Scripture aloud to yourself. You will be happily surprised by doing so!

The Lawsuit

As a good place to begin we suggest you read Isaiah 3:13–26. This constitutes an allegorical literary form called a "covenant lawsuit" (Hebrew, *rîb*). In this and the scores of other lawsuit allegories in the Prophetic Books (e.g., Hos 3:3–17; 4:1–19; etc.), God is portrayed imaginatively as the plaintiff, prosecuting attorney, judge, and bailiff in a court case against the defendant, Israel. The full lawsuit form contains a summons, a charge, evidence, and a verdict, though these elements may sometimes be implied rather than explicit. In Isaiah 3 the elements are incorporated as follows: The court convenes, and the lawsuit is brought against Israel (vv. 13–14a). The indictment or accusation is spoken (vv. 14b–16). Since the evidence shows that Israel is clearly guilty, the judgment sentence is announced (vv. 17–26). Because the covenant has been violated, the sorts of punishments listed in the covenant will come upon Israel's women and men: disease, destitution, deprivation, death. The figurative style of this allegory is a dramatic and effective way of communicating to Israel that they are going to be punished because of their disobedience, and that the punishment will be severe. This special literary form helps get the prophet's special message across.

The Woe

Another common literary form is that of the "woe oracle." "Woe" was the word ancient Israelites cried out when facing disaster or death, or when they mourned at a funeral. Through the prophets, God makes predictions of imminent doom using the device of the "woe," and no Israelite could miss the significance of the use of that word. Woe oracles contain, either explicitly or implicitly, three elements that uniquely characterize this form: an announcement of distress (the word "woe," for example), the reason for the distress, and a prediction of doom.

Here you might read Habakkuk 2:6–8 to see one of several instances in this prophetic book of a "woe oracle" spoken against the nation of Babylon. Babylon, a brutal, imperialistic superpower in the ancient Fertile Crescent, was making plans to conquer and crush Judah at the end of the seventh century BC when Habakkuk spoke God's words against it. Personifying Babylon as a thief and extortionist (the *reason*), the oracle *announces* woe and *predicts* disaster (when all those whom Babylon has oppressed will one day rise against it). Again, this form is allegorical (though not all woe oracles are; cf. Mic 2:1–5; Zeph 2:5–7).

The Promise
Yet another common prophetic literary form is "the promise" or "salvation oracle." You will recognize this form whenever you see these elements: reference to the future, mention of radical change, and mention of blessing. A typical promise oracle may be seen in Amos 9:11–15; it contains these elements. The *future* is mentioned as "In that day" (v. 11). The *radical change* is described as the restoration and repair of "David's fallen shelter" (v. 11), the exaltation of Israel over Edom (v. 12), and the return from exile (vv. 14–15). *Blessing* comes via the covenantal categories mentioned (life, health, prosperity, agricultural abundance, respect, and safety). All these items are included in this oracle, though health is implicit rather than explicit. The central imagery is of agricultural abundance. Crops, for example, will be so enormous that the harvesters still will not be finished by the time the sowers start planting again (v. 13)! For other examples of promise oracles, see Isaiah 45:1–7; Jeremiah 31:1–9; and Hosea 2:16–20, 21–23.

The Enactment Prophecy
Because of the power of visual aids to enhance the impact and memorability of oral presentations, God sometimes told prophets not merely to speak his word but also to accompany that word with symbolic actions that would vividly reinforce the concepts contained in what the prophets spoke.

For example, Isaiah's brief prophecy against Egypt and Cush (ch. 20) describes how God instructed Isaiah to go "stripped and barefoot for three years" (v. 3) to symbolize the prediction that "the king of Assyria will lead away stripped and barefoot the Egyptian captives and Cushite exiles" (v. 4). In this instance, Isaiah's symbolic enactment first of all depicted the fact that exiles were allowed to wear only what today would be called underwear as they gathered for their long march of deportation—an action intended both to humiliate them and to prevent them from concealing weapons in their garments. But this action also took advantage of the fact that the Hebrew verb *gālāh* refers to both "exile" and "strip," a double entendre to reinforce the prophecy in the minds of Isaiah's audience.

Did Isaiah actually appear publicly in his underwear for three years? Yes, but almost certainly only at particular times during the three-year period. He had many prophecies to deliver during those three years and could not likely have limited himself to this one enactment for the entire time. But whenever anyone did see Isaiah in public "stripped and barefoot," a central point of his prophecy was reinforced: If the Assyrians, far to the north and east of Israel, were going to capture and deport Egypt and Cush, located far to the south and west of Israel, how could Israel, right in the middle, expect to escape unharmed?

Several other prophets made good use of enactment prophecies. For example, God told Ezekiel, himself among the first wave of exiles in Babylon, to build a tiny model of Jerusalem and then "face" toward it the way the Babylonian army faced Jerusalem (Ezek 4:1–4). This symbolized the siege of the city, which Ezekiel prophesied would eventually be successful so that Jerusalem would be conquered by the Babylonians—against total disbelief by his fellow exiles.

Similarly, Zechariah used an enactment prophecy to symbolize the oppression of God's people by ruthless monarchs. This is recorded toward the end of the collection of oracles (11:4–17), where he is described as playing the roles of two "shepherds" (kings) over the hapless "flock" (Israel). Such an enactment also prepares the reader for the expectation of the true Good Shepherd, Jesus Christ, who will deliver and bless rather than take advantage of his people (Zech 12–14).

The Messenger Speech

This form is the most common of all the forms in the Prophetic Books and often occurs alongside of, or as part of, one of the other prophetic speech forms. It is signaled by standard wordings (called "messenger formulae") such as "This is what the LORD says" or "says the LORD" or "This is the word of the LORD concerning . . ." or the like. Such formulae as these were used by messengers in diplomatic and business settings in the ancient world to remind recipients that what the messenger was saying was not something they were making up but was in fact the exact words of the one who had sent them to deliver the message (cf. Num 20:14; 1 Sam 11:9; 2 Sam 11:25).

Thus the prophets often remind their audiences via the messenger speech form that they are merely spokespersons for God, not independent creators of the words of their prophecies. Typical examples of messenger speeches can be seen in such diverse prophetic oracles as Isaiah 38:1–8; Jeremiah 35:17–19; Amos 1:3–2:16; and Malachi 1:2–5.

From these brief examples, we hope you can see how an informed sense of prophetic literary devices will help you comprehend the message of God more accurately. Learn the forms by referring to the commentaries (see appendix), and you will be glad you did!

The Prophets as Poets

Many people have little appreciation for poetry. Poetry seems a strange and confusing way to express things, as though it were designed to make ideas less, rather than more, intelligible. Our present culture tends to place little emphasis on poetry, except in popular music, which normally contains the sort of poor quality poetry called "doggerel." In some present-day cultures, however, and in most ancient ones, poetry was a highly prized mode of expression. Whole national epics and key historical and religious memories were preserved in poetry. We say "preserved" because one major advantage of poetry over prose is that it is more readily memorized. A poem has a certain rhythm (also called meter), certain balances (also called parallelism or stichometry), and a certain overall structure. It is relatively regular and orderly. Once learned well, poetry is not as easily forgotten as is prose.

The poetic prose sometimes used by the prophets is a special, formal style employing these same characteristics, though less consistently. Because it is so much more regular and stylized than common spoken language (colloquial prose), it, too, is better remembered. For convenience, we will also speak of it with the general term "poetry."

In ancient Israel, poetry was widely appreciated as a means of learning. Many memories that were important enough to be recalled were considered appropriate for composition in poetry. Just as people today can reproduce from memory the words of songs (i.e., the poems called "lyrics") much more easily than we can reproduce sentences from books or speeches, the Israelites found it relatively simple to commit to memory and to recall things composed in poetry. God made good use of this helpful phenomenon in an age where reading and writing were rare skills and where the private ownership of written documents was virtually unknown. Thus the larger parts of the prophetic oracles were usually expressed in poetic form. People were used to poetry and could remember those prophecies; they would ring in their ears.

All the Prophetic Books contain a substantial amount of poetry, and several are exclusively poetic. Before you read these books, therefore, you may find it very helpful to read an introduction to Hebrew poetry. We especially recommend either the article titled "Poetry" in the *New Bible Dictionary* (Downers Grove, Ill.: InterVarsity Press, 1996); or chapters 6 and 7 in Tremper Longman III, *How to Read the Psalms* (Downers Grove, Ill.: InterVarsity Press, 1988, pp. 89–110). But any Bible dictionary will have at least one informative article on poetry. As a small hint of the benefits to be realized from knowing how Hebrew poetry functions, we suggest you learn these three features of the repetitive style of Old Testament poetry:

1. *Synonymous parallelism.* The second or subsequent line repeats or reinforces the sense of the first line, as in Isaiah 44:22:

> I have swept away your offenses like a cloud,
> your sins like the morning mist.

2. *Antithetical parallelism.* The second or subsequent line contrasts the thought of the first, often reinforcing the first line by the contrast, as in Hosea 7:14:

> They do not cry out to me from their hearts
> but wail on their beds.

3. *Synthetic parallelism.* The second or subsequent line adds to the first line in any manner that provides further information, as in Obadiah 21:

Deliverers will go up on Mount Zion
to govern the mountains of Esau.
And the kingdom will be the LORD's.

Remember that the presentation of ideas in poetry need not confuse you as long as you read carefully and knowledgeably. Poetry is just as comprehensible as prose when you know the rules.

SOME HERMENEUTICAL SUGGESTIONS

If the task of exegesis is to set the Prophetic Books within their own historical contexts and to hear what God was saying to Israel through them, then what can be said at the hermeneutical level? What is God's word to us through these inspired poetic oracles, spoken in another time to God's ancient people? First, we would point out that much of what was said in chapter 4 about the hermeneutics of the Epistles applies here as well. Once we hear what God said to them, even if our circumstances differ considerably, we will often hear it again in our own settings in a rather direct way. We would argue that God's judgment always awaits those who "sell ... the needy for a pair of sandals" (Amos 2:6), or who use religion as a cloak for greed and injustice (cf. Isa 1:10–17), or who have mixed modern idolatries (such as self-justification) with the gospel of Christ (cf. Hos 13:2–4). These sins of an earlier time are sins in the new covenant as well. They violate the two great commandments that both the old and new covenants share (see ch. 9).

But beyond these kinds of applications, there are three further matters that we feel would be helpful for us to address: one a caution, another a concern, and still another a benefit.

A Caution: The Prophet as Foreteller of the Future

Toward the beginning of this chapter we noted that it was not the prophets' primary task to predict the distant future. They did indeed predict future events, but for the most part *that* future is now past. That is, they spoke of coming judgment or salvation in the relatively immediate future of ancient Israel, not our own future. We cautioned that to see their prophecies fulfilled we must look back on times that for them were still future but for us are past. This hermeneutical principle needs to be illustrated.

As an example of the prophets' messages being concentrated on the near rather than the distant future, we suggest you read through Ezekiel 25–39. Notice that the various oracles contained in that large block of material concern mostly the fate of nations other than Israel, though Israel is also included. It is important to see that God refers to the fate of these nations, and that the fulfillment came *within decades* of the time the prophecies were delivered, that is, mostly during the sixth century BC. There are individual exceptions to this, of course. For example, at one point Ezekiel actually describes the new-covenant age and the blessings God will pour out on the church via the Messiah (37:15–28). But most of the prophecies, including symbolic Gog and Magog of chapters 38 and 39 (consult a commentary on these chapters) concern Old Testament times and events.

Too great a zeal for identifying New Testament events in Old Testament prophetic oracles can yield strange results. Isaiah's reference to kings who "will bow down before you with their faces to the ground" (49:23) has sounded just enough like the three magi who visited the infant Jesus (Matt 2:1–11) to encourage many to assume that Isaiah's words are messianic. Such an interpretation embarrassingly ignores the *context* (both kings and queens are mentioned; the issue of the passage is the restoration of Israel after its Babylonian exile), the *intent* (the language of the oracle intends to show how great Israel's respect will be when God restores Israel), the *style* (the poetry symbolizes the respect of the nations via images of their rulers as foster parents to Israel and licking the dust at the nation's feet), and the *wording* (magi are wise men/astrologers, not kings). We must be careful that we do not make prophetic oracles, or any part of Scripture, say what we would like it to say. Rather, we must try to hear what *God* intends it to say.

It should be noted, of course, that some of the prophecies of the near future were set against the background of the great eschatological future, and sometimes they seem to blend. We will speak to this again in our final chapter (13.) For now let it be noted that the reason for this is that the Bible regularly sees God's acts in temporal history in light of his overall plan for all of human history. Thus the temporal is to be seen in light of the eternal plan. It is like looking at two discs, with a smaller one in front of a larger, straight on; then from the perspective of subsequent history to see them from a side view and thus see how much distance there is between them.

Prophetic Perspective of Chronological Events

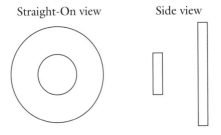

Straight-On view   Side view

Thus there are some descriptions in the Prophetic Books that may belong to the final events of the age (e.g., Joel 3:1–3; Zeph 3:8–9; Zech 14:9). But the temporal judgments that are often spoken of in conjunction with these final events must not be pushed into the future as well.

One further point should be mentioned. Eschatological language by its very nature is often metaphorical. Sometimes these metaphors express poetically the language of the final events but are not necessarily intended to be predictions of those events per se. An example is found in the well-known "dry bones" oracle in Ezekiel (37:1–14). Using the language of the resurrection of the dead, an event we know will occur at the *end* of the age, God predicts through Ezekiel the return of the nation of Israel from the exile in Babylon *in the sixth century BC* (vv. 12–14). Thus an event that to us is past (as described in Ezra 1–2) is predicted metaphorically with eschatological language as though it were an end-time event.

A Concern: Prophecy and Second Meanings

At a number of places in the New Testament, reference is made to Old Testament passages that do not appear to refer to what the New Testament writers seem to suggest they do. That is, these passages seem to have a clear meaning in their original Old Testament setting and yet are used in connection with a different meaning by a New Testament writer.

As an example, consider the two stories of how Moses and the Israelites were miraculously given water from rocks in the wilderness—once at Rephidim (Exod 17:1–7) and once at Kadesh (Num 20:1–13). The stories are, it appears, simple enough and abundantly clear in their original contexts. But in his first letter to the believers in Corinth (10:4), Paul seems to identify the experience of the Israelites as an encounter with Christ. He says that "they drank from the spiritual rock that accompanied them, and that rock was Christ." In each Old Testament story there is no hint that the rock is anything other than a rock. Paul gives the rock a second meaning, identifying it as "Christ." This second meaning is commonly called the *sensus plenior* (fuller meaning).

Upon reflection, one can see that Paul is drawing an analogy. He is saying, in effect, "That rock was to them as Christ is to us—a source of sustenance in the same way that Christ at his table sustains us." Paul's language at the beginning of this analogy (vv. 2–4) is highly metaphorical. He wants the Corinthians to understand that the experience of the Israelites in the desert can be understood in an analogous way to their own experience with Christ, especially at the Lord's Table.

To be sure, we modern readers are quite unlikely on our own to notice this analogy in the way that Paul described it. If Paul had never written these words, would we have made the identification of cloud and sea with baptism (v. 2) or the rock with Christ (v. 4)? In other words, would we, on our own, be able with any degree of certainty to determine the *sensus plenior* or secondary meaning? The answer is no. The Holy Spirit inspired Paul to write about this analogical connection between the Israelites in the desert and life in Christ without following the usual rules about *context, intent, style,* and *wording* (see above, "The Prophet as Foreteller of the Future"). The Holy Spirit directed Paul to describe the fact that the Israelites got water more than once from rocks, with the figurative, unusual language that a rock had "accompanied them," an idea already present in Jewish rabbinic lore. Other details of the descriptive language Paul uses in the presenting paragraph (vv. 1–4)—nonliteral terms like "[all] our ancestors" (v. 1) and "spiritual food and ... drink" (vv. 3–4)—are likewise strikingly unusual.

We, however, are simply not inspired writers of Scripture. What Paul did we are not authorized to do. The allegorical connections he was inspired to find between the Old Testament and the New Testament are trustworthy. But nowhere does the Scripture say to us, "Go and do likewise." Thus the principle: *Sensus plenior (fuller meaning) is a function of inspiration, not illumination.* The same Holy Spirit who inspired an Old Testament author to write a certain set of words or a passage can inspire a New Testament writer to bypass the usual considerations of context, intent, style, and wording and identify that set of words or that passage as having a contemporary application. But *we* are not inspired writers; we are illumined readers. Inspiration is the original motivation to record the Scripture in a certain way; illumination is the insight to understand what the Scripture's authors wrote. We cannot rewrite or redefine Scripture by our illumination. We can only perceive a *sensus plenior* with any certainty, therefore, *after the fact*. Unless something is identified as a *sensus plenior* in the New Testament, it cannot confidently be identified as such from the Old Testament by us on our own authority.

Study Bibles, commentaries, handbooks, and Bibles with reference columns will all tend to identify Old Testament prophetic passages that have a second, often analogical, meaning in the New Testament. Some typical instances where the New Testament gives a second meaning are Matthew 1:22–23 (Isa 7:14); Matthew 2:15 (Hos 11:1); Matthew 2:17–18 (Jer 31:15); and John 12:15 (Zech 9:9).

We need take only one of these—Matthew 2:15—to illustrate the phenomenon of an analogical meaning being assigned to a prophetic passage. A powerful oracle toward the end of Hosea thus begins (11:1),

> When Israel was a child, I loved him,
> and out of Egypt I called my son.

Hosea, of course, is picking up the language of Exodus, where Yahweh calls Israel his "firstborn son." In Hosea, the *context* is Israel's rescue from Egypt by way of the exodus (4:22). The *intent* is to show how God loved Israel from the beginning as his own "child." Good exegesis of Hosea indicates that there is no reason to think that Hosea was referring to the coming Messiah.

In time, however, the language of Israel as God's "son" had also come to be applied to its king, as the one who "stood in for" Israel (see 2 Sam 7:14; Ps 2:7; 89:27; 110:1). Matthew is writing his gospel at a time when this double usage of "son" language (Israel and its king) had already been applied to Christ, the exalted Son who now sits at God's right hand (see Rom 8:32–34; Col 1:13–15). It is this usage that Matthew is reflecting when he *reuses* this moment in Hosea to refer to the "flight to Egypt" of the young Jesus with his family. Matthew is not suggesting that Hosea was "prophesying" that the Messiah would someday come "out of Egypt." Rather, he is seeing an *analogical "fulfillment"* in which the Messiah as God's true "Son" now *reenacts* Israel's own history as God's "firstborn son." This kind of "second meaning," therefore, should not be thought of as playing games with the Old Testament; rather, as God's inspired servant, Matthew is retelling the story of Israel, God's son, as that which has been reenacted by God's true and greater Son.

We also may be able to see such analogies as we read the story of Jesus; but it is unlikely as a valid hermeneutics that we can legitimately use the language of "fulfillment" in this way without Matthew's own inspiration by the Spirit.

A Final Benefit: The Dual Emphasis on Orthodoxy and Orthopraxy

Orthodoxy is correct belief. Orthopraxy is correct living. Through the prophets, God called the people of ancient Israel and Judah to a balance of right belief and right living. This, of course, remains the very balance that the new covenant requires as well (cf. Eph 2:8 – 10; James 1:27; 2:18). What God wanted from Israel and Judah is in a general sense the same as what he wants from us. The Prophetic Books can serve constantly as reminders to us of God's determination to enforce his covenant. For those who obey the stipulations of the new covenant (loving God and loving one's neighbor), the final, eternal result will be blessing, even though the results in the present world are not guaranteed to be so encouraging. For those who disobey, the result can be only curse, regardless of how well one fares during life on earth. Malachi's warning (Mal 4:6), we suggest, still stands.

CHAPTER 11

The Psalms: Israel's Prayers and Ours

The book of Psalms, a collection of inspired Hebrew prayers and hymns, is probably for most Christians the best-known and most-loved portion of the Old Testament. The fact that the book of Psalms is often appended to copies of the New Testament and that psalms are used so often in worship and meditation has given this particular book a certain prominence for modern readers.

But frequently the psalms, as beloved as they are, present special difficulties for understanding, since the poetic features of rhyme and repetitive meter (factors that indeed allow poetry to be far more memorable than most prose) take very different forms in Hebrew poetry, and, more importantly, are virtually always lost in English translation. Further difficulty with interpreting the psalms arises primarily from their nature—what they are. Because the Bible is God's word, many Christians automatically assume that all it contains are words *from* God *to* people. Thus they fail to recognize that the Bible also contains words spoken *to* God or *about* God—which is what the psalms do—and that these words, too, are God's Word. That is, because psalms are basically prayers and hymns, by their very nature they are addressed to God or express truth about God in song.

This reality presents us with a unique problem of hermeneutics in Scripture. *How* do these words spoken *to* God function as a word *from* God to us? Since they are not propositions or imperatives or stories that get us in touch with God's story, they do not function primarily for the teaching of doctrine or moral behavior. Yet they are profitable when used for the purposes intended by God, who inspired them, by helping us to express ourselves to God and to consider God's ways. The psalms, therefore, are of great benefit to the believer who looks to the Bible for help in expressing joys and sorrows, successes and failures, hopes and regrets, or simply to worship.

But the psalms are frequently applied poorly, if not in an altogether wrong way, precisely because they are often so poorly understood. Not all of them are as easy to follow logically, or to apply to the twenty-first century, as perhaps the best known of them all, Psalm 23. In its symbolism God is portrayed as a shepherd, and the psalmist (and thus ourselves) as his sheep. God's willingness to care for us by pasturing us in the appropriate places (i.e., meeting our every need, generously protecting us and benefiting us) is evident to those who are familiar with the psalm. And, of course, the psalmist knew well what very few modern readers know, that sheep are probably among the dumbest animals ever to walk on our planet. Despite the verb that comes to us in English from this occupation, one does not easily "herd" sheep. Our guess is that this frequent analogy in Scripture was not intended to flatter us! Rather, it serves as a constant reminder as to how greatly we need the great Shepherd's tender, loving care.

But other psalms do not yield their meaning so easily at first glance. For example, how is one to use a psalm that seems to be negative throughout (e.g., Ps 88) and seems to express the misery of the speaker? Is this something that should be used in a church service? Or is it for private use only? And what of a psalm that tells about the history of Israel and God's blessings on it? Can a modern Christian, for example, make good use of this sort of psalm? Or is it reserved only for Jews? Or how about psalms that predict the work of the Messiah? Or what of psalms that laud the benefits of wisdom? What about the several psalms that discuss the glory of Israel's human kings? Since very few people in the world now live under royalty, it would seem especially difficult to make sense of this latter sort of psalm. And finally, what does one do with the desire that Babylonian infants should be dashed against the rocks (137:8–9)?

It would require a lengthy book to discuss all the types of psalms and all their possible uses. In this chapter we provide some guidelines by which you can be in a better position to appreciate and use the psalms both in your personal life and in the life of your local church. You may also want to look at *How to 2*, pages 130–43, to get a sense of how they work as a collection—in five "books."

SOME PRELIMINARY EXEGETICAL OBSERVATIONS

As a distinct kind of literature, psalms require special care in reading and interpreting—in this case, the reader will need to understand their *nature* and their various *types*, as well as their *forms* and *functions*.

The Psalms as Poetry

The most important item to remember in reading or interpreting psalms is that they are poems—musical poems. We have already briefly discussed the nature of Hebrew poetry in the preceding chapter (pp. 204–06; if you have not read these pages, you will want to do so now), but there are three additional points that need to be made in connection with the Psalter.

1. *Hebrew poetry, by its very nature, was addressed to the mind through the heart* (i.e., much of the language is intentionally emotive). Because of this feature common to biblical poetry, a reader must be careful not to "overexegete" psalms by finding special meanings in specific words or phrases where the poet will have intended none. For example, you will recall that the nature of Hebrew poetry always involves some form of parallelism and that one common form is that called synonymous parallelism (where the second line repeats or reinforces the sense of the first line; see p. 205). In this type of parallelism, the two lines together express the poet's meaning, and the second line is not trying to say something new or different. Consider, for example, the opening of Psalm 19:

> The heavens declare the glory of God;
> the skies proclaim the work of his hands.
> Day after day they pour forth speech;
> night after night they reveal knowledge.

Here, in two sets of synonymous parallelism, the inspired poet is glorifying God as Creator. Notice how the NIV translators have tried to help you see the parallels by capitalizing only the first line in each couplet and using a semicolon between the two lines.

The poet's point in plain prose is, "God is revealed in his creation, especially in the heavenly bodies." But our plain-prose sentence is totally colorless next to the magnificent poetry of the psalm, which both says it better and in a more memorable way. Note that the four lines are not trying to say four different things, although the second set adds the new idea that during both the day and the night the heavens reveal their maker. In the first set the psalmist is not trying to say that the "heavens" do one thing and the "skies" another; together the two lines speak of one glorious reality, that creation itself demonstrates God's glory and wonders.

2. *The psalms themselves are* musical *poems*. A musical poem cannot be read in the same way as an epistle or a narrative or a section of law. It is intended to appeal to the emotions, to evoke feelings that straight propositional expression seldom does, and thus to stimulate a response on the part of the individual that goes beyond a mere cognitive understanding of certain facts—this, after all, is the very reason musical poems are so well-loved, and so easily remembered. None of us would ever say in normal conversation, "glorious things of thee are spoken, Zion, city of our God." But for those of us who know John Newton's hymn well, we can both immediately pick up the next line, "He whose word cannot be broken, formed thee for his own abode," and put ourselves into the poetry. The church is God's dominion, not ours, and we can rest in that greater reality. So with psalms; while they contain and reflect doctrine, they are not intended to be repositories for doctrinal exposition. Thus it is dangerous to read a psalm as though it taught a system of doctrine, in the same way that it is dangerous to do this with narrative.

For example, who of us in singing Martin Luther's hymn "A Mighty Fortress Is Our God" (based on Psalm 46:1) would assume that God is in fact some kind of a fortification or impenetrable building or wall? We understand that "mighty fortress" is a figurative way of thinking about God. In the same way, when the psalmist says, "And in sin my mother conceived me" (Ps 51:5 NASB), the writer is hardly trying to establish the doctrine that conception is sinful, or that all conceptions are sinful, or that his mother was a sinner by getting pregnant, or that original sin applies to unborn children, or any such notion. The psalmist has employed hyperbole—purposeful exaggeration—in order to express strongly and vividly that he is a sinner, with a long history of such. Thus the present NIV has put it well: "Surely I was sinful at birth, sinful from the time my mother conceived me." This is poetry, not theology, where the psalmist expressed poetically that his sinful ways did not begin recently! To make it say something more than that is simply to abuse poetry, not to mention Scripture itself. Thus, when you read a psalm, be careful that you do not try to derive from it concepts that were never intended by the musical poet who was inspired to write it. Let it do what it was originally intended to do, such as prompting you to stop momentarily, and recognize the incredible greatness and goodness of God.

3. *The vocabulary of poetry is purposefully metaphorical.* Thus one must take care to look for the intent of the metaphor. In the book of Psalms, mountains leap like rams (114:4; singing about God's presence at Mount Sinai, narrated in Exod 19:16–25!); enemies spew out swords from their lips (59:7; who has not felt the sharp pain of slander or lies?); and God is variously seen as a shepherd, fortress, shield, rock, etc. It is extremely important that you learn to "listen" to the metaphors and understand what they signify, and from time to time, pause to reflect on the truths they convey, including God's vast love for us all.

It is also important that one not press metaphors or take them literally. If someone were to take Psalm 23 literally, for example, they might make the rather excessive mistake of assuming that God wants us to be and act like sheep, or else wants us to live a rural, pastoral life. In so doing the psalm would become a treatise against city life. To read any of the psalms well, you need to appreciate symbolic language (metaphor and simile) for what it is intended to evoke and then to "translate" it into the reality it is pointing to.

The Psalms as Literature

As musical poems, psalms are also a form of literature, with certain distinct literary features. Being aware of these should aid your reading and enjoyment.

1. *Psalms are of several different types.* This is so important to your understanding that we will elaborate on the basic types later in the chapter. The Israelites themselves, of course, were fully acquainted with all these types. They knew the difference between a psalm of lament (whereby an individual or a group could express grief before the Lord and appeal for help) and a psalm of thanksgiving (whereby individuals or groups expressed joy in the mercy God had already shown them). But since psalms are not an ordinary part

of our culture, you may need regularly to ask yourself before you start reading any given psalm: What *type* of psalm am I reading?

2. *Each psalm is also characterized by its formal structure.* One item that distinguishes the various types of psalms from each other is that each type has its own structural characteristics. With some understanding of the formal structure of a psalm, you will be able to recognize such features as the transitions from topic to topic or the way the psalmist apportions the attention paid to given issues, and thus have an appreciation for the message the psalm conveys. This will be especially apparent in our exegetical sampling presented later on.

3. *Each type of psalm was intended to have a given function in the life of Israel.* This matter will also receive special attention below. For now one must remember that each psalm has an intended purpose. The royal psalms, for example, were composed to be sung at the celebration of Israel's kingship as God endowed it, and not, for example, at weddings(!).

4. *There are also various patterns within the psalms.* The psalmists frequently took delight in certain arrangements or repetitions of words and sounds, as well as stylistic plays on words. Moreover, some psalms are acrostics; that is, the initial letters of each line or verse work through the twenty-two letters of the Hebrew alphabet. Psalm 119 is an example of an acrostic psalm, where each letter of the alphabet begins a set of eight verses (note how these are set off in the NIV). Its pattern of enumeration and repetition effectively guides the reader through a long list of the believers' benefits from and responsibilities toward the law of God.

5. *Each psalm has its own integrity as a literary unit.* Psalms are to be treated as wholes, not atomized into single verses or, as is often the case with proverbs, thought of as so many pearls on a string, each to be enjoyed for its own sake apart from its relationship to the whole. As you read a given psalm, learn to follow its flow and balance. Each psalm has a pattern of development by which its ideas are presented, developed, and brought to some kind of conclusion.

This last matter needs special emphasis. Because of the literary unity of any given psalm, one must be especially careful to keep individual verses in their context in the psalm, not seeing them only in their own light and not treating them as though they needed no context in which to be interpreted. For example, consider Psalm 51:16: "You do not delight in sacrifice, or I would bring it; you do not take pleasure in burnt offerings." Taken out of context, this may seem to suggest that the sacrificial system has no real importance under the former covenant. But how, then, does this fit with what is said at the end: "Then you will delight in the sacrifices of the righteous, in burnt offerings offered whole; then bulls will be offered on your altar" (v. 19)?

The answer is, of course, that in the full context of the psalm, David is acknowledging that sacrifices without genuine contrition and repentance mean simply to go through the motions. What God delights in is the contrite heart that accompanies the sacrifices. So to read the earlier line (v. 16) on its own is to miss its point *in this psalm*. Our point is that there is a framework of meaning that helps us to define the earlier words (v. 16), and thus to understand them according to their real intent rather than according to some intent we may assign them because we do not know the context. Decontextualizing any part of a psalm is to betray the psalmist, and will often lead to wrong conclusions. Whenever one takes even a part of a piece of literature and uses it wrongly, and especially so with poetry(!), that literature will be unable to do what it was intended to do, and so God's purposes in inspiring it are thwarted.

THE USE OF THE PSALMS IN ANCIENT ISRAEL

The psalms were functional songs composed for use in worship by the ancient Israelites. By *functional* we mean that they served the crucial function of making connection between the worshiper and God. Although some of them appear to have been intended for use by individual worshipers (e.g., Ps 63), many of them were intended for corporate use (e.g., Pss 74; 147–150). Indeed, psalms were commonly used as worship aids by Israelites when they brought sacrifices to the temple in Jerusalem. Based on some of the titles (e.g., Pss 80 and 81), it seems likely that professional singers sometimes sang psalms during the time people were worshiping. However, it is obvious that the knowledge of the psalms spread widely beyond the temple, and that people began to sing them in all sorts of situations where the wordings expressed their own attitudes and circumstances. The psalms were eventually collected into groupings called "books." There are five such books (Book 1: Pss 1–41; Book 2: Pss 42–72; Book 3: Pss 73–89;

Book 4: Pss 90–106; Book 5: Pss 107–150). For the significance of this grouping, see *How to 2*, pages 130–43.

Understandably, it is not possible to date most of the psalms with certainty. The ambiguity, however, is not in this case a significant exegetical problem. The psalms are remarkably applicable to *all* "times and climes." As with great hymns, their uses in ancient Israel are instructive to us but do not confine us to the worship and prayer of a past age. As they speak to the heart of a believer or group of believers gathered together in worship, the pan-cultural, pan-geographic value of the psalms is demonstrated.

Because certain groups of psalms have special characteristics, it is likely that they were collected originally into smaller groupings (e.g., psalms of David; "Hallelujah" psalms [146–150]), which have now been included together within the five major books. But these categories are less significant in terms of the present organization of the book of Psalms, because so many different types are scattered throughout the present order of the Psalter.

According to the titles, which are not part of the original psalms and therefore are not considered inspired, David wrote almost half the psalms, seventy-three in all. Moses wrote one (Ps 90), Solomon wrote two (Pss 72 and 127), and the "sons" of Asaph and of Korah, etc., also wrote several ("sons of" being a Hebraism for an ongoing "school" of musicians).

After the Israelites returned from exile and rebuilt the temple, the book of Psalms was apparently made a formal collection, almost a "temple hymnal," with the untitled Psalms 1 and 2 being placed at the beginning as an introduction to the whole and Psalm 150 at the end as a conclusion. From the New Testament we see that Jews in general, and Jesus and his disciples in particular, knew the psalms well. The psalms continued to be part of their worship. Paul encourages the early Christians to encourage one another with "psalms, hymns and songs from the Spirit" (Eph 5:19; Col 3:16). At least the first two of these terms can refer to the book of Psalms, although in giving this advice Paul may also have had in mind other types of early Christian music.

THE TYPES OF PSALMS

It is possible to group psalms into seven different categories. Though these categories may overlap somewhat or have subcategories, they serve well to classify the psalms and thus to guide the reader toward good use of them.

Laments

Laments constitute the largest group of psalms in the Psalter, which in itself probably says something about our common humanity. There are more than sixty, including individual and corporate laments. *Individual* laments (e.g., 3; 22; 31; 39; 42; 57; 71; 88; 120; 139; 142), which either express or presuppose deep trust in Yahweh, help a person to express struggles, suffering, or disappointment to the Lord. *Corporate* laments (e.g., 12; 44; 80; 94; 137) do the same for a group of people rather than for an individual. Are you discouraged? Is your church going through a difficult period? Are you part of a family or group, small or large, that wonders why things are not going as well as you had expected? If so, the use of laments is potentially a valuable adjunct to your own expression of concern to the Lord. Indeed, one of the more moving experiences in the life of one of the authors was to hear Psalm 88 read aloud in a chapel service within hours of the horrific events of September 11, 2001. Times were often hard for the ancient Israelites. The laments in the book of Psalms express with a deep, honest fervor the distress that people felt.

Thanksgiving Psalms

These psalms were used, as the name suggests, in circumstances very opposite from those of the laments. Such psalms expressed joy to the Lord because something had gone well, because circumstances were good, or because people had reason to render thanks to God for his faithfulness, protection, and benefits. The thanksgiving psalms help a person or a group express thoughts and feelings of gratitude. In all, there are six community (group) psalms of thanksgiving (65; 67; 75; 107; 124; 136) and ten individual psalms of thanksgiving (18; 30; 32; 34; 40; 66; 92; 116; 118; 138) in the Psalter.

Hymns of Praise

These psalms—without particular reference to personal miseries or joys, whether previous or recent—center on the praise of

God for who God is, for God's greatness and beneficence toward the whole earth as well as God's own people. The Eternal One may be praised as Creator of the universe, as in Psalms 8; 19; 104; and 148; or may be praised as the protector and benefactor of Israel, as in Psalms 66; 100; 111; 114; and 149; or may be praised as the Lord of history, as in Psalms 33; 103; 113; 117; and 145–147. God deserves praise. These psalms are especially adapted for individual or group praise in worship. They help us "sing praises to our God," something that is truly "pleasant and fitting" (Ps 147:1).

Salvation-History Psalms

These few psalms (78; 105; 106; 135; 136) have as their focus a review of the history of God's saving works among the people of Israel, especially his deliverance of them from bondage in Egypt and his creation of them as a people. Israel, from whom eventually came Jesus the Christ and through whom the message of God was mediated, is, of course, a special nation in human history, and its story is celebrated in these salvation-history psalms. You will notice that each has a different purpose (celebration, thanksgiving, warning, etc.).

Psalms of Celebration and Affirmation

Several kinds of psalms are included in this category. A first group is the covenant renewal liturgies, such as Psalms 50 and 81, which are designed to lead God's people to a renewal of the covenant first given to them on Mount Sinai. These psalms can serve effectively as worship guidelines for a service of renewal. Psalms 89 and 132 are often categorized as Davidic covenant psalms, which praise the importance of God's choice of the lineage of David. Inasmuch as this lineage eventually leads into the birth of our Lord, these psalms provide background for his messianic ministry.

There are nine psalms in the Psalter that deal especially with the kingship. These we call royal psalms (2; 18; 20; 21; 45; 72; 101; 110; 144). One of them (18) is a royal thanksgiving psalm and one of them (144) a royal lament. The kingship in ancient Israel was an important institution because through it God provided stability and protection. Though most of Israel's kings were unfaithful, God nevertheless could use any of them for good purposes. The Eternal One works through intermediaries in society, and the praise of the function of these intermediaries is what we find in the royal psalms.

Related to the royal psalms are the so-called "enthronement psalms" (24; 29; 47; 93; 95–99). It is likely that these psalms celebrated the enthronement of the king in ancient Israel, a ceremony that may have been repeated yearly. Some scholars have argued that they represent also the enthronement of the Lord himself and were used as liturgies for some sort of ceremony that celebrated this, although the evidence for this is scant.

Finally, there is a category called the Songs of Zion, or Songs of the City of Jerusalem (46; 48; 76; 84; 87; 122). According to the predictions of God through Moses to the Israelites while they were yet in the wilderness (e.g., Deut 12), Jerusalem became the central city of Israel, the place where the temple was built as the visible expression of God's presence with his people and the place from which the kingship of David exercised authority. Jerusalem as the "holy city" receives special attention and celebration in these songs. Inasmuch as the book of Revelation makes use of the symbol of a new Jerusalem (the new heaven that descends to earth), these psalms remain useful in Christian worship.

Wisdom Psalms

Eight psalms (36; 37; 49; 73; 112; 127; 128; 133) can be placed in this category. We may note also that Proverbs 8 is itself a psalm, praising, as these others do, the merits of wisdom and the wise life. These psalms may be read profitably along with the book of Proverbs. (See the section on Proverbs in ch. 12.)

Songs of Trust

These ten psalms (11; 16; 23; 27; 62; 63; 91; 121; 125; 131) center their attention on the fact that God can be trusted and that, even in times of despair, God's goodness and care for his people ought to be expressed. God delights in knowing that those who believe in him trust him for their lives and for what he will choose to give them. These psalms help us express our trust in God, whatever our circumstances.

For those who wish to explore further the different categories of the psalms and to understand the characteristics that determine how psalms are categorized, we recommend Bernhard Anderson with Steven Bishop, *Out of the Depths: The Psalms Speak for Us Today,* 3rd ed. (Louisville, Ky.: Westminster John Knox, 2000); or Tremper Longman III, *How to Read the Psalms* (Downers Grove, Ill.: InterVarsity Press, 1988). These books not only contain additional details of how the psalms functioned in ancient Israel but also make further suggestions for the way they might function in the lives of believers today.

AN EXEGETICAL SAMPLING

In order for us to illustrate how knowing a psalm's form and structure helps us appreciate its message, we have chosen two psalms for close examination. One is a personal lament; the other is a thanksgiving psalm.

Psalm 3: A Lament

By carefully comparing all the lament psalms, scholars have been able to isolate six elements that appear in one way or another in virtually all of them. These elements, in their typical order, are as follows:

1. *Address.* The psalmist identifies the one to whom the psalm is prayed. This is, of course, the Lord.
2. *Complaint.* The psalmist pours out a complaint honestly and forcefully, identifying what the trouble is and why God's help is being sought.
3. *Trust.* The psalmist immediately expresses trust in God, which serves as the presuppositional basis for his complaint. (Why pour out a complaint to God if you don't trust him?) Moreover, you must trust God to answer your complaint in keeping with the bigger picture, God's own greater purposes predicated on God's grace, not necessarily the answer that you yourself would come up with.
4. *Deliverance.* The psalmist cries out to God for deliverance from the situation described in the complaint.
5. *Assurance.* The psalmist expresses the assurance that God will deliver. This assurance is somewhat parallel to the expression of trust.
6. *Praise.* The psalmist offers praise, thanking and honoring God for the blessings of the past, present, and/or future.

Psalm 3

> [1]LORD, how many are my foes!
>   How many rise up against me!
> [2]Many are saying of me,
>   "God will not deliver him."
>
> [3]But you, LORD, are a shield around me,
>   my glory, the One who lifts my head high.
> [4]I call out to the LORD,
>   and he answers me from his holy mountain.
>
> [5]I lie down and sleep;
>   I wake again, because the LORD sustains me.
> [6]I will not fear though tens of thousands
>   assail me on every side.
>
> [7]Arise, LORD!
>   Deliver me, my God!
> Strike all my enemies on the jaw;
>   break the teeth of the wicked.
>
> [8]From the LORD comes deliverance.
>   May your blessing be on your people.

In this psalm, the six elements of a lament are to be identified as follows:

1. *Address.* This is the cry "LORD" (Hebrew *yhwh*, from which we render "Yahweh") of verse 1. Note that the address need not be lengthy or fancy. Simple prayers will always do! Note also that the address is repeated in parallel form in verse 7. The cry is directed not just to anyone or any group, but to the only true God, the only one who has both the power and love to respond perfectly to the need of the petitioner.

2. *Complaint.* This comprises the remainder of verse 1 and all of verse 2. David describes the foes (who in these psalms can function as personified symbols of virtually any misery or problem) and how bleak his situation seems. *Any* difficulty can be expressed this way.

3. *Trust.* Here verses 3–6 are all part of the expression of trust in the Lord. Who God is, how God answers prayer, how God's people are kept secure even when their situation is apparently hopeless—all this represents evidence that God is trustworthy.

4. *Deliverance.* In verse 7a ("Arise, LORD! Deliver me, my God!") David expresses his (and *our*) plea for help. Notice how the direct request for aid has been held until this point in the psalm, coming *after* the expression of trust. This order is not required but is normal. A balance between asking and praising seems to characterize the laments, and this should be instructive to us relative to our own prayers.

5. *Assurance.* The remainder of verse 7 ("Strike all my . . .") constitutes the statement of assurance. You may ask: What sort of assurance is communicated by this pugilistic picture of God? In fact, the language is, again, metaphorical rather than literal. "You have already knocked out all my real problems" would be a suitable paraphrase, since the "enemies" and the "wicked" stand for the problems and distresses David felt then and we feel now. By this vivid picture, the defeat of that which oppresses us is envisioned. But remember that this part of the psalm is not promising that God's people will be trouble free. It expresses the assurance that in God's own time our really significant problems will be taken care of according to the divine plan for us.

6. *Praise.* Verse 8 lauds God for his faithfulness. Yahweh (the LORD) is declared to be *the* deliverer, and in the request for divine blessing, he is implicitly declared to be *the* one who blesses.

Much can be learned from a lament such as Psalm 3. The importance of balanced prayer is at the top of the list. Requests should be balanced by appreciation; complaints by expressions of confidence. Note also how freely and strongly David is inspired to word the complaint and the appeal. This example of honesty leads us to be more willing to express ourselves to God openly without covering over our problems.

The psalm, however, is not designed specifically to instruct but to be used as a guide. We can read and reflect on this very psalm when we are at wit's end, discouraged, seemingly surrounded by problems, feeling defeated. Such a psalm will help us to express our thoughts and feelings and to rely on God's faithfulness, just as it did for the ancient Israelites. God has placed it in the Bible so that it may help us commune with him and cast all our anxiety on him because he cares for us (1 Pet 5:7).

The group lament psalms, sometimes called "community laments," follow the same six-step pattern. A family or church or other group facing difficult circumstances can use these psalms in a way analogous to the way the individual uses a psalm like Psalm 3.

Psalm 138: A Thanksgiving Psalm

Thanksgiving psalms have a different structure, as may be expected, because they have a different purpose in what they express. The elements of the thanksgiving psalm are as follows:

1. *Introduction.* Here the psalmist's testimony of how God has helped is summarized.
2. *Distress.* The situation from which God gave deliverance is portrayed.
3. *Appeal.* The psalmist reiterates the appeal that has been made to God.
4. *Deliverance.* The deliverance God provided is described.
5. *Testimony.* A word of praise for God's mercy is given.

As you can see from this outline, the thanksgiving psalms concentrate on appreciation for past mercies. A thanksgiving psalm usually thanks God for what he has already done. The order of these five elements may vary considerably, however—after all, this kind of outline is our discovery, not a rigid form a psalmist felt compelled to fit the musical poem into. A firmly fixed order would unduly limit the creativity of the inspired author.

Psalm 138

> ¹I will praise you, LORD, with all my heart;
>   before the "gods" I will sing your praise.
> ²I will bow down toward your holy temple
>   and will praise your name
>   for your unfailing love and your faithfulness,
> for you have so exalted your solemn decree
>   that it surpasses your fame.
> ³When I called, you answered me;
>   you greatly emboldened me.
>
> ⁴May all the kings of the earth praise you, LORD,
>   when they hear what you have decreed.
> ⁵May they sing of the ways of the LORD,
>   for the glory of the LORD is great.

⁶Though the LORD is exalted, he looks kindly on the lowly;
    though lofty, he sees them from afar.
⁷Though I walk in the midst of trouble,
    you preserve my life;
you stretch out your hand against the anger of my foes,
    with your right hand you save me.
⁸The LORD will vindicate me;
    your love, LORD, endures forever—
    do not abandon the works of your hands.

In this psalm, the five elements of a thanksgiving psalm are to be identified as follows:

1. *Introduction.* In verses 1–2 David expresses his intention to praise God for the love and faithfulness he has shown, as well as for the fact that God's greatness in and of itself deserves acclamation.

2. *Distress.* In verse 3 the distress is unspecified—it may be any sort of difficulty in which David called to the Lord. Accordingly, the psalm is of use to any Christian who wishes to thank God for any sort of help.

3. *Appeal.* The appeal is also contained in verse 3. God is praised for having graciously responded to David's (unspecified) distress.

4. *Deliverance.* Here verses 6–7 are most pertinent. The fact that God paid attention to David, an undeserving supplicant, preserved his life in the midst of trouble (perhaps many times, since "preserve" is in the present tense), and rescued him from his "foes" serves to express for us our own appreciation for God's faithful help to us in the past.

5. *Testimony.* Verses 4–5 and 8 all constitute David's (and our) testimonial to God's goodness. God is so beneficent that he deserves praise from even the great of the earth (vv. 4–5). God may be counted on and appealed to in connection with carrying out his promises and intentions. God's love never stops (v. 8).

What grand expectations of our relationship to God a thanksgiving song like Psalm 138 contains! How useful it can be in marshaling our own thoughts and feelings when we reflect on the faithfulness God has shown us over the years.

If you wish to pursue the contents of other types of psalms than those discussed here, you will find either Anderson's or Longman's book helpful. Many of the same results can be obtained, however, from simply reading several psalms of a given type and then analyzing on your own the common characteristics they contain. The most important thing is to realize that the psalms do differ from one another, and that a wise discernment of the types will lead to a wise use of the psalms themselves.

A SPECIAL NOTE ON THE "IMPRECATORY PSALMS"

One reason the psalms have had so much appeal to God's people in all ages is their comprehensiveness of language. A full range of human emotion, even extreme emotion, is found. No matter how sad you are, the psalmist helps you express your sadness, with abject pathos if necessary (e.g., Ps 69:7–20; 88:3–9). No matter how glad you are, the psalmist helps you express that as well (e.g., Ps 23:5–6; 98; 133). The obviously exaggerated language (hyperbole) is hard to outdo!

Neither sadness nor gladness, of course, is sinful. But bitterness, anger, and hatred may lead one to sinful thoughts or actions, such as the desire or the attempt to harm others. It is surely true that expressing one's anger verbally—letting it out in words directly, as it were—is better than letting it out in violent actions. Parts of certain psalms help us in just this way, and with an added dimension. They guide or channel our anger *to and through* God verbally rather than to or at anyone else—verbally or physically. Psalms that contain verbalizations to God of anger at others are sometimes called imprecatory psalms.

Why deny that we sometimes have such anger toward others? Through the imprecatory psalms, God invites us "in your anger, do not sin" (Ps 4:4, as cited in Eph. 4:26). We must fulfill the New Testament teaching, "Do not let the sun go down while you are still angry, and do not give the devil a foothold" (Eph 4:26–27), by expressing our anger directly to and through God rather than by seeking to return evil to those who have done evil to us. Imprecatory psalms harness our anger and help us express it (to God) by using the same sorts of obvious, purposeful exaggeration known to us from other types of psalms.

The imprecatory parts of psalms are almost always found in laments. Psalm 3, described in detail above, contains in verse 7 an imprecation that, like most others found in the book of Psalms, is brief and therefore not likely to be highly offensive. But some imprecations are rather lengthy and harsh (see parts of Pss 12; 35; 58; 59; 69; 70; 83; 109; 137; 140). Consider, for example, Psalm 137:7–9:

> [7]Remember, LORD, what the Edomites did
>   on the day Jerusalem fell.
> "Tear it down," they cried,
>   "tear it down to its foundations!"
>
> [8]Daughter Babylon, doomed to destruction,
>   happy is the one who repays you
>   according to what you have done to us.
> [9]Happy is the one who seizes your infants
>   and dashes them against the rocks.

Psalm 137 is a lament for the suffering endured by the Israelites in the exile; their capital, Jerusalem, had been destroyed, and their land had been taken from them by the Babylonians, aided and encouraged by the Edomites (cf. the book of Obadiah), who greedily helped themselves to the spoils. Heeding God's word, "It is mine to avenge; I will repay" (Deut 32:35; cf. Rom 12:19) the composer of this lament calls for judgment *according to the covenant curses* (see the discussion in ch. 10). Included in these curses is provision for the annihilation of the whole wicked society, including family members (Deut 32:25; cf. Deut 28:53–57). Nothing in Scripture teaches, of course, that this *temporal* judgment should be seen as indicating anything about the *eternal* destiny of such family members.

What the psalmist has done here is to tell God about the feelings of the suffering Israelites, using hyperbolic language of the same extreme sort found in the covenant curses themselves. The fact that the psalmist seems to be addressing the Babylonians directly is simply a function of the style of the psalm — he also addresses Jerusalem directly in verse 5. It is God who is the actual hearer of these angry words (v. 7), just as it should be God, and God alone, who hears *our* angry words. Understood in their context as part of the language of the laments and used rightly to channel and control our potentially sinful anger, the imprecatory psalms can indeed help keep us from harboring or displaying anger against others (see Matt 5:22).

The imprecatory psalms do not contradict Jesus' teaching to love our enemies. We tend wrongly to equate "love" with "having a warm feeling toward." Jesus' teaching, however, defines love actively. It is not so much how you *feel* about a certain person but what you *do* for that person that shows love (Luke 10:25–37). The biblical command is to *do* love, rather than to *feel* love. In a related way, the imprecatory psalms help us, when we feel anger, not to do anger. We may honestly express our anger to God, no matter how bitterly and hatefully we feel it, and let God take care of justice against those who misuse us. The foe who continues to do evil in the face of our forbearance is in big trouble indeed (Rom 12:20). The proper function of these psalms, then, is to help us not to be "overcome by evil" but to free us from our anger, that we might "overcome evil with good" (Rom 12:21).

A final word: The term "hate" in the book of Psalms has been commonly misunderstood. While this Hebrew word does in some contexts mean "despise," it can also mean "be unwilling or unable to put up with" or "reject" (as God toward Esau in Mal 1:3). Both are standard definitions in the Hebrew lexicons for this word. Thus when the psalmist says, "I have nothing but hatred for them" (Ps 139:22), he is expressing in the strongest possible way his utter dismay and inability to put up with those who hate God. Therefore, on this account as well there should be no presumption that the language of the imprecatory psalms violates the Bible's teaching elsewhere, including Matthew 5:22, nor that it offers us a loophole to hate someone in the usual English sense of the word "hate."

SOME CONCLUDING HERMENEUTICAL OBSERVATIONS

Since Christians for generations have almost instinctively turned to the Psalter in times of need, perplexity, or joy, we hesitate to offer a "hermeneutics of the psalms," lest we somehow make them too pedestrian. Nonetheless, some observations are in order—hopefully so as to make them still a greater joy to read, sing, or pray.

First, we should note that the Christian "instinct" (common sense) just alluded to provides the basic answer to the question with which we began this chapter: How do these words spoken *to* God function for us as a word *from* God? The answer: Precisely in the ways they functioned for Israel in the first place—as opportunities to speak to God with the help of words he inspired others to use to speak to him in times past.

Three Basic Benefits of the Psalms

From the use of the psalms both in ancient Israel and in the New Testament church, we can see three important ways in which Christians can use them.

First, *the psalms can serve as a guide to worship.* By this we mean that the worshiper who seeks to praise God or to appeal to God or to remember God's benefits can use the psalms as a formal means of expression of his or her thoughts and feelings. A psalm is a carefully composed literary preservation of words designed to be spoken. When a psalm touches on a topic or a theme that we wish to express to the Lord, it can help us express our concerns in spite of our own lack of skill to find the right words.

Second, *the psalms demonstrate to us how we can relate honestly to God*—how to be honest and open in expressing joy, disappointment, anger, or other emotions. On this point they do not so much provide doctrinal instruction as they give, by example, instruction in the godly articulation of even our strongest feelings.

Third, *the psalms demonstrate the importance of reflection and meditation on that which God has done for us.* They invite us to prayer, to controlled thinking on and discussion of God's Word (that is what meditation is), and to reflective fellowship with other believers. Such actions help shape in us a life of purity and charity. The Psalms, like no other literature, lift us to a position where we can commune with God, capturing a sense of the greatness of his kingdom and a sense of what living with our heavenly Father for eternity will be like. Even in our darkest moments, when life has become so painful as to seem unendurable, God is with us. "Out of the depths" (Ps 130:1) we wait and watch for the Lord's deliverance, knowing we can trust God in spite of our feelings. To cry to God for help is not a judgment on God's faithfulness but an affirmation of it.

A Caution

We conclude this chapter with a very important caution: *The psalms do not guarantee a pleasant life.* It is a misunderstanding — an overliteralization — of the language of the psalms to infer from some of them that God promises to make his believers happy and their lives trouble-free. David, who expresses in the book of Psalms God's blessing in the strongest terms, lived a life that was filled with frequent tragedy and disappointment, as 1 and 2 Samuel describe. Yet he praises and thanks God enthusiastically at every turn, even in laments, just as Paul advises us to do, even in the midst of hard times (Col 1:12; 2:7; 3:17). Our heavenly Father deserves praise for his greatness and goodness in spite of and in the midst of our misery. This life holds no certainty of freedom from distress.

CHAPTER 12

Wisdom: Then and Now

Hebrew wisdom is a category of literature that is unfamiliar to most present-day Christians. Though a significant portion of the Old Testament is devoted to wisdom writings, contemporary believers sometimes either misunderstand or misapply this material, losing benefits that God intended for them. When properly understood and used, however, wisdom is a helpful resource for Christian living. When misused, it can provide a basis for selfish, materialistic, shortsighted behavior—just the opposite of what God intended.

Three Old Testament books are commonly classified under the category of "wisdom": Proverbs, Job, and Ecclesiastes. In addition, as we noted in the preceding chapter, a number of the psalms are often classified in this category. Finally, Song of Songs (sometimes called Song of Solomon), can also come under the category of wisdom, as we will point out below. Not everything in these books is, strictly speaking, concerned with wisdom; nevertheless, they in general contain the type of material that bears the wisdom label.

THE NATURE OF WISDOM

What exactly is wisdom, biblically speaking? A brief definition runs as follows: "Wisdom is the ability to make godly choices in life." You achieve this goal by applying God's truth to your life, so that your choices will indeed be godly. This sounds reasonable enough, and not the sort of thing that should confuse Christians. The problem arises when the Old Testament wisdom material is misunderstood, and thus misapplied. In such cases people will often make choices that are not always godly. This chapter intends to help you refine your understanding and application of wisdom. To get there we begin with some common abuses—how not to read and use this literature.

Abuse of Wisdom Literature

Traditionally, the wisdom books have been misused in three ways:

1. People often read these books only in bits and pieces and thus fail to see that they have an overall message. Snatches of wisdom teaching taken out of context can sound profound and seem practical, which often results in misapplication. Take, for example, the phrase in Ecclesiastes that there is "a time to be born and a time to die" (3:2). This is part of a lyrical poem set in the context of the transitory/elusive nature of human life; it is about how the ebb and flow of human life and activity are set by God and thus outside of human control—since all die when their "time" comes, no matter how bad or good their life is. Unfortunately, some Christians have thought that this very human observation was intended to teach that God protectively picks out our life span for us; but in context, this is definitely *not* what this author was saying.

2. People sometimes misunderstand the terms and categories of Hebrew wisdom, as well as its styles and literary modes; this also can lead to misuse. Consider this proverb, for example, "Stay away from a fool, for you will not find knowledge on their lips" (14:7). What is a contemporary Christian to do with this? Does this mean that followers of Jesus should choose not to associate with those who have mental disabilities or are uneducated or mentally ill? Of course not! That would indeed make fools of us in the more modern sense! In Proverbs, however, "fool" is basically a referent to someone whom today we might refer to as an "infidel"—the person who lives life according to selfish, indulgent whims and who acknowledges no higher authority than oneself. And the "staying away" is inextricably linked with the purpose ("for you will not find knowledge"). In other words, the proverb teaches that if you are seeking knowledge, you should not look for it in the "fool"— the one who lives life apart from God (Pss 14:1; 53:1).

3. Especially in a wisdom discourse like Job, people often fail to understand what the book is all about, and thus also fail to follow the line of argument. Accordingly, they cite as biblical truth what

was intended by this great author as an *incorrect* understanding of life. Consider these words, in this case, coming from one of Job's so-called "comforters": "All his days the wicked man suffers torment, the ruthless man through all the years stored up for him" (15:20). Would you take this to be an inspired teaching that evil people cannot really be happy? Job himself did not! Indeed, he energetically refuted it. These words are part of a speech by Job's self-appointed "comforter" Eliphaz, who is trying to convince Job that the reason he is suffering so much is the direct result of some evil on his part. Later in the book God vindicates the words of Job and condemns the words of Eliphaz (42:7–8). But unless you follow the *whole* discourse of Job, you will not know this, and thus perhaps both misunderstand and misapply what this "comforter" has mistakenly assumed to be true of Job.

Our procedure in this chapter will be to discuss what wisdom literature is and what it is not, and then to make some observations about how to understand these books on their own terms and thus to use them well. We will pay most attention to Proverbs, because it is the book we judge to be used the most often and therefore most often *mis*used (abused?). Indeed, our experience is that many contemporary Christians tend to avoid reading either Job or Ecclesiastes.

Who Is Wise?

We began by noting that "wisdom" is the ability to make godly choices in life. There is thus a personal side to wisdom. Wisdom is not something theoretical and abstract—it is something that exists only when a *person* thinks and acts according to truth when making the many choices that life demands. The Old Testament recognizes, therefore, that some people have more wisdom than others and that some people have so devoted themselves to gaining wisdom that they themselves can be called "wise" (Hebrew ḥākām). The wise person was highly practical, not merely theoretical. Such a person was interested in being able to formulate the sorts of plans—that is, make the sorts of choices—that would help produce God's desired results in their life.

There is a very real sense in which the entire progress of our lives may be viewed as the result of choices. In fact, almost everything we do is to some degree a matter of choice. When to get up in the morning, what to do first, where to work, whom to speak to, how to speak to them, what to accomplish, when to start and stop things, what to eat, what to wear, whom to associate with, where to go, with whom to go — all these actions are the result of decisions. Some of the decisions are made on the spot (what to have for lunch, for example); others may have been made long ago so that they need not be remade daily (where to live, whom to marry, what kind of work to engage in). Others may be the result of God's choices and not our own (Gen 45:8), while yet others may be only partly voluntary on our part (Prov 16:33). Nevertheless, choices chart the course of life.

The ancients knew this, and thus wisdom literature abounded in most ancient cultures. Non-Israelite wisdom also had as its goal the making of the best choices, the purpose being to achieve the best life. What the inspired biblical wisdom added to this was the crucial idea that the only good choices are godly choices. Thus from the faithful Israelite perspective, "*the fear of the LORD is the beginning of wisdom*" (Prov 9:10; Ps 111:10 [emphasis added]), which does not mean, of course, to be "afraid" of God, but to understand and approach God full of awe and wonder. After all, how can you make godly choices if you do not believe and obey God? The very first step, then, in biblical wisdom is knowing God — not abstractly or theoretically, but in the concrete sense of committing your life to God. Then your general direction will be correct, and as you learn specific guidelines and perspectives for making godly choices, a more precise sense of direction for wise living can follow.

Wisdom, therefore, as the Bible defines it (Hebrew *ḥokmāh*) has nothing to do with IQ. It is not a matter of cleverness and quickness or skill in expression, or even age, though personal experience is a valuable teacher if interpreted in light of revealed truth. Rather, it is a matter of orientation to God, out of which comes the ability to please God, our heavenly Father. This is why in the New Testament James says that God gives wisdom to those who ask for it (1:5). This is a promise not that we can become smarter by prayer, but that God will help us to become more godly in our choices, if we ask. James defines the kind of wisdom God gives (Jas 3:13–18), and then goes on to contrast it with the worldly wisdom by which a person seeks to know how to get ahead of others.

Responsible, successful living was the goal. Sometimes such wisdom was applied to technical matters like construction (cf.

Bezalel, the tabernacle architect, "filled ... with the Spirit of God in wisdom" [Exod 31:3 NASB]) or navigation (Ezek 27:8–9). Wisdom was also sought by people who had to make decisions affecting the welfare of others. National leaders such as Joshua (Deut 34:9), David (2 Sam 14:20), and Solomon (1 Kgs 3:9; et al.) were described as having been given wisdom by God so that their rule might be effective and successful. We are reminded of the personal side of the skill of wise people by the fact that the human heart is described as the focal point of wisdom (cf. 1 Kgs 3:9, 12). The "heart" in the Old Testament refers to the moral and volitional faculties, as well as the intellectual.

Wisdom literature, then, tends to focus on people and their behavior—how successful they are at making godly choices and whether or not they are learning how to apply God's truth to the experiences they have. It is not so much the case that people seek to learn how to *be* wise but rather that they seek to *get* wise. Anyone who seeks to apply God's truth daily and learn from their experience can become wise eventually. But there is a great danger in seeking wisdom simply for one's own advantage or in a way that does not honor God above all: "Woe to those who are wise in their own eyes" (Isa 5:21). Moreover, God's wisdom always surpasses human wisdom (Isa 29:13–14; cf. 1 Cor 1:18–2:5).

Teachers of Wisdom

In ancient Israel, some individuals devoted themselves not only to gaining wisdom but also to teaching others how to gain it. These wisdom instructors were simply called "wise men" (1 Chron 27:32; Eccl 2:16) or "wise women" (2 Sam 20:16; Prov 14:1), though they eventually occupied a position in Israelite society somewhat parallel to that of the priest and the prophet (Jer 18:18). This special class of wise men and women arose at least as early as the beginning of the kingship period in Israel (i.e., about 1000 BC; cf. 1 Sam 14:2) and functioned as teacher-counselors to people who sought their wisdom. Some were inspired by God to help write portions of the Old Testament.

We note also that the wise person served as a sort of substitute parent to the person seeking wisdom from them. Even before the exodus from Egypt, Joseph was made by God a "father" to Pharaoh (Gen 45:8), and later the prophet Deborah is called a "mother" in Israel (Judg 5:7). Thus often in the book of Proverbs we see the wise teacher addressing their pupil as "my child" ("my son" is not the best translation). Parents sent their children to be educated in wisdom attitudes and lifestyles by such wisdom teachers, and these teachers taught their pupils as they would their own children.

Wisdom in the Home
Wisdom, however, has always been taught more at home than in any other setting. Modern parents teach their children all sorts of wisdom, virtually every day and often without realizing it, as they try to help them make the right choices in life. Whenever a parent gives a child rules to live by, from "Don't play in the street" to "Try to choose nice friends" to "Be sure to dress warmly enough," the parent is actually teaching wisdom. Most parents want their children to be happy, self-sufficient, and of benefit to others. A good parent spends time shaping the behavior of their children in this direction, talking to them regularly about how to behave. In Proverbs, especially, this same sort of practical advice is given. But Proverbs subordinates all its advice to God's wisdom, just as a Christian parent should try to do. The advice may be strongly practical and concerned with secular issues, but it should never fail to acknowledge that the highest good a person can achieve is to do God's will.

Wisdom among Colleagues
One way people refine their ability to make the right choices in life is by discussion and debate. This sort of wisdom is arrived at sometimes by lengthy discourse, either in a monologue intended for others to read and reflect on (e.g., Ecclesiastes) or in a dialogue among various persons seeking to inform each other's opinions on truth and life (e.g., Job). The kind of wisdom that predominates in the book of Proverbs is called proverbial wisdom, whereas the kind found in Ecclesiastes and Job is usually called speculative wisdom. The kind found in Song of Songs may be called lyric wisdom. We will discuss these in more detail below. For now, just remember that even so-called speculative wisdom is highly practical and empirical (centered in experience) rather than merely theoretical.

Wisdom Expressed through Poetry
Students and teachers alike in Old Testament times used a variety of literary techniques as aids to remembering their wisdom. God inspired the wisdom portions of the Bible according to such

techniques, so that they might be learnable and easily memorized. As noted in the two preceding chapters, poetry has careful wordings, cadences, and stylistic qualities that make it easier to commit to memory than prose, and thus poetry also became the medium of Old Testament wisdom. Proverbs, Ecclesiastes, Job, and Song of Songs, as well as the wisdom psalms and other bits of wisdom in the Old Testament, are composed, therefore, mostly in poetry. Among the particular techniques used are parallelisms (cf. p. 205)—whether synonymous (e.g., Prov 7:4), antithetical (Prov 10:1), or synthetic (Prov 21:16); acrostics (Prov 31:10–31); alliteration (Eccl 3:1–8); numerical sequences (Prov 30:15–31); and countless comparisons (such as similes and metaphors, e.g., Job 32:19; Song 4:1–6). Formal parables, allegories, riddles, and other poetic techniques are also found in wisdom material.

The Limits of Wisdom

It is important to remember that not all wisdom in the ancient world was godly or orthodox. Throughout the ancient Near East there was a class of wise teachers and scribes who were supported, often by royalty, in the task of collecting, composing, and refining wisdom proverbs and discourses. Much of this wisdom generally resembles the Old Testament wisdom writings, though it lacks the firm emphasis on the Lord as the origin of wisdom (Prov 2:5–6) and the purpose of wisdom as to please him (Prov 3:7).

Moreover, wisdom does not cover all of life. Intensely practical, it tends not to touch on the theological or historical issues so important elsewhere in the Bible. And skill at wisdom does not guarantee that it will be properly used. Jonadab's wise advice to Amnon (2 Sam 13:3) was rendered in an evil cause; Solomon's great wisdom (1 Kgs 3:12; 4:29–34) helped him gain wealth and power but could not keep him from turning away from faithfulness to the Lord in his later years (1 Kgs 11:4). Only when wisdom as a skill is subordinated to obedience to God does it achieve its proper ends in the Old Testament sense.

WISDOM IN PROVERBS

The book of Proverbs is the primary locus of "prudential wisdom"—that is, memorable aphorisms (maxims) people can use to help themselves make responsible choices in life. In contrast to Ecclesiastes and Job, which use *speculative* wisdom as a way of wrestling with the great issues of life, *proverbial* wisdom concentrates mostly on *practical attitudes and behavior in everyday life*. As a generalization, one can say that Proverbs teaches "old-fashioned basic values." A good parent does not want their child to grow up unhappy, disappointed, lonely, socially rejected, in trouble with the law, immoral, inept, or broke. It is neither selfish nor unrealistic for a parent to wish a child a reasonable level of success in life — including social acceptance, moral uprightness, and freedom from want. The book of Proverbs provides a collection of pithy advisory statements designed to do just that. There is no guarantee, of course, that a life will always go well for a young person. What Proverbs does say is that, all things being equal, there *are* basic attitudes and patterns of behavior that will help a person grow into responsible adulthood.

Proverbs continually presents a sharp contrast between choosing the life of wisdom and choosing the life of folly. What characterizes the life of folly? Such things as violent crime (1:10 – 19; 4:14 – 19), careless promising or pledging (6:1 – 5), laziness (6:7 – 11), malicious dishonesty (6:12 – 15), and sexual impurity, which is especially odious to God and harmful to an upright life (2:16 – 19; 5:3 – 20; 6:23 – 35; 7:4 – 27; 9:13 – 18; 23:26 – 28). Besides urging the opposites of these as the life of wisdom, Proverbs also urges such things as caring for the poor (2:22, 27), respect for government leaders (23:1 – 3; 24:21 – 22), the importance of disciplining children (23:13 – 14), moderation in consumption of alcoholic beverages (23:19 – 21, 29 – 35), and regard for one's parents (23:22 – 25).

Specifically religious language is seldom used in Proverbs; it is present (cf. 1:7; 3:5 – 12; 15:3, 8 – 9, 11; 16:1 – 9; 22:9, 23; 24:18, 21; et al.), but it does not predominate. Not everything in life has to be *religious* to be godly. Indeed, Proverbs can help serve as a corrective to the extremist tendency to spiritualize everything, as though there were something wrong with the basic material, physical world, as though God had seen that it was "bad" rather than "good" when he first looked at the world he had created.

Uses and Abuses of Proverbs

The Hebrew word for proverbs is *mĕšālîm,* having to do with "figures of speech," "parables," or "specially contrived sayings."

A proverb, therefore, is a *brief, particular* expression of a truth. The briefer a statement is, the less likely it is to be totally precise and universally applicable. We know that long, highly qualified, elaborate, detailed statements of fact are often not only difficult to understand but very difficult to remember. The proverbs then are phrased in a catchy way, so as to be memorable. Indeed, in Hebrew many of the proverbs have some sort of rhythm, sound repetition, or vocabulary qualities that make them particularly easy to learn.

Consider the English proverbs "Look before you leap" and "A stitch in time saves nine." The repetition of single-syllable words beginning with the letter *l* in the first case and the rhythm and rhyme of single-syllable words in the second case are elements that give these proverbs a certain catchiness. They are not as easy to forget as would be the following statements: "In advance of committing yourself to a course of action, consider your circumstances and options"; and "There are certain corrective measures for minor problems that, when taken early on in a course of action, forestall major problems from arising." These latter formulations are more precise but lack the punch and effectiveness of the two well-known wordings, not to mention the fact that they are much harder to remember. "Look before you leap" is a pithy, inexact statement; it could easily be misunderstood, or thought to apply only to jumping. It does not say where or how to look, what to look for, or how soon to leap after looking, and it is not even intended to apply literally to jumping!

So it is with Hebrew proverbs. They must be understood reasonably and taken on their own terms. A proverb does not state everything about a truth, but rather points *toward* it. They are, taken literally, often technically inexact. But as learnable guidelines for the shaping of selected behavior, they are unsurpassed. Consider Proverbs 6:27–29:

> [27]Can a man scoop fire into his lap
>   without his clothes being burned?
> [28]Can a man walk on hot coals
>   without his feet being scorched?
> [29]So is he who sleeps with another man's wife;
>   no one who touches her will go unpunished.

Taken in isolation, the last line could be easily misapplied: What if someone accidentally touches another man's wife — will he be punished? Or, what about people who commit adultery and get away with it? But such "interpretations" quite miss the point. First, this last line concludes a couplet in which the second line is to be understood in light of the first one (see p. 214). Second, proverbs tend to use *figurative* language and express things *suggestively* rather than in detail. The word "touches" in this line is clearly a euphemism for sexual relations (cf. Gen 20:6; 1 Cor 7:1; see pp. 242–49). The point you should get from the whole proverb is that committing adultery is like playing with fire. God will see to it that sooner or later, in this life or the next, the adulterer will be hurt by their actions. To take it otherwise is to distort the Holy Spirit's inspired message. Thus a proverb should not be taken too literally or too universally if its message is to be helpful.

For another example, consider Proverbs 9:13–18:

> 13Folly is an unruly woman;
>   she is simple and knows nothing.
> 14She sits at the door of her house,
>   on a seat at the highest point of the city,
> 15calling out to those who pass by,
>   who go straight on their way,
> 16"Let all who are simple come to my house!"
>   To those who have no sense she says,
> 17"Stolen water is sweet;
>   food eaten in secret is delicious!"
> 18But little do they know that the dead are there,
>   that her guests are deep in the realm of the dead.

This pithy proverb includes a whole allegory (a story pointing to something other than itself by implicit comparisons) in a few verses. Here folly, the opposite of wise living, is personified as a prostitute trying to entice passersby into her house. The fool is characterized by his fascination with forbidden pleasures (v. 17). But the end result of a life of folly is not long life, success, or happiness—it is death. "Stay away from folly!" is the message of this brief allegory. "Don't be taken in! Walk right past those temptations [spelled out in various ways in other proverbs] that folly makes seem attractive!" The wise, godly, moral person will choose a life free from the selfishness of folly. Proverbs like this are somewhat like parables in that they express their truth in a symbolic way.

Another example can be found a bit later in a well-known and often cited proverb:

> Commit to the LORD whatever you do,
>   and your plans will succeed.
>   *Prov 16:3 (NIV 1984)*

This is the sort of proverb that is most often misinterpreted. Not realizing that proverbs tend to be inexact statements pointing to the truth in figurative ways, people often assume that this is a direct, clear-cut, always applicable promise from God—that if a person dedicates their plans to God, those plans *must* succeed. People who reason this way, of course, may all too often be disappointed. They can dedicate some perfectly selfish or idiotic scheme to God, then if it happens to succeed, even briefly, they can assume that God blessed it. A hasty marriage, a rash business decision, an ill-thought-out vocational decision—all can be dedicated to God but can eventually result in misery. Or a person might commit a plan to God only to have it fail; then the person would wonder why God did not keep his promise, why he went back on his inspired word. In either case they have failed to see that the proverb is not a categorical, always applicable, ironclad promise, but a more general truth; it teaches that lives committed to God and lived according to his will succeed *according to God's definition of success.* Thus the NIV renders line 2 as "and he will establish your plans." But according to the world's definition of success, the result may be just the opposite. The story of Job eloquently reminds us of this.

When these proverbs, then, are taken on their own terms and understood as the special category of suggestive, general truth that they are, they become important and useful adjuncts for living.

SOME HERMENEUTICAL GUIDELINES

Here, then, in capsule form are some summary guidelines for understanding proverbial wisdom.

1. Proverbs Are Not Legal Guarantees from God

Proverbs set forth a wise way to approach certain selected practical goals, but do so in terms that cannot be treated like a divine guarantee of success. The particular blessings, rewards, and opportunities mentioned in Proverbs are *likely* to follow if one will choose the wise courses of action outlined in the poetic, figurative language of the book. But nowhere does Proverbs teach *automatic* success.

Remember that inspired Scripture also includes both Ecclesiastes and Job, which remind us that there is very little that is automatic about the good or bad events that may take place in our lives.

Consider these examples:

> Do not be one who shakes hands in pledge,
>   or puts up security for debts;
> if you lack the means to pay,
>   your very bed will be snatched from under you.
>   *Proverbs 22:26–27*

> If a ruler listens to lies,
>   all his officials become wicked.
>   *Proverbs 29:12*

> The LORD tears down the house of the proud,
>   but he sets the widow's boundary stones in place.
>   *Proverbs 15:25*

If you were to take the extreme step of considering the first of these as an all-encompassing command from God, you might not buy a house so as never to incur a mortgage (a secured debt). Or you might assume that God promises that if you default on something like a credit card debt, you will eventually lose all your possessions—including your bed(s). Such literalistic, extreme interpretations would miss the point of the proverb, which states poetically and figuratively that *debts should be taken on cautiously because foreclosure can be very painful.* The proverb frames this truth in specific, narrow terms (shaking hands, losing a bed, etc.) that are intended to point toward the broader principle rather than to express something technically. In Bible times, righteous people incurred debts without any violation of this proverb because they understood its real point.

The second example (29:12) is also not to be taken literally. It does not guarantee, for example, that if you are a government official, you have no choice but to become wicked if your boss (the governor, president, or whoever) listens to some people who do not tell him the truth. It intends to convey a different message: Rulers who want to hear lies instead of the truth will gather people around them who will say what they want to hear. And the end result can be a corrupt government. Thus the ruler who insists on hearing the truth, even though it is painful, helps keep the government honest. The words of the proverb point to this principle in a parabolic way rather than in a literal, technical sense.

The third example (15:25) is perhaps the most obviously non-literal in intention. We know both from our own experience and from the witness of the Scriptures that there are indeed proud people whose houses are still standing and that there are widows who have been abused by greedy creditors or by fraud (cf. Mark 12:40; Job 24:2–3; et al.). So what does the proverb mean if it does not intend to convey the impression that the Lord is actually a house smasher or boundary guard? It means that God opposes the proud and is on the side of the needy ("widows," "the fatherless," and "foreigners" are terms that stand for *all* dependent people; cf. Deut 14:29; 16:11; 26:12, 13; et al.). When this proverb is compared with other moments in Scripture (Proverbs 23:10–11 and Luke 1:52–53), its meaning becomes much clearer. It is a miniature parable designed by the Holy Spirit to point beyond the "house" and the "widow" to the general principle that God will *eventually* right this world's wrongs, abasing the arrogant and compensating those who have suffered for the sake of righteousness (cf. Matt 5:3–4).

2. Proverbs Must Be Read as a Collection

Each inspired proverb must be balanced with others and understood in comparison with the rest of Scripture. As the third example above (15:25) illustrates, the more one reads a proverb in isolation, the less clear its interpretation may be. An individual proverb, if misunderstood, may lead you to attitudes or behavior far more inappropriate than would be the case if you read Proverbs as a whole. Moreover, you must guard against letting their intensely practical concern with material things and this world make you forget the balancing value of other Scriptures that warn against materialism and worldliness. Do not engage in the kind of wisdom Job's friends did, equating worldly success with righteousness in God's eyes. This is an unbalanced reading of selected proverbs. Do not try to find in Proverbs justification for living a selfish life or for practices that do not comport with what the Scriptures teach otherwise. And remember that the proverbs are often grouped in various ways, so that one jumps from topic to topic in reading through them.

Consider also these two proverbs:

> One who is wise can go up against the city of the mighty
> and pull down the stronghold in which they trust.
>
> *Proverbs 21:22*

> The mouth of an adulterous woman is a deep pit;
> a man who is under the LORD's wrath falls into it.
>
> *Proverbs 22:14*

If you are wise, do you go out to attack a well-defended city and thereby do something good for God? If you have displeased God, is there a danger that you will suffocate inside the (very large) mouth of an adulteress?

Most people would answer no to these questions, adding "Whatever they mean, they can't mean that!" But many of the same people will insist that a following proverb (22:26) is to be taken literally to prohibit borrowing on the part of Christians, or that an earlier proverb about children obeying their parents (6:20) means that a person must always obey his or her parents *at any age, no matter how wrong the advice of the parents may be.* By failing to balance proverbs against one another and against the rest of Scripture (let alone common sense) people can do themselves and others great injustice, not to mention harm.

In the first proverb above (21:22), the point is that wisdom can be stronger even than military might. This is a hyperbolic statement. In style it is not unlike the modern proverb, "The pen is mightier than the sword." It is not a command. It is a symbolic, figurative portrayal of the power of wisdom. Only when one relates this proverb to the many other proverbs that praise the usefulness and effectiveness of wisdom (e.g., 1:1–6; chs. 2–3; 8; 22:17–29; et al.) does one get its message. Here *overall context* is crucial in the interpretation.

The other proverb cited above (22:14) likewise needs comparison to its overall context. A large number of proverbs stress the importance of careful thought and speech (e.g., 15:1; 16:10, 21, 23–24, 27–28; 18:4; et al.). What one says, in other words, is usually far more incriminating than what one hears (cf. Matt 15:11, 15–20). You may not be able to control what you hear, but you can almost always control what you say. This particular proverb can be paraphrased as follows: "What an adulteress practices and talks about are as dangerous to you as falling into a deep pit would be. Avoid such circumstances if you wish to avoid God's wrath." An appreciation of the full contexts of the individual proverbs will help to interpret and apply them well.

3. Proverbs Are Worded to Be Memorable, Not to Be Theoretically Accurate

No proverb is a complete statement of truth. No proverb is so perfectly worded that it can stand up to the unreasonable demand that it apply in every situation at every time. The more briefly and parabolically a principle is stated, the more common sense and good judgment are needed to interpret it properly—but the more effective and memorable it is (cf. the example, "Look before you leap," cited above). Proverbs try to impart knowledge that can be *retained* rather than philosophy that can impress a critic. Thus the proverbs are designed either to stimulate an image in your mind (the mind remembers images better than it remembers abstract data) or to include sounds pleasing to the ear (i.e., repetitions, assonance, acrostics, et al.). As an example of the use of imagery, consider the following proverb (15:19):

> The way of the sluggard is blocked with thorns,
> but the path of the upright is a highway.

Here we read language designed to point not to the types of plants found in certain lazy people's favorite routes but to point beyond itself to the principle that diligence is better than sloth.

The portrayal of extreme devotion of the wife of noble character described in the epilogue or closing frame of the book (31:10–31) is the result of an acrostic ordering. Each verse begins with a successive letter of the Hebrew alphabet, memorable and pleasing to the ear in Hebrew, but resulting in what could seem to the callous critic or the literalistic reader to be a pattern of life impossible for any mortal woman to follow. But if one gets the point that such a description as Proverbs 31:22 is purposely designed to emphasize by exaggeration the joy that a good wife brings to her family and community, the proverbial wisdom does its job admirably well. The words (and images) of the passage tend to stick with the reader, providing useful guidance when needed. That is what proverbs are intended by God to do.

4. Some Proverbs Need to Be "Translated" to Be Appreciated

A good many proverbs express their truths according to practices and institutions that no longer exist, although they were common to the Old Testament Israelites. Unless you think of these proverbs in terms of their true modern equivalents (i.e., carefully "translate" them into practices and institutions that exist today), their meaning may seem irrelevant or be lost to you altogether (cf. ch. 4). Consider these two examples:

> One who loves a pure heart and who speaks with grace
>   will have the king for a friend.
>
> *Proverbs 22:11*

> Better to live on a corner of the roof
>   than share a house with a quarrelsome wife.
>
> *Proverbs 25:24*

Most of us do not live in societies where there are kings. And we do not have the flat-roof houses of Bible times, where lodging on a roof was not only possible but common (cf. Josh 2:6). Does reading these proverbs therefore constitute a waste of time? Not at all, if one can only see the transcultural issues expressed in their culturally specific language. The essential message of the first example cited above (22:11) is easy to comprehend as long as we recognize that a true modern equivalent for "have the king for his friend" would be something like "make a positive impression on people in leadership positions." The proverb *always* meant that anyway. The "king" stands as a synecdoche (one of a class) for all leaders. The specific parabolic language of the proverb is intended to point beyond itself to the truth that leaders and responsible persons are generally impressed both by honesty and by careful discourse.

The meaning of the second proverb above (25:24) is also not so difficult to discern if one makes the necessary "translation" from that culture to ours. We could even paraphrase: "It's better to live in a garage than in a spacious house with a woman you never should have married." Here one needs to remember that the advice of most proverbs is given as if to young persons starting out in life. The proverb is not intended to suggest literally what to do if you, a male, find your wife to be quarrelsome. It is intended to advise that people be careful in the selection of a mate. Such a selection is a transcultural decision for which the proverb, correctly understood, provides sound, godly advice (cf. Matt 19:3–11; 1 Cor 7:1–14, 25–40). Everyone should recognize that a hasty marriage, based largely on physical attraction, can turn out to be an unhappy marriage.

For convenience, we conclude by listing in summary form some rules that will help you make proper use of proverbs and be true to their divinely inspired intent.

1. Proverbs are often parabolic (i.e., figurative, pointing beyond themselves).
2. Proverbs are intensely practical, not theoretically theological.
3. Proverbs are worded to be memorable, not technically precise.
4. Proverbs are not designed to support selfish behavior—just the opposite!
5. Proverbs strongly reflecting ancient culture may need sensible "translation" so as not to lose their meaning.
6. Proverbs are not guarantees from God but poetic guidelines for good behavior.
7. Proverbs may use highly specific language, exaggeration, or any of a variety of literary techniques to make their point.
8. Proverbs give good advice for wise approaches to certain aspects of life but are not exhaustive in their coverage.
9. Wrongly used, proverbs may justify a crass, materialistic lifestyle. Rightly used, proverbs will provide practical advice for daily living.

WISDOM IN JOB

The book of Job is one of the greatest literary treasures in the world. It comes to us as a carefully structured dialogue between Job and his well-meaning but desperately wrong "comforters"—Bildad, Zophar, Eliphaz, and Elihu. But if one does not pay attention to who is speaking at any given point, you will find here all sorts of wrong advice and incorrect conclusions, especially if what is said comes from the lips of any of Job's comforters. This dialogue has a very important goal: to establish convincingly in the mind of the reader that what happens in life does not always happen either because God desires it or because it is fair. The "foil" for this truth is to be found primarily in the advice of the comforters. They regularly represent the viewpoint that God is not simply involved in the daily affairs of life but that God is in fact constantly meting out his judgment through the events of this life. Indeed,

they say to Job that what happens to anyone in life—good or ill—
is a *direct* result of whether that person has pleased God or not.
They are horrified when Job protests that he did nothing wrong
to deserve the sorts of miseries (illness, bereavement, impoverish-
ment) that have struck him. Their message is that when life goes
well for a person, it is a sign that they have chosen to do what
is good, but when things go badly, surely the person has sinned
against God and God has responded by imposing affliction.

Jesus' disciples were capable of this sort of logic (John 9:1–3),
as are many Christians today. It seems so natural to assume that if
God is in control of the world, everything that happens must be
God's doing, according to God's will. We must remember, however, that the Scriptures do not teach us this. They teach rather
that the world is fallen, corrupted by sin, and under the domina-
tion of Satan (cf. John 12:31), and that many things happen in life
that are not as God wishes them to be. Specifically, suffering is not
necessarily the result of sin (cf. Rom 8:18–23).

In order to read the book in keeping with its own purposes,
you may wish to consult *How to 2*, pages 121–24. Job, a godly
man, knew that he had done nothing to deserve the wrath of God.
In his frequent speeches (chs. 3; 6–7; 9–10; 12–14; 16–17; 19;
21; 23–24; 26–31) he asserts his innocence eloquently and also
expresses his frustration at the horrors he has had to endure. He
cannot understand why such things have happened to him. His
colleagues are horrified to hear such talk—to them it is blas-
phemy. They persist at trying to convince him that he is offending
God by his protestations. One by one they urge him repeatedly to
confess his sin—whatever it is—and admit that God administers
a fair and just world in which we get what our choices deserve.
Just as tenaciously, and even more eloquently, Job argues that life
is unfair, that the world as it is now is not the way it ought to be.

Elihu, the final "comforter" to arrive on the scene, defends
God's superior knowledge and ways. This is the closest to an
answer for Job that anyone has yet been able to provide, and it
looks as though Job is going to have to settle for Elihu's partly
satisfying, partly infuriating answer, when suddenly God himself
speaks to Job and the others (chs. 38–41). God both corrects
Job and puts the situation in perspective, but he also vindicates
Job over against the "wisdom" of his colleagues (42:7–9). As to
the question of whether everything in life is fair or not, Job had

prevailed; it is not. As to Job's wondering, *Why me?* God had prevailed; his ways are far above our ways, and his allowing suffering in our lives does not mean that he does not know what he is doing or that his right to do it should be questioned. His choices are always superior to ours.

This is true wisdom at its finest. The reader of the book of Job learns what is simply the world's wisdom—seemingly logical but actually wrong—and what constitutes God's wisdom and builds confidence in God's sovereignty and righteousness. Thus the dialogue and the storyline combine to produce the Old Testament's paramount exemplar of speculative wisdom.

As you read Job, be sure not to miss the overall structure of the book. The poetic dialogues of the book (3:1–42:6) are framed by a prose prologue (chs. 1–2) that tells you in advance why Job was tested so severely (God planned it all so that Job's refusal to give up on God would honor God and thwart the adversary, Satan) and by a prose epilogue (42:7–17) in which Job is openly vindicated and rewarded, in direct contrast to his comforters. This framing structure gives the reader information that Job and his comforters lacked as they debated. It doesn't "spoil" the story, but it helps one keep the story in proper perspective: this is not just a story about someone's suffering, but about God's gracious superintendence of suffering and the way that innocent suffering can truly glorify God (1 Pet 2:20).

WISDOM IN ECCLESIASTES

Ecclesiastes is a wisdom monologue that often puzzles Christians, especially if they read it amiss and assume that because it is Scripture everything said here is from God's perspective. There is good reason for the reader to be puzzled, because Ecclesiastes is a very difficult book to read, with several passages that seem self-contradictory and others that seem contradictory to the whole of biblical revelation.

This confusion has led to polar-opposite interpretations, as can be seen from two of the recommended commentaries in the appendix (whose authors happen to be close friends with one another). Professor Longman (along with one of us) understands most of Ecclesiastes to be an expression of cynical wisdom, which serves as a kind of "foil" regarding an outlook on life that should be avoided; Professor Provan (along with the other one of us) understands the book more positively, as an expression of how one should enjoy life under God in a world in which all die in the end. This latter point of view is the one you will find in *How to 2*, pages 154–60. It is important for you, therefore, in approaching Ecclesiastes to have an overall strategy for reading it. And whatever else, it is imperative here—as with Proverbs and Job—that you not take phrases and lines out of their context and give them a meaning that lies quite outside the author's purpose.

Thus an important part of reading the book's assertions in their proper context is to appreciate its structure. We have already pointed out that the book of Job is framed by a prologue and epilogue, which are different in kind from the dialogues placed between them. Something similar is true of Ecclesiastes as well. The opening prologue (1:1–11) and the closing epilogue (12:8–14) are written *about* the "Teacher" (Hebrew *qōhelet* = "congregation gatherer"), not *by* him. The Teacher speaks in the first person, whereas the prologue and epilogue speak about him in the third person. They frame what the Teacher says both by summarizing his message (note how similar 1:2 and 12:8 are as these introduce the opening and closing parts of the frame) and by informing the reader that what the Teacher says can be very valuable for learning wisdom (12:9–11). But the wise reader must not take the Teacher's specific conclusions as the final word. The final, proper perspective is the overview provided by the last two verses of the epilogue (12:13–14), including "Fear God and keep his commandments, for this is the duty of all mankind."

At issue ultimately in reading Ecclesiastes—both in the case of the frame and also the Teacher's words—is to come to terms with the frequently used and very important word *hebel* ("vanity," NRSV; "meaningless," NIV; "futility," NJB), which occurs thirty-seven times in this book (out of seventy-three in the entire OT). The word itself means "vapor" or "breath/wisp of air" (cf. Ps 39:5; Prov 31:30; Isa 57:13). But the question is, what does it mean for the Teacher? Does he intend it to go in the direction of the ephemeral/fleeting nature of all things? Or does he intend it to be a way of speaking about the "meaninglessness/uselessness" of all things? Or is it perhaps a bit of both?

How one answers this question depends in part on how one understands the other things that the Teacher says in the purposely rambling style that makes up the heart of the book. Five realities dominate his thinking: (1) God is the single, indisputable reality, the Creator of all and the One from whom all of life comes as a gift, including its—for the Teacher—burdensome nature; (2) God's ways are not always, if ever, understandable; (3) on the human side, "what is done under the sun" doesn't add up at all, in that the way things should be are not always—if ever—the way things actually are; (4) most things that happen are just repetitive, part of the endless cyclical flow of life ("there is nothing new under the Sun," the ancient equivalent of "same old, same old"). And, even worse, they don't last long enough to count for much (the *hebel*, vapor, vanishes quickly); (5) the great equalizer is death, which happens to all people alike. At the heart of all this is the Teacher's lack of hope in a resurrection of the dead. Once dead, that's it; and this is what makes life itself seem so *hebel* ("fleeting" and therefore sometimes also "in vain").

The Teacher's own point seems to be that, even if the only real certainty about this present life is the certainty of the grave, one should still live life, *hebel* as it is, as a gift from God (e.g., 3:12–14). Thus all is not lost, even in his frequently despairing outlook. Joy in this life does not come ultimately from "getting" (securing profit from what one does), but in the journey itself, the life that God has given. In such a world, joy and satisfaction are to be found in living the rhythms of life without trying to be in control or to "make gain" of what is merely transitory.

In spite of this more positive assessment of the Teacher's message than is often made, however, one can look at much of his opinion of life as a foil (i.e., as a contrast to what the rest of the Bible teaches). By this understanding of how the book teaches wisdom, the final part of the frame, Ecclesiastes 12:13–14, can be seen as concluding the book with a corrective, orthodox warning:

> Now all has been heard;
>   here is the conclusion of the matter:
> Fear God and keep his commandments,
>   for this is the duty of all mankind.
> For God will bring every deed into judgment,
>   including every hidden thing,
>   whether it is good or evil.

According to the foil theory, the bulk of the book—everything but the frame (the prologue and epilogue) represents a brilliant, artful argument for the way one would still find positive things to look at in life *if* God played a more distant role and *if* there were no life after death. If you are looking for a prescription for living in a deistic world with no afterlife—a world where there is a God, but he leaves people pretty much alone to live and die by their own devices—Ecclesiastes provides it. The aim of the book, by this understanding, is to represent the sort of "wisdom" that Solomon could produce after he had degenerated from orthodoxy (1 Kgs 11:1–13), a view of life that is supposed to leave you cold because, in spite of its evident divine providences, it remains relatively fatalistic and discouraging—and therefore makes you long for the alternative of a real covenant relationship with the living God.

What is lacking in the book by either interpretation, of course, are many of the great themes of Scripture with their assurances of God's own faithfulness toward those who trust in him. But this is perhaps to ask too much of this expression of speculative wisdom, which is not so much trying to provide answers as it is to remind its readers of the hard questions—ones that ultimately point us to Christ's death and resurrection for the answer.

WISDOM IN SONG OF SONGS

Song of Songs is a lengthy love song, a ballad about human romance, written in the style of ancient Near Eastern lyric poetry. We may call it lyric wisdom. Love songs as such have had a long history, including in Israel (see Ezek 33:32). But how does a love song fit the category of wisdom, and why is such love poetry in the Bible at all? The answer is actually quite simple: First, it was associated with Solomon (1:1; 3:6–11; 8:11–12; on this issue see *How to 2*, p. 162), whose name in Israel was synonymous with wisdom. But at a deeper level it deals explicitly with a category of wisdom found in Proverbs: the "wise choice" of marital and sexual fidelity.

God has created human beings with a large number of brain cells devoted to love and sex. This is a fact of our humanity and a part of God's design that was declared "good" (Gen 1:31). Unfortunately, as with everything else, the fall also corrupted this dimension of our humanity. Instead of its being a constant source of joy and blessing in monogamous marriage, as God intended, sexual love is often a means of selfish personal gratification involving all sorts of lusts and exploitation. But these things need not be.

True romance can be celebrated to God's glory in keeping with his original design; and this is what Song of Songs is about.

To be sure, the book has had a long history of odd interpretation in the form of allegorizing. Because readers were uncomfortable with its forthright, explicit exultation of human sexual love, many early interpreters—both Jewish and Christian—looked for a way around it. They found it in the allegorical "love songs" in the Prophetic Books—one way the prophets told the story of God's love for his people, Israel, and how that love was rejected or abused (e.g., Isa 5:1–7; Hos 2:2–15). Since some of the same kind of language and imagery used by the prophets in these songs is also used throughout Song of Songs, they concluded that the book was also an allegory. In an age when it was a common practice to allegorize virtually all of Scripture (see p. 108), some early church fathers argued that the Song of Songs should be read as an allegory of Christ's love for the church. Indeed, an early church council (AD 550) forbade any other interpretation, so that it has prevailed until recent times.

But even on the surface that is obviously *not* what the Song of Songs is about. Rather, it centers on human love—love between a man and a woman, celebrating both this love itself and their attraction for one another. After all, nothing in the Prophetic Books reads like this(!):

> How beautiful you are, my darling!
>> Oh, how beautiful!
>> Your eyes behind your veil are doves.
> Your hair is like a flock of goats
>> descending from the hills of Gilead.
> Your teeth are like a flock of sheep just shorn,
>> coming up from the washing.
> Each has its twin;
>> not one of them is alone.
> Your lips are like a scarlet ribbon;
>> your mouth is lovely.
> Your temples behind your veil
>> are like the halves of a pomegranate.
> Your neck is like the tower of David,
>> built with courses of stone;
> on it hang a thousand shields,
>> all of them shields of warriors.

Song of Songs 4:1–4

This is the language of a man's adoration of his loved one in which he compares features of her appearance to beautiful images in life. He is not talking, of course, about things that are strictly similar in appearance but things that are similarly impressive visually. And so it goes throughout the book. Nothing in the prophetic love songs compares with Song of Songs 5:2–6, where the woman recounts a dream in which she was asleep and could not wake up and move fast enough to keep from missing the man she loved when he called for her ("I slept but my heart was awake" is a poetic way of saying "I was dreaming"). Here the dream serves to heighten the emphasis on the attraction she feels for the man she loves and how frustrating it is when she misses a chance to be with him (cf. also 3:1–5).

There are many other kinds of expressions of love and fondness in the Song of Songs in addition to visual comparisons and dream sequences: statements of the ardor of love (e.g., 1:2–4), advice and challenge from observers of the romance (e.g., 1:8; 5:9), romantic invitations from the man to the woman and vice versa (e.g., 7:11–13; 8:13), purposely exaggerated boasts about the greatness of the woman by the man and vice versa (e.g., 2:8–9), the need to resist temptation to be unfaithfully attracted to anyone else (e.g., 6:8–9), and declaration that a lover's attraction can be stronger even than the splendor of so great a king as Solomon himself (e.g., 3:6–11 following on 2:16–3:5; cf. 8:11–12). All these are cast in the form of musical poetry, celebrating human love in a monogamous relationship as God's good gift.

Here, then, are some of the considerations we think will help you use the Song of Songs in the way Scripture intends (see further, *How to 2*, pp. 161–65):

First, try to appreciate the overall ethical context of Song of Songs. Monogamous, heterosexual marriage was the proper context for sexual activity according to God's revelation in the Old Testament, and God-fearing Israelites would regard the book in that light. The attitude of the book itself is the very antithesis of unfaithfulness, either before or after marriage. Marriage consummates and continues love between a man and a woman. This is what the Song of Songs points toward.

Second, be aware of the genre of the Song of Songs. Its closest parallels are indeed the love poetry of the Old Testament and elsewhere in the ancient Near East, the context of which was not just love of any kind but attraction in marriage. Love songs were probably sung routinely at wedding banquets and had great meaning for those involved. They speak of attraction, fidelity, warding off the temptation to cheat, the preciousness of love, its joys and pleasures, and the dangers of infidelity.

Third, read the Song of Songs as *suggesting* godly choices rather than merely *describing* these choices in a mundane manner. This is similar to what we have already said about interpreting proverbs—they carry truth as suggestions and generalizations rather than precise statements of universal fact. In Scripture some parallels to the Song of Songs can be found in the prologue to Proverbs (chs. 1–9). There one finds poems about the attractiveness of wisdom and the counter-attractiveness of folly, in a manner that suggests lyrically rather than propositionally what our right choices ought to be.

Fourth, be aware that the Song of Songs focuses on very different values from those of our modern culture. Today "experts" talk about sex *techniques* but almost never about virtuous *romance*, the attraction of a man and a woman to each other that leads to and continues in lifelong marriage. Some "experts" advocate self-indulgence; the Song of Songs emphasizes just the opposite. Our culture encourages people to fulfill themselves, whatever their sexual tastes and desires, whereas the Song of Songs is concerned with how one person can respond faithfully to the attractiveness of another and fulfill the needs of the other. In most of the modern world, romance is thought of as something that precedes marriage, and is based primarily on feelings or pleasure. In the Song of Songs, romance is something that actually characterizes marriage, even forty-three years later, as in the case of one of the authors, and sixty years later, as in the case of the other. Let it be so.

CHAPTER 13

Revelation: Images of Judgment and Hope

When turning to the book of Revelation from the rest of the New Testament, the ordinary modern reader may feel as though they are entering a foreign country. Instead of narratives and letters containing plain statements of fact and imperatives, one comes to a book full of angels, trumpets, and earthquakes; of beasts, dragons, and bottomless pits.

The hermeneutical problems are intrinsic. The book is in the canon; for us it is God's Word, inspired of the Holy Spirit. Yet when we come to it to hear this word, most of us in the church today hardly know what to make of it. The author sometimes speaks forthrightly: "I, John, your brother and companion in the suffering and kingdom and patient endurance that are ours in Jesus, was on the island of Patmos because of the word of God and the testimony of Jesus" (1:9). He writes to seven known churches in known cities with recognizable first-century conditions.

At the same time, however, there is a rich, diverse symbolism, some of which is manageable (judgment in the form of an earthquake; 6:12–17), while some is more obscure (the two witnesses; 11:1–10). Most of the problems stem from the symbols, plus the fact that the book often deals with future events, while at the same time it is set in a recognizable first-century context. The problem is also related to the thoroughgoing way that John sees everything in light of the Old Testament, which he cites or echoes over 250 times, so that every significant moment in his narrative is imaged almost exclusively in Old Testament language (see *How to 2*, pp. 428–29).

We do not pretend to be able to resolve all the matters, nor do we imagine that all of our readers will be happy with everything we say. It seems necessary to say at the outset that no one should approach Revelation without a proper degree of humility! There are already too many books on "Revelation Made Easy." But it is not easy. As with the difficult passages in the Epistles (see pp. 71–73), one should be less than dogmatic here, especially since there are at least five major schools of interpretation, not to mention significant variations within each of the schools.

But we are also bold enough to think we have more than an inkling as to what John was up to. So we will lead you into some hermeneutical suggestions that make sense to us. But exegesis comes first, and in this case exegesis is especially crucial, for this is a book on which a lot of popular books and pamphlets have been written. In almost every case, these popular books do no exegesis at all. They jump immediately to hermeneutics, which usually takes the form of fanciful speculations that John himself could never possibly have intended or understood.

The very best introduction to Revelation—how it "works" as a book, its basic point of view, and its theological contribution to the Bible—is by Richard Bauckham, *The Theology of the Book of Revelation* (Cambridge: Cambridge University Press, 1993); for an "easy read" commentary intended for the lay reader, you may wish to look at Professor Fee's *Revelation* in the New Covenant Commentary Series (2011), where what is given here is spelled out in a bit more detail.

THE NATURE OF REVELATION

As with most of the other biblical genres, the first key to the exegesis of the book of Revelation is to examine the kind of literature it is. In this case, however, we face a different kind of problem, for Revelation is a unique, finely blended combination of three distinct literary types: apocalypse, prophecy, and letter. Furthermore, the basic type—apocalypse—is a literary form that does not exist in our own day. In previous cases, even if our own examples differ somewhat from the biblical ones, we nonetheless have a basic understanding of what an epistle or a narrative, a psalm or a proverb, is. But we simply have nothing quite like this. Thus it is especially important in this case to have a clear picture of the literary type we are dealing with.

Revelation as Apocalypse

The book of Revelation is primarily an apocalypse. It is only one—though a very special one, to be sure—of dozens of apocalypses that were well-known to Jews and Christians from about 200 BC to AD 200. These other apocalypses, which of course are not canonical, were of a variety of kinds, yet they all, including Revelation, have some common characteristics. These common characteristics are as follows:

1. The taproot of apocalyptic is the Old Testament prophetic literature, especially as it is found in Ezekiel, Daniel, Zechariah, and parts of Isaiah. As was the case in some prophetic literature, apocalyptic was concerned about coming judgment and salvation. But apocalyptic was born either in persecution or in a time of great oppression. Therefore, its great concern was no longer with God's activity *within* history. The apocalyptists looked exclusively forward to the time when God would bring a violent, radical *end* to history, an end that would mean the triumph of good and the final judgment of evil.

2. Unlike most of the Prophetic Books, apocalypses are literary works from the beginning. The prophets were primarily spokespersons for Yahweh, whose spoken oracles were later committed to writing and collected in a book. But an apocalypse is a form of *literature*. It has a particular written structure and form. John, for example, is told to "*write*, therefore, what you have *seen*" (1:19, emphasis added), whereas the prophets were mostly told to *speak* what they were told or had seen.

3. Most frequently the "stuff" of apocalyptic is presented in the form of visions and dreams, and its language is cryptic (having hidden meanings) and symbolic. Therefore, most of the apocalypses contained literary devices that were intended to give the book a sense of hoary age. The most important of these devices was pseudonymity, that is, they were given the appearance of having been written by ancient worthies (Enoch, Baruch, et al.), who were told to "seal it up" for a later day, the "later day" of course being the age in which the book was now being written.

4. The images of apocalyptic are often forms of fantasy rather than of reality. By way of contrast, the nonapocalyptic prophets and Jesus also regularly used symbolic language, but most often it involved real images—for example, salt (Matt 5:13), vultures and carcasses (Luke 17:37), senseless doves (Hos 7:11), half-baked

bread (Hos 7:8), et al. But most of the images of apocalyptic belong to fantasy—for example, a beast with seven heads and ten horns (Rev 13:1), a woman clothed with the sun (12:1), locusts with scorpions' tails and human heads (9:10), et al. The fantasy may not necessarily appear in the items themselves (we understand beasts, heads, and horns) but in their unearthly combination.

5. Because they were literary, most of the apocalypses were very formally stylized. There was a strong tendency to divide time and events into neat packages. There was also a great fondness for the symbolic use of numbers. As a consequence, the final product usually has the visions in carefully arranged, often numbered sets. Frequently these sets, when put together, express something (e.g., judgment) without necessarily trying to suggest that each separate picture follows hard on the heels of the former.

The book of Revelation fits all these characteristics of apocalyptic but one. And this one difference is so important that in some ways it becomes a world of its own: *Revelation is not pseudonymous.* John felt no need to follow the regular formula here. He made himself known to his readers and through the seven letters (chs. 2–3) he spoke to known churches of Asia Minor, people who were his contemporaries and companions in suffering. Moreover, he was told *not* to "seal up the words of the prophecy of this scroll, because the time is near" (22:10).

Revelation as Prophecy

The major reason John's apocalypse is not pseudonymous is probably related to his own sense of the end as already/not yet (see pp. 151–53). He is not, with his Jewish predecessors, simply anticipating the end. He knew that it had already begun with the coming of Jesus. Crucial to this understanding is the advent of the Spirit. The other apocalyptists wrote in the name of former prophetic figures because they lived in the age of the "quenched Spirit," awaiting the prophetic promise of the outpoured Spirit in the coming age. Thus they were in an age when prophecy had ceased.

John, on the other hand, belongs to the new era. He was "in the Spirit" when he was told to write what he saw (1:10–11). He calls his book "this prophecy" (1:3; 22:18–19) and says that the "testimony about Jesus," for which he and the churches are suffering (20:4; cf. 1:9), "is the Spirit of prophecy" (19:10). This probably means that the message of Jesus, attested by him and to which John and the churches bear witness, is the clear evidence that the prophetic Spirit had come.

What makes John's apocalypse different, therefore, is first of all this combination of apocalyptic and prophetic elements. On the one hand, the book is cast in the apocalyptic mold and has most of the literary characteristics of apocalypse. It is born in persecution and intends to speak about the end with the triumph of Christ and his church, and it is a carefully constructed piece of literature, using cryptic language and rich symbolism of fantasy and numbers.

On the other hand, John clearly intends this apocalypse to be a prophetic word to the church. His book was not to be sealed for the future. It was a word from God for their present situation. You will recall from chapter 10 that to prophesy does not primarily mean to foretell the future but rather to speak forth God's word in the present, a word that usually had as its content coming judgment or salvation. In Revelation, even the seven letters bear this prophetic imprint. Here, then, is God's prophetic word to some churches in the latter part of the first century who are undergoing persecution from without and some decay from within.

Revelation as Epistle

Finally, it must be noted that this combination of apocalyptic and prophetic elements has been cast in the form of a letter. For example, if you were to begin by reading how John both opens (1:4–7) and concludes (22:21) you will note that all the characteristics of the letter form are present. Furthermore, John speaks to his readers in the first person/second person formula (I ... you). Thus in its final form the Revelation is sent by John as a letter to the seven churches of Asia Minor.

The significance of this is that, as with all epistles, there is an *occasional* (see pp. 60–61, 90–91) aspect to Revelation. It was occasioned at least in part by the needs of the specific churches to which it is addressed. Therefore, to interpret, we must try to understand its original historical context.

THE NECESSITY OF EXEGESIS

It may seem strange that after twelve chapters in this book, we should still feel constrained to contend for the necessity of exegesis. But it is precisely the lack of sound exegetical principles that has caused so much unfortunate and speculative interpretation of Revelation to take place. What we want to do here, then, is simply to repeat, with Revelation in mind, some of the basic exegetical principles we have already delineated in this book, beginning with chapter 3.

1. The first task of the exegesis of Revelation is to seek the author's, and there with the Holy Spirit's, original intent. As with the Epistles, *the primary meaning of Revelation is what John intended it to mean, which in turn must also have been something his readers could have understood it to mean.* Indeed, the great advantage they would have over us is their familiarity with their own historical context (which caused the book to be written in the first place) and their greater familiarity with apocalyptic forms and images. At the same time they had a thoroughgoing acquaintance with the Old Testament that most contemporary Christians lack, so that they would immediately have heard and recognized the source of John's echoes and allusions to the Old Testament and understood what he was doing with them.

Since the book of Revelation intends to be prophetic, one must be open to the possibility of a secondary meaning, inspired by the Holy Spirit but not fully seen by the author or his readers. However, such a second meaning lies beyond exegesis in the broader area of hermeneutics. Therefore, the task of exegesis here is to understand what John was intending his original readers to hear and understand.

2. One must be especially careful of overusing the concept of the "analogy of Scripture" in the exegesis of Revelation. The analogy of Scripture means that Scripture is to be interpreted in the light of other Scripture. We hold this to be self-evident, based on our stance that all of Scripture is God's word and has God as its ultimate source. However, to interpret Scripture by Scripture must not be tilted in such a way that one *must* make other Scriptures the hermeneutical keys to unlock Revelation.

Thus, it is one step to recognize John's new use of images from Daniel or Ezekiel or to see the analogies in apocalyptic images from other texts. But one may not assume, as some schools of interpretation do, that John's readers had to have read Matthew or 1 and 2 Thessalonians, and that they already knew from their reading of these texts certain keys to understanding what John had written. Therefore, any keys to interpreting the book of Revelation must be *intrinsic* to the text of Revelation itself or otherwise available to the original recipients from *their own historical context.*

3. Because of the apocalyptic/prophetic nature of the book, there are some added difficulties at the exegetical level, especially having to do with the imagery. Here are some suggestions in this regard:

a. *One must have a sensitivity to the rich background of ideas that have gone into the composition of Revelation.* The chief source of these ideas and images is the Old Testament, but John also has derived images from apocalyptic and even from ancient mythology. But these images, though deriving from a variety of sources, do not necessarily mean what they meant in their sources. They have been broken and transformed under inspiration and thus blended together into this "new prophecy."

b. *Apocalyptic imagery is of several kinds.* In some cases the images, like the donkey and elephant in American political cartoons, are constant. The beast out of the sea, for example, is a standard image for a world empire, not for an individual ruler. On the other hand, some images are fluid. The "Lion" of the tribe of Judah turns out in fact to be a "Lamb" (Rev 5:5–6)—the *only* Lion there is in Revelation. The woman in chapter 12 is clearly a positive image, yet the woman in chapter 17 is evil.

Likewise some of the images clearly refer to specific counterparts. The seven lampstands in the prologue (1:12–20) are identified as the seven churches, and the dragon in chapter 12 is Satan. On the other hand, many of the images are probably general. For example, the four horsemen of chapter 6 probably do not represent any specific expression of conquest, war, famine, and death, but rather represent this expression of human fallenness as the source of the church's suffering (6:9–11) that in turn will be a cause of God's judgment (6:12–17).

All of this is to say that the images are the most difficult part of the exegetical task. Because of this, two further points are especially important:

c. *When John himself interprets his images, these interpreted images must be held firmly and must serve as a starting point for understanding other images.* There are six such interpreted images: The one like a son of man (1:13) is Christ, who alone "was dead, and ... [is] alive for ever and ever!" (1:18). The golden lampstands (1:20) are the seven churches. The seven stars (1:20) are the seven angels, or messengers, of the churches (unfortunately, this is still unclear because of the use of the term "angel," which may in itself be yet another image). The great dragon (12:9) is Satan. The seven heads (17:9) are the seven hills on which the woman sits (as well as seven kings, thus becoming a fluid image). The prostitute (17:18) is the great city, clearly indicating Rome.

d. *One must see the visions as wholes and not allegorically press all the details.* In this matter the visions are like the parables. The whole vision is trying to say something; the details are either (1) for dramatic effect (6:12–14) or (2) to add to the picture of the whole so that the readers will not mistake the points of reference (9:7–11). Thus the details of the sun turning black like sackcloth and the stars falling like figs probably do not "mean" anything. They simply make the whole vision of the earthquake more impressive. However, the locusts with crowns of gold, human faces, and women's long hair (9:7–11) help to fill out the picture in such a way that the original readers could hardly have mistaken what was in view—the barbarian hordes at the outer edges of the Roman Empire, who served as a constant threat to the Empire and were thus duly feared.

4. John expects his readers to hear his echoes of the Old Testament as the continuation—and consummation—of that story. You will find this happening at every turn. For example, the presentation of Christ begins with a doxology to him (1:5b–6) that echoes the sacrificial system and uses the language of Exodus 19:6 to refer to the church as the new people of God, redeemed by Christ. This is followed by an announcement of his coming, which is a collage from Daniel 7:13 and Zechariah 12:10. The picture of Christ that follows is based primarily on Daniel 10:6 but is a superb collage of that passage with Daniel 7:9, 13; Isaiah 49:2; Ezekiel 1:24. In Revelation 5 the presentation of Christ climaxes as the "Lion of the tribe of Judah" (cf. Gen 49:9), the "Root of David" (cf. Isa 11:1), turns out to be a "Lamb, looking as if it had been slain" (from the Passover and sacrificial system). Similarly the preliminary, temporal judgments pictured in the first seven trumpets (chs. 8–9) echo several of the plagues that fell on Egypt in Exodus 7–10, while the final judgment of Rome in chapters 17–18 is expressed in language and pictures from the several prophetic judgments on Babylon and Tyre in Isaiah, Jeremiah, and Ezekiel—and Rome itself is called Babylon.

Good exegesis of the book of Revelation, therefore, requires one to be constantly aware of these Old Testament echoes, since in the vast majority of instances the Old Testament context of these echoes gives you clues as to how John intends his own images and pictures to be understood.

5. One final note: Apocalypses in general, and Revelation in particular, seldom intend to give a detailed chronological account of the future. Their message tends to transcend this kind of concern. John's larger concern is that, despite present appearances, God is in control of history and the church. And even though the church will experience suffering and death, it will be triumphant in Christ, who will judge his enemies and save his people. All of the visions must be seen in terms of this greater concern.

THE HISTORICAL CONTEXT

As with most of the other genres, the place to begin one's exegesis of Revelation is with a provisional reconstruction of the situation in which it was written. To do this well, you need to do here what we have suggested elsewhere—try to read it all the way through in one sitting. Read for the big picture. Do not try to figure out everything. Let your reading itself be a happening, as it were. That is, let the visions roll past you like waves on the shore, one after another, until you have a feel for the book and its message.

Again, as you read, make some mental or brief written notes about the author and his readers. Then go back a second time and specifically pick up all the references that indicate John's readers are companions in his suffering (1:9). These are the crucial historical indicators.

For example, in the seven letters, note 2:3, 8–9, 13; 3:10, plus the repeated "to those who are victorious." The fifth seal (6:9–11), which follows the devastation wrought by the four horsemen, reveals Christian martyrs who have been slain because of the "word" and the "testimony" (exactly why John is in exile [1:9]). In 7:14 the great multitude, who will never again suffer (7:16), has "come out of the great tribulation." Suffering and death are again linked to bearing "Jesus' testimony" in 12:11 and 17. And in chapters 13–20 the suffering and death are specifically attributed to the "beast" (13:7; 14:9–13; 16:5–6; 18:20, 24; 19:2).

This motif is the key to understanding the historical context and fully explains the occasion and purpose of the book. John himself was in exile for his faith. Others were also experiencing suffering—one had even died (2:13)—for the testimony of Jesus. While John was "in the Spirit," he came to realize that their present suffering was only the beginning of woes for those who would refuse "to worship the beast." At the same time John was not altogether sure that all the church was ready for what was ahead of them. So he wrote this "prophecy" that he had seen.

The main themes are abundantly clear: The church and the state are on a collision course; and initial victory will appear to belong to the state. Thus he warns the church that suffering and death lie ahead; indeed, it will get far worse before it gets better (6:9–11). He is greatly concerned that they do not capitulate in times of duress (14:11–12; 21:7–8). But this prophetic word is also one of encouragement—for God is in control of all things. Christ holds the keys to history, and he holds the churches in his hands (1:17–20). Thus the church triumphs even through death (12:11). God will finally pour out his wrath on those who caused this suffering and death and bring eternal rest to those who remain faithful. In that context, of course, Rome was the enemy that would be judged.

It should be noted here that one of the keys for interpreting the book of Revelation is the distinction John makes between two crucial words or ideas—"tribulation" and "wrath." To confuse these and make them refer to the same thing will cause one to become hopelessly muddled as to what is being said.

Tribulation (suffering and death) is clearly a part of what the church was enduring and was yet to endure. God's wrath, on the other hand, is his judgment that is to be poured on those who have afflicted God's people. It is clear from every kind of context in Revelation that God's people will *not* have to endure God's awful wrath when it is poured out on their enemies, but it is equally clear that they will indeed suffer at the hands of their enemies. This distinction, it should be noted, is precisely in keeping with the rest of the New Testament. See, for example, 2 Thessalonians 1:3–10, where Paul boasts of the Thessalonians' "persecutions and trials" (the same Greek word as "tribulation"), but he also notes that God will eventually judge those "who trouble you" (the verb form of "tribulation").

You should note also how the opening of seals 5 and 6 (6:9–17) raises the two crucial questions in the book. In seal 5 the Christian martyrs cry out, "How long, Sovereign Lord,... until you judge the inhabitants of the earth and avenge our blood?" The answer is twofold: (1) They must "wait a little longer" because there are to be many more martyrs; (2) judgment is nonetheless absolutely certain, as the sixth seal indicates.

In seal 6, when God's judgment comes, the judged cry out, "Who can withstand [the coming wrath of the Lamb]?" The answer is given in chapter 7: those whom God has sealed, who "have washed their robes and made them white in the blood of the Lamb" (7:14).

THE LITERARY CONTEXT

To understand any one of the specific visions in the book of Revelation it is especially important not only to wrestle with the background and meaning of the images (the *content* questions) but also to ask how this particular vision *functions* in the book as a whole. In this regard Revelation is much more like the Epistles than the Prophets. The latter are collections of individual oracles, not always with a clear functional purpose in relation to one another. In the Epistles, as you will recall, one must "think paragraphs," because every paragraph is a building block for the whole argument. So also it is with Revelation. The book is a creatively structured whole, and each vision is an integral part of that whole.

Since Revelation is the only one of its kind in the New Testament, we will try to guide you all the way through it rather than simply offer a model or two. It should be noted, of course, that the basic structure is clear and not an object of debate; differences come in how one interprets said structure (see *How to 2*, pp. 426–36).

The book unfolds like a great drama in which the earliest scenes set the stage and the cast of characters, and the later scenes presuppose all the earlier scenes and must be so understood for us to be able to follow the plot.

Chapters 1–3 thus set the stage and introduce us to most of the significant *characters.* First comes John himself (1:1–11), who is the "seer" and will be the narrator throughout. He was exiled for his faith in Christ, and he had the prophetic insight to see that the present persecution was only a forerunner of what was to be.

Second, there is Christ (1:12–20), whom John describes in magnificent images derived from Daniel 10 and elsewhere as the Lord of history and the Lord of the church. God has not lost control, despite present persecution, for Christ alone holds the keys of death and Hades.

Third, there is the church (2:1–3:22). In letters to seven real, but also representative, churches, John encourages and warns the church. Persecution is already present; the church is promised more. But there are many internal disorders that also threaten its well-being. Those who are victorious are given the promises of final glory.

Chapters 4–5 further help to *set the stage*. With breathtaking visions, set to worship and praise, the church is told that God reigns in sovereign majesty (ch. 4). To believers who may be wondering whether God is really there, acting on their behalf, John reminds them that God's "Lion" is a "Lamb," who himself redeemed humankind through suffering (ch. 5). And so all heaven bursts forth in praise to "him who sits on the throne and to the Lamb."

Chapters 6–7 begin the unfolding of the actual drama itself. Three times throughout the book visions are presented in carefully structured sets of seven (chs. 6–7; 8–11; 15–16). In each case the first four items go together to form one picture; in 6–7 and 8–11 the next two items also go together to present two sides of another reality. These are then interrupted by an interlude of two visions, before the seventh item is revealed. In chapters 15–16 the final three group together without the interlude precisely because they lead directly into the final visions of chapters 17–22. Note how this works out in chapters 6–7:

1. White horseman = Conquest
2. Red horseman = War
3. Black horseman = Famine
4. Pale horseman = Death
5. The martyrs' question: "How long?"
6. The earthquake (God's judgment): "Who can withstand [the wrath]"
   a. 144,000 sealed
   b. A great multitude
7. God's wrath: the seven trumpets of chapters 8–11

Chapters 8–11 reveal the content of God's temporal judgments on Rome. The first four trumpets, echoing the plagues of Egypt (Exod 7–10), indicate that part of this judgment will involve great disorders in nature; trumpets five and six indicate that it will also come from the barbarian hordes and a great war. After the interlude, which expresses God's own exaltation of his "witnesses" even though they die, the seventh trumpet sounds the conclusion: "The kingdom of the world has become the kingdom of our Lord and of his Messiah" (Rev 11:15).

Thus we have been brought through the suffering of the church and the judgment of God on the church's enemies to the final triumph of God. But the visions are not finished. In chapters 8–11 we have been given the big picture; chapters 12–22 offer details of this judgment and triumph. What has happened is something like looking at Michelangelo's Sistine Chapel. At first, one is simply awestruck at the sight of the whole of the chapel; only later one can inspect the parts and see the magnificence that has gone into every detail.

Chapter 12 is the theological key to the book. In two visions we are told of Satan's attempt to destroy Christ and of his own defeat instead. Thus, within the recurring New Testament framework of the already/not yet, Satan is revealed as a defeated foe (already) whose final end has not yet come. Therefore, there is rejoicing because "now [has] come the salvation ... of our God," (Rev 12:10) yet there is woe to the church because Satan knows his time is limited and he is taking vengeance on God's people.

Chapters 13–14 then show how for John's church this vengeance took the form of the Roman Empire, with its emperors who were demanding religious allegiance. But the empire and the emperors are doomed (chs. 15–16). The book concludes as a "tale of two cities" (chs. 17–22). The city of earth (Rome) is condemned for its part in the persecution of God's people. This is followed by the city of God, where God's people dwell eternally.

Within this overall structure several of the visions present considerable difficulties, both as to the meaning of their content and of their function in context. For these questions you should consult one of the better commentaries (see appendix).

THE HERMENEUTICAL QUESTIONS

The hermeneutical difficulties with the book of Revelation are much like those of the Prophetic Books surveyed above in chapter

10. As with all other genres, God's word to us is to be found first of all in his word to them. But in contrast to the other genres, the Prophets and Revelation often speak about things that in their case were yet to be.

Often what was "yet to be" had a temporal immediacy to it, which from our historical vantage point has now already taken place. Thus Judah *did* go into captivity, and they were restored, just as Jeremiah prophesied; and the Roman Empire *did* in fact come under temporal judgment, partly through the barbarian hordes, just as John saw.

For such realities the hermeneutical problems are not too great. We can still hear as God's word the reasons for the judgments. As we may properly assume that God will always judge those who trample on the heads of the poor and sell the needy for a pair of sandals (Amos 2:6–7), we may rightly assume that God's judgment will be poured out on those nations who have murdered Christians, just as it was on Rome.

Furthermore, we can still hear as God's word—indeed, *must* hear—that discipleship goes the way of the cross, that God has not promised us freedom *from* suffering and death but triumph *through* it. As Martin Luther rightly put it in the hymn "A Mighty Fortress": "The prince of darkness grim, we tremble not for him ... the body they may kill, God's truth abideth still: His kingdom is forever." Thus Revelation is God's word of comfort and encouragement to Christians who suffer, especially believers who suffer at the hands of the state, precisely because they are Christians. God is in control. The slain Lamb has triumphed over the dragon (Rev 12:7–12).

All of this needs to be heard again and again in the church—in every geographical setting and in every age. And to miss this, is to miss the book altogether.

But our hermeneutical difficulties do not lie in hearing this word, the word of warning and comfort that is the point of the book. Our difficulties lie with that other phenomenon of prophecy, namely that the "temporal" word is often so closely tied to the final eschatological realities (see pp. 206–11). This is especially true in the book of Revelation. The fall of Rome in chapter 18 seems to appear as the first chapter in the final wrap-up, and many of the pictures of "temporal" judgment are interlaced with words or ideas that also imply the final end as a part of the picture. There seems to be no way one can deny the reality of this. The question is, what do we do with it? We have already spoken to this question in chapter 10. Here we simply offer a few suggestions.

1. We need to learn that pictures of the future are just that—pictures. The pictures express a reality, but they are not themselves to be confused with reality, nor are the details of every picture necessarily to be "fulfilled" in some specific way. Thus when the first four trumpets proclaim calamities on nature as a part of God's judgment, we must not necessarily expect a literal fulfillment of all the details of these pictures. Their point, made by the deliberate echo of God's plagues against Pharaoh, is to encourage believers under Rome's soon-coming oppression that God's "plagues" will fall on Rome as well.

2. Some of the pictures that were intended primarily to express the certainty of God's judgment must not also be interpreted to mean "*soon-ness*," at least "soon-ness" from our limited perspective. Thus when Satan is defeated at Christ's death and resurrection and is "hurled to the earth" to wreak havoc on the church, he knows his time is "short." But "short" does not necessarily mean "very soon," as if, for example, John thought that these things must happen during his lifetime, but something much more like "limited." There will, in fact, come a time when he will be bound forever, but of that day and hour no one knows.

3. The pictures where the "temporal" is closely tied to the "eschatological" should not be viewed as simultaneous—even though the original readers themselves may have understood them in this way (cf. pp. 206–11). The eschatological dimension of the judgments and of the salvation should alert us to the *possibility* of a "not yet" dimension to many of the pictures. On the other hand, there seem to be no fixed rules as to how we are to extract or to understand that still (for us) future element. What we must be careful not to do is to spend too much time speculating as to how any of our own contemporary events may be fitted into the pictures of Revelation. The book was *not* intended to prophesy the existence of Communist China, for example, or to give us literal details of the conclusion of history.

4. Although there are probably many instances where there is a second, yet-to-be-fulfilled dimension to the pictures, we have been given no keys as to how we are to pin these down. In this regard the New Testament itself exhibits a certain amount of ambi-

guity. The antichrist figure, for example, is a particularly difficult one. In Paul's writings (2 Thess 2:3–4) he is a definite figure; in Revelation 13–14 he comes in the form of the Roman emperor. In both cases, his appearance seems to be eschatological. Yet in 1 John, all of this is reinterpreted in a generalized way to refer to the false prophets who had invaded the church (1 John 2:20–23). How, then, are *we* to understand this figure with regard to our own future?

Historically, the church has seen (in a certain sense, properly so) a variety of world rulers as an expression of antichrist. Adolf Hitler surely fit the picture, as did Idi Amin for a generation of Ugandans. In this sense many antichrists continue to come (1 John 2:18). But what of a specific worldwide figure who will accompany the final events of the end? Does Revelation 13–14 tell us that such is to be? Our own reply is, not necessarily; however, we are open to the possibility. It is the ambiguity of the New Testament texts themselves that leads to our caution and lack of dogmatic certainty.

5. The pictures that were intended to be totally eschatological are still to be taken so. Thus the pictures of 11:15–19 and 19:1–22:21 are entirely eschatological in their presentation. This we should affirm as God's word yet to be fulfilled. But even these are *pictures*; the fulfillment will be in God's own time, in his own way—and will undoubtedly be infinitely greater than even these marvelous pictures.

Just as the opening word of Scripture speaks of God and creation, so the concluding word speaks of God and consummation. If there are some ambiguities for us as to *how* all the details are to work out, there is no ambiguity as to the certainty that God *will* work it all out—in his time and in his way. Such certainty should serve for us as warning and encouragement, as it did for the book's original recipients.

Until Christ comes, we live out the future in the already, and we do so by hearing and obeying his word. But there comes a day when such books as this will no longer be needed, for, "No longer will they teach their neighbors ... because they will all know me" (Jer 31:34). And with John, and the Spirit and the bride, we say, "Amen. Come, Lord Jesus."

Appendix:
The Evaluation and
Use of Commentaries

Throughout this book we have regularly suggested that there are times when you will want to consult a good commentary. We do not apologize for this. A good commentary is every bit as much a gift to the church as are good sermons, good video, audio and web resources, or good counselors.

Our purpose in this appendix is simple. After some words on how you may go about evaluating a commentary as to its exegetical value, we will list one or more of the better commentaries for each of the biblical books. There is an inherent problem in such a list, of course, in that excellent commentaries are regularly appearing. We are listing what is available as of our writing. As new commentaries come out, you can evaluate them according to the procedures given here.

THE EVALUATION OF COMMENTARIES

If you are a serious Bible student, you will eventually want to secure or have access to a good commentary for each book of the Bible. There really is no completely satisfactory one-volume commentary. One-volume commentaries are usually designed to do the very work we have tried to teach you to do on your own throughout this book. They briefly give the historical context and then trace the meaning of the text in terms of its literary context. This indeed has its value, but much of this you can find in the

Zondervan Handbook to the Bible, for example. What you want a commentary for is basically to supply three things: (1) helps on sources and information about the historical context, (2) answers to those manifold content questions, and (3) thorough discussions of difficult texts as to the possibilities of meaning, along with supporting arguments.

How, then, does one evaluate a commentary? First, you do *not* evaluate on the basis of your agreement with the author. If the commentary is really a good one, and if you have done your own exegesis well, more often than not you and the better commentaries will be in agreement. But agreement is not the basic criterion.

Moreover, you do *not* evaluate on the basis of its "turning you on." The point of a commentary is *exegesis*—what the text *means*—not homiletics—preaching the text in our day. You may make good use of books of this kind in trying to discover how to use a text in the present scene. As preachers, we ourselves confess to the usefulness of such books to get one's mind to thinking about the present age. *But these are not commentaries,* even if they are excellent models for how to apply the Bible in the here and now. Our concern here is not with these books but with exegetical commentaries alone.

There are at least seven criteria you should use in judging a commentary. Not all of these are of the same kind, nor are all of them of equal importance. But all of these combine to help at the one crucial point: Does this commentary help you understand what the biblical text actually said?

The first two criteria are basically points of information that you will want to know about the commentary.

1. Is the commentary exegetical, homiletical, or a combination of both? This simply reiterates what we have just said above. Remember, what you really want in a commentary is exegesis. If it also has hermeneutical suggestions, you may find this helpful, but what you want are answers to your content questions—and content questions are primarily exegetical.

2. Is it based on the Greek or Hebrew text, or on an English translation? It is not bad for a commentary to be based on a translation, *as long as the author knows the text in the original language and uses this knowledge as the real source of their comments.* Note well: You can use most commentaries based on the Greek

or Hebrew text. Sometimes you will have to "read around" the Greek or Hebrew, but you can usually do this with minimal loss.

The next criterion is the MOST IMPORTANT, and it is the real place to bring your evaluation.

3. When a text has more than one possible meaning, does the author discuss *all* the possible meanings, evaluate them, and give reasons for his or her own choice? For example, in chapter 2 we gave an illustration from 1 Corinthians 7:36 for which there are at least three possible meanings. A commentary does not fully inform you unless the author discusses all three possibilities, gives reasons for and against each, then explains his or her own choice.

The next four criteria are important if you are going to get all the help you need.

4. Does the author discuss text-critical problems? You have already learned the importance of this in chapter 2.

5. Does the author discuss the historical background of the idea of the text at important places?

6. Does the author give bibliographic information so you can do further study if you wish?

7. Does the introduction section in the commentary give you enough information about the historical context to enable you to understand the occasion of the book?

The best way to get at all this is simply to pick one of the really difficult texts in a given biblical book and see how helpful a commentary is in giving information and answering questions, and especially how well it discusses all possible meanings. One can initially evaluate the worth of a commentary on 1 Corinthians, for example, by seeing how the author discusses 7:36 or 11:10. For the Pastoral Epistles, check 1 Timothy 2:15. For the book of Genesis, 2:17 would constitute a "checkpoint." For Isaiah, it might be 7:14–17. And so on.

The final judgment, of course, is how well the author puts his or her information together in understanding the text in its context. Some commentaries that are mines of historical and bibliographic data are unfortunately not always adept at explaining the biblical writer's meaning in context.

Before we give our lists, let us repeat: You do not begin your Bible study with a commentary! You go to the commentary after you have done your own work. The reason you eventually consult a commentary is to find answers to the content questions that have arisen in your own study. At the same time, of course, the commentary will alert you to questions you failed to ask but perhaps should have.

Please be warned that the commentaries we list here do not always represent theological viewpoints with which we agree. We are not recommending their *conclusions* but rather their alertness to the kinds of issues we have mentioned above. Use them with care and caution. We have recommended evangelical commentaries only when in our opinion they were clearly the most exegetically useful for you.

OLD TESTAMENT COMMENTARIES

There are several complete and up-to-date Old Testament commentary series that meet the criteria we have described and are evangelical in theological outlook: The Expositor's Bible Commentary (7 vols., Grand Rapids, MI: Zondervan); the Tyndale Old Testament Commentaries (28 vols., Downers Grove, IL: InterVarsity Press); the New American Commentary (28 vols., Nashville, TN: Broadman & Holman); and the Word Biblical Commentary (34 vols., Grand Rapids, MI: Zondervan). The latter contains among its volumes a mixture of evangelical and non-evangelical commentaries, and each must therefore be evaluated on its own merits. A three-volume series on the Minor Prophets (*The Minor Prophets,* Grand Rapids, MI: Baker) is also available. The century-old Keil and Delitzsch (K-D) remains one of the best complete series you can purchase for the Old Testament. The Tyndale Old Testament Commentaries, a series that continues to be revised and updated, represent perhaps the best starter set of commentaries anyone could purchase.

Other commendable series are also underway, mostly but not entirely complete. They include: The New International Commentary on the Old Testament (Grand Rapids, MI: Eerdmans), The NIV Application Commentary series (Grand Rapids, MI: Zondervan), and the Understanding the Bible Commentary Series: Old Testament (16 vols., Grand Rapids, MI: Baker). As individual volumes in these series are published, look them over. When any of the series becomes complete, consider buying it, whether in book or in electronic form.

Genesis

For the general reader: James McKeown, *Genesis* (Two Horizons Old Testament Commentary Series); Grand Rapids, MI: Eerdmans, 2008.

For the advanced student: Kenneth A. Matthews, *Genesis* (NAC), 2 vols.; Nashville, TN: Broadman & Holman, 1996, 2005; Bruce K. Waltke, *Genesis: A Commentary*; Grand Rapids, MI: Zondervan, 2001; Gordon Wenham, *Genesis* (WBC), 2 vols.; Dallas, TX: Word, 1987, 1994.

Exodus

For the general reader: Peter Enns, *Exodus* (NIVAC); Grand Rapids, MI: Zondervan, 2000; Walter Kaiser Jr., *Exodus* (EBC); Grand Rapids, MI: Zondervan, 1992.

For the advanced student: Douglas Stuart, *Exodus* (NAC); Nashville, TN: Broadman and Holman, 2006.

Leviticus

For the general reader: Mark F. Rooker, *Leviticus* (NAC); Nashville, TN: Broadman & Holman, 2000; Allen Ross, *Holiness to the Lord: A Guide to the Exposition of the Book of Leviticus*; Grand Rapids, MI: Baker, 2006.

For the advanced student: Gordon Wenham, *The Book of Leviticus* (NICOT); Grand Rapids, MI: Eerdmans, 1994.

Numbers

For the general reader: David Stubbs, *Numbers* (Brazos Theological Commentary on the Bible); Grand Rapids, MI: Brazos Press, 2009; Gordon Wenham, *Numbers* (TOTC); Downers Grove, IL: IVP Academic, 2008.

For the advanced student: Timothy R. Ashley, *The Book of Numbers* (NICOT); Grand Rapids, MI: Eerdmans, 1993; R. Dennis Cole, *Numbers* (NAC); Nashville, TN: Broadman & Holman, 2000.

Deuteronomy

For the general reader: Daniel Block, *Deuteronomy* (NIVAC); Grand Rapids, MI: Zondervan, 2012.

For the advanced student: Duane Christensen, *Deuteronomy* (WBC), rev. ed., 2 vols.; Nashville, TN: Nelson, 2001, 2002;

Peter Craigie, *The Book of Deuteronomy* (NICOT); Grand
Rapids, MI: Eerdmans, 1976; Eugene H. Merrill, *Deuteronomy*
(NAC); Nashville, TN: Broadman & Holman, 1994.

Joshua

For the general reader: Richard Hess, *Joshua* (TOTC);
Downers Grove, IL: IVP Academic, 2008.

For the advanced student: David M. Howard Jr., *Joshua*
(NAC); Nashville, TN: Broadman & Holman, 1998.

Judges

For the general reader: K. Lawson Younger, *Judges* (NIVAC);
Grand Rapids, MI: Zondervan, 2002.

For the advanced student: Daniel I. Block, *Judges, Ruth* (NAC);
Nashville, TN: Broadman & Holman, 1999; Barry Webb,
Judges (NICOT); Grand Rapids, MI: Eerdmans, 2012.

Ruth

For the general reader: Iain Duguid, *Esther & Ruth* (REC);
Phillipsburg, NJ: P & R Publishing, 2005.

For the advanced student: Daniel I. Block, *Judges, Ruth* (NAC);
Nashville, TN: Broadman & Holman, 1999; Robert Chisholm
Jr., *A Commentary on Judges and Ruth*; Grand Rapids, MI:
Kregel Academic, 2013; Robert L. Hubbard Jr., *The Book of
Ruth* (NICOT); Grand Rapids, MI: Eerdmans, 1988.

1, 2 Samuel

For the general reader: Bill T. Arnold, *1 & 2 Samuel* (NIVAC);
Grand Rapids, MI: Zondervan, 2003; Joyce Baldwin, *1 and
2 Samuel* (TOTC); Downers Grove, IL: InterVarsity Press,
1988.

For the advanced student: Robert Bergen, *1, 2 Samuel* (NAC);
Nashville, TN: Broadman & Holman, 1996; Robert P.
Gordon, *1 and 2 Samuel*; Grand Rapids, MI: Zondervan,
1986; David Tsumura, *The First Book of Samuel* (NICOT);
Downers Grove, IL: IVP Academic, 2007.

1, 2 Kings

For the general reader: Iain Provan, *1 & 2 Kings* (UBCS);
Grand Rapids, MI: Baker, 1993; Donald J. Wiseman, *1 and
2 Kings* (TOTC); Downers Grove, IL: InterVarsity, 1993.

For the advanced student: Paul House, *1, 2 Kings* (NAC);
Nashville,, TN: Broadman & Holman, 1995.

1, 2 Chronicles

For the general reader: Andrew Hill, *1 & 2 Chronicles*
(NIVAC); Grand Rapids, MI: Zondervan, 2008.

For the advanced student: Raymond Dillard, *2 Chronicles*
(WBC); Dallas, TX: Word, 1988; Richard Pratt, *1 &
2 Chronicles*, Fearn, UK: Mentor, 1999; J. A. Thompson,
1, 2 Chronicles (NAC); Nashville, TN: Broadman &
Holman, 1994.

Ezra – Nehemiah

For the general reader: Derek Kidner, *Ezra & Nehemiah*
(TOTC); Downers Grove, IL: IVP Academic, 2009; Gary
V. Smith, *Ezra, Nehemiah, Esther* (Cornerstone Biblical
Commentary); Carol Stream, IL: Tyndale House, 2010.

For the advanced student: Mervin Breneman, *Ezra, Nehemiah,
Esther* (NAC); Nashville, TN: Broadman & Holman, 1993;
H. G. M. Williamson, *Ezra – Nehemiah* (WBC); Dallas, TX:
Word, 1985.

Esther

For the general reader: Debra Reid, *Esther* (TOTC); Downers
Grove, IL; IVP Academic, 2008.

For the advanced student: Frederic W. Bush, *Ruth, Esther*
(WBC); Dallas, TX: Word, 1996.

Job

For the general reader: Francis Anderson, *Job* (TOTC);
Downers Grove, IL: IVP Academic, 2008.

For the advanced student: John E. Hartley, *The Book of Job*
(NICOT); Grand Rapids, MI: Eerdmans, 1988; Elmer
Smick, *Job* (EBC); Grand Rapids, MI: Zondervan, 1988.

Psalms

For the general reader: Craig C. Broyles, *Psalms* (UBCS);
Peabody, MA: Hendrickson, 1999.

For the advanced student: Peter Craigie and Marvin Tate,
Psalms 1 – 50; Marvin Tate, *Psalms 51 – 100*; Leslie Allen,

Psalms 101–150 (WBC); Dallas, TX: Word, 2004, 1991, 2002 respectively; Willem VanGemeren, *Psalms* (EBC), rev. ed.; Grand Rapids, MI: Zondervan, 2008; Bruce Waltke and James Houston, *The Psalms as Christian Worship*; Grand Rapids, MI: Eerdmans, 2010.

Proverbs

For the general reader: David A. Hubbard, *Proverbs* (Mastering the Old Testament); Dallas, TX: Word, 1989; Tremper Longman III, *Proverbs* (BCOT); Grand Rapids, MI: Baker, 2006.

For the advanced student: Duane A. Garrett, *Proverbs, Ecclesiastes, Song of Songs* (NAC); Nashville, TN: Broadman & Holman, 1993; Bruce Waltke, *The Book of Proverbs* (NICOT), 2 vols.; Grand Rapids, MI: Eerdmans, 2004, 2005.

Ecclesiastes

For the general reader: Iain Provan, *Ecclesiastes/Song of Songs* (NIVAC); Grand Rapids, MI: Zondervan, 2001.

For the advanced student: Craig Bartholomew, *Ecclesiastes* (BCOT); Grand Rapids, MI: Baker, 2009; Duane A. Garrett, *Proverbs, Ecclesiastes, Song of Songs* (NAC); Nashville, TN: Broadman & Holman, 1993; Tremper Longman III, *The Book of Ecclesiastes* (NICOT); Grand Rapids, MI: Eerdmans, 1998.

Song of Songs

For the general reader: G. Lloyd Carr, *The Song of Solomon* (TOTC); Downers Grove, IL: InterVarsity Press, 1984.

For the advanced student: Duane Garrett and Paul House, *Song of Songs/Lamentations* (WBC); Nashville, TN: Thomas Nelson, 2004; Tremper Longman III, *Song of Songs* (NICOT); Grand Rapids, MI: Eerdmans, 2001.

Isaiah

For the general reader: Alec Motyer, *The Prophecy of Isaiah*; Downers Grove, IL: InterVarsity Press, 1993.

For the advanced student: John Oswalt, *The Book of Isaiah* (NICOT), 2 vols.; Grand Rapids, MI: Eerdmans, 1981,

1998; Gary Smith, *Isaiah* (NAC), 2 vols.; Nashville, TN: Broadman & Holman, 2007, 2009.

Jeremiah

For the general reader: Derek Kidner, *The Message of Jeremiah* (BST); Downers Grove, IL: IVP Academic, 2004.

For the advanced student: Leslie Allen, *Jeremiah* (OTL); Louisville, KY: Westminster John Knox, 2008; John A. Thompson, *The Book of Jeremiah* (NICOT); Grand Rapids, MI: Eerdmans, 1995.

Lamentations

For the general reader: Robin Parry, *Lamentations* (Two Horizons Commentary); Grand Rapids, MI: Eerdmans, 2010.

For the advanced student: Delbert R. Hillers, *Lamentations* (AB); New York, NY: Doubleday, 1992; F. B. Huey Jr., *Jeremiah, Lamentations* (NAC); Nashville, TN: Broadman & Holman, 1993.

Ezekiel

For the general reader: Douglas Stuart, *Ezekiel* (The Preacher's Commentary); Nashville, TN: Thomas Nelson, 2002.

For the advanced student: Daniel I. Block, *Ezekiel* (NICOT) 2 vols.; Grand Rapids, MI: Eerdmans, 1997, 1998; Margaret Odell, *Ezekiel* (Smyth & Helwys Bible Commentary); Macon, GA: Smyth & Helwys, 2005.

Daniel

For the general reader: Iain Duguid, *Daniel* (REC); Phillipsburg, NJ: P & R Publishing, 2008.

For the advanced student: Stephen R. Miller, *Daniel* (NAC); Nashville, TN: Broadman & Holman, 1994; Andrew Steinmann, *Daniel* (CC); St. Louis, MO: Concordia Publishing House, 2008.

Hosea

For the general reader: Derek Kidner, *The Message of Hosea* (BST); Downers Grove, IL: IVP Academic, 2004.

For the advanced student: Duane A. Garrett, *Hosea, Joel* (NAC); Nashville, TN: Broadman & Holman, 1996; Douglas Stuart, *Hosea – Jonah* (WBC); Dallas, TX: Word, 1987.

Amos

For the general reader: Gary Smith, *Hosea, Amos, Micah* (NIVAC); Grand Rapids, MI: Zondervan, 2001.

For the advanced student: Francis Anderson and David Noel Freedman, *Amos* (AB); New Haven, CT: Yale University Press, 1989; R. Reed Lessing, *Amos* (CC); St. Louis, MO: Concordia, 2009; Jeffrey Niehaus, *Amos* (The Minor Prophets); Grand Rapids, MI: Baker, 1992.

Obadiah

For the general reader: David Baker, *Obadiah, Jonah, Micah* (TOTC); Downers Grove, IL: InterVarsity Press, 1988.

For the advanced student: Jeffrey Niehaus, *Obadiah* (The Minor Prophets); Grand Rapids, MI: Baker, 1992; Paul Raabe, *Obadiah* (AB); New Haven, CT: Yale University Press, 1996; Douglas Stuart, *Hosea – Jonah* (WBC); Dallas, TX: Word, 1987.

Jonah

For the general reader: T. Desmond Alexander, *Obadiah, Jonah, Micah* (TOTC); Downers Grove, IL: IVP Academic, 2009; Joyce Baldwin, *Jonah* (The Minor Prophets); Grand Rapids, MI: Baker, 1993.

For the advanced reader: Douglas Stuart, *Hosea – Jonah* (WBC); Dallas, TX: Word, 1987.

Micah

For the general reader: Dale Ralph Davis, *Micah* (EP Study Commentary); Darlington, UK: Evangelical Press, 2010.

For the advanced student: Kenneth L. Barker, *Micah* (NAC); Nashville, TN: Broadman & Holman, 1999; Bruce Waltke, *A Commentary on Micah*; Grand Rapids, MI: Eerdmans, 2008.

Nahum

For the general reader: David Baker, *Nahum, Habakkuk, Zephaniah* (TOTC); Downers Grove, IL: IVP Academic, 2009.

For the advanced student: Waylon Bailey, *Nahum* (NAC); Nashville, TN: Broadman & Holman, 1999; Tremper

Longman III, *Nahum* (The Minor Prophets); Grand Rapids, MI: Baker, 1993.

Habakkuk

For the general reader: John Currid, *The Expectant Prophet: Habakkuk Simply Explained* (Welwyn Commentaries); Darlington, UK: EP Books, 2009.

For the advanced student: Carl Armerding, *Habakkuk* (EBC); Grand Rapids, MI: Zondervan, 1985; F. F. Bruce, *Habakkuk* (The Minor Prophets); Grand Rapids, MI: Baker, 1993.

Zephaniah

For the general reader: David Baker, *Nahum, Habakkuk, Zephaniah* (TOTC); Downers Grove, IL: InterVarsity Press, 1989.

For the advanced student: J. Alec Motyer, *Zephaniah* (The Minor Prophets); Grand Rapids, MI: Baker, 1998; Richard Patterson, *Nahum, Habakkuk, Zephaniah*; Richardson, TX: Biblical Studies Press, 2013.

Haggai

For the general reader: Mark Boda, *Haggai, Zechariah* (NIVAC); Grand Rapids, MI: Zondervan, 2004.

For the advanced student: Eugene Merrill, *Haggai, Zechariah, Malachi*; Richardson, TX: Biblical Studies Press, 2013; J. Alec Motyer, *Haggai* (The Minor Prophets); Grand Rapids, MI: Baker, 1998.

Zechariah

For the general reader: Barry Webb, *The Message of Zechariah* (BST); Downers Grove, IL: IVP Academic, 2004.

For the advanced student: George Klein, *Zechariah* (NAC); Nashville, TN: Broadman & Holman, 2008; Thomas McComiskey, *Zechariah* (The Minor Prophets); Grand Rapids, MI: Baker, 1998.

Malachi

For the general reader: Iain Duguid, *Haggai, Zechariah, Malachi* (EP Study Commentary); Darlington, UK: Evangelical Press, 2010.

For the advanced student: Ray Clendenen, *Zechariah, Malachi* (NAC); Nashville, TN: Broadman & Holman, 2004; Douglas Stuart, *Malachi* (The Minor Prophets); Grand Rapids, MI: Baker, 1998; Pieter Verhoef, *The Books of Haggai and Malachi* (NICOT); Grand Rapids, MI: Eerdmans, 1994.

NEW TESTAMENT COMMENTARIES

For years many people have found help in reading William Barclay's *The Daily Study Bible* (Louisville, KY: Westminster John Knox), which covers the whole New Testament in seventeen volumes. This work is now being replaced by Tom Wright's " … *for Everyone*" series (e.g., *Matthew for Everyone;* London: SPCK, 2001+). But for a detailed, specific study we recommend the following (asterisks indicate commentaries that are particularly outstanding):

Matthew

For the general reader: Craig S. Keener, *Matthew* (IVP New Testament Commentary Series); Downers Grove, IL: InterVarsity Press, 1997.

For the advanced student: R. T. France, *Matthew* (NICNT); Grand Rapids, MI: Eerdmans, 2007; Donald A. Hagner, *Matthew* (WBC), 2 vols.; Dallas, TX: Word, 1993, 1995.

Mark

For the general reader: James R. Edwards, *The Gospel According to Mark* (Pillar NT Commentary); Grand Rapids, MI: Eerdmans, 2002; Morna D. Hooker, *The Gospel According to St. Mark* (BNTC); Peabody, MA: Hendrickson, 1991.

For the advanced student: R. T. France, *The Gospel of Mark* (NIGTC); Grand Rapids, MI: Eerdmans, 2002.

Luke

For the general reader: Craig A. Evans, *Luke* (NIBC); Peabody, MA: Hendrickson, 1990.

For the advanced student: Joel B. Green, *The Gospel of Luke* (NICNT); Grand Rapids, MI: Eerdmans, 1997; Luke Timothy Johnson, *The Gospel of Luke* (SP); Collegeville, MN: Liturgical Press, 1991.

John

For the general reader: D. A. Carson, *The Gospel According to John* (Pillar NT Commentary); Grand Rapids, MI: Eerdmans, 1990; J. R. Michaels, *The Gospel of John* (NICNT); Grand Rapids, MI: Eerdmans, 2011.

For the advanced student: *Raymond E. Brown, *The Gospel According to John* (AB), 2 vols. New York, NY: Doubleday, 1966, 1970.

Acts

For the general reader: I. Howard Marshall, *The Acts of the Apostles* (TNTC); Grand Rapids, MI: Eerdmans, 1980.

For the advanced reader: Luke T. Johnson, *The Acts of the Apostles* (SP); Collegeville, MN: Liturgical Press, 1992.

Romans

For the general reader: Douglas Moo, *The Epistle to the Romans* (NICNT); Grand Rapids, MI: Eerdmans, 1993.

For the advanced student: Leon Morris, *The Epistle to the Romans*; Grand Rapids, MI: Eerdmans, 1988.

1 Corinthians

For the general reader: Gordon D. Fee, *The First Epistle to the Corinthians* (NICNT); Grand Rapids, MI: Eerdmans, 2nd. ed., 2013; Richard B. Hays, *First Corinthians* (*Int*); Louisville, KY: John Knox, 1997.

2 Corinthians

For the general reader: Paul Barnett, *The Second Epistle to the Corinthians* (NICNT); Grand Rapids, MI: Eerdmans, 1997; Linda L. Belleville, *2 Corinthians* (IVP NT Commentary); Downers Grove, IL: InterVarsity Press, 1996.

For the advanced reader: Jan Lambrecht, *Second Corinthians* (SP); Collegeville, MN: Liturgical Press, 1999.

Galatians

For the general reader: James D. G. Dunn, *The Epistle to the Galatians* (BNTC); Peabody, MA: Hendrickson, 1993; Gordon D. Fee, *Galatians* (Pentecostal Commentary); Dorset, England: Deo Publishing, 2007.

For the advanced reader: Ben Witherington III, *Grace in Galatia*; Grand Rapids, MI: Eerdmans, 1998.

Ephesians
For the general reader: F. F. Bruce, *The Epistles to the Colossians, to Philemon, and to the Ephesians* (NICNT); Grand Rapids, MI: Eerdmans, 1984; Peter T. O'Brien, *The Letter to the Ephesians* (Pillar NT Commentary); Grand Rapids, MI: Eerdmans, 1999.

Philippians
For the general reader: Markus Bockmuhl, *The Epistle to the Philippians* (BNTC); Peabody, MA: Hendrickson, 1997; Gordon D. Fee, *Paul's Letter to the Philippians* (NICNT); Grand Rapids, MI: Eerdmans, 1995; Gordon D. Fee, *Philippians* (IVP NT Commentary); Downers Grove, IL: InterVarsity Press, 1999.

Colossians
For the general reader: F. F. Bruce, *The Epistles to the Colossians, to Philemon, and to the Ephesians* (NICNT); Grand Rapids, MI: Eerdmans, 1984; N. T. Wright, *Colossians and Philemon* (TNTC); Grand Rapids, MI: Eerdmans, 1986.
For the advanced student: James D. G. Dunn, *The Epistles to the Colossians and to Philemon* (NIGTC); Grand Rapids, MI: Eerdmans, 1996.

1, 2 Thessalonians
For the general reader: Gordon D. Fee, *1 and 2 Thessalonians* (NICNT); Grand Rapids, MI: Eerdmans, 2007; Gene L. Green, *The Letters to the Thessalonians* (Pillar NT Commentary); Grand Rapids, MI: Eerdmans, 2002; I. Howard Marshall, *1 and 2 Thessalonians* (NCBC); Grand Rapids, MI: Eerdmans, 1983.

1, 2 Timothy, Titus
For the general reader: Gordon D. Fee, *1 and 2 Timothy, Titus* (NIBC); Peabody, MA: Hendrickson, 1988; Philip H. Towner, *1–2 Timothy and Titus* (IVP NT Commentary); Downers Grove, IL: InterVarsity, 1994.
For the advanced student: William D. Mounce, *Pastoral Epistles* (WBC); Nashville, TN: Nelson, 2000.

Hebrews

For the general reader: F. F. Bruce, *The Epistle to the Hebrews* (NICNT); Grand Rapids, MI: Eerdmans, 1990; Donald A. Hagner, *Hebrews* (NIBC); Peabody, MA: Hendrickson, 1990; David A. DeSilva, *Perseverance in Gratitude*; Grand Rapids, MI: Eerdmans, 2000.

For the advanced student: William L. Lane, *Hebrews* (WBC), 2 vols.; Dallas, TX: Word, 1991.

James

For the general reader: Peter H. Davids, *James* (NIBC); Peabody, MA: Hendrickson, 1989; Douglas J. Moo, *The Letter of James* (Pillar NT Commentary); Grand Rapids, MI: Eerdmans, 2000.

1 Peter

For the general reader: *Peter H. Davids, *The First Epistle of Peter* (NICNT); Grand Rapids, MI: Eerdmans, 1990.

For the advanced student: J. R. Michaels, *1 Peter* (WBC); Dallas, TX: Word, 1988.

2 Peter

For the general reader: J. N. D. Kelly, *A Commentary on the Epistles of Peter and of Jude* (HNTC); New York, NY: Harper & Row, 1969.

For the advanced student: *Richard J. Bauckham, *Jude, 2 Peter* (WBC); Dallas, TX: Word, 1983.

1, 2, 3 John

For the general reader: Colin G. Kruse, *The Letters of John* (Pillar NT Commentary); Grand Rapids, MI: Eerdmans, 2000; *I. Howard Marshall, *The Epistles of John* (NICNT); Grand Rapids, MI: Eerdmans, 1978.

For the advanced student: Stephen S. Smalley, *1, 2, 3 John* (WBC); Dallas, TX: Word, 1984.

Jude

For the general reader: J. N. D. Kelly, *A Commentary on the Epistles of Peter and of Jude* (HNTC); New York, NY: Harper & Row, 1969.

For the advanced student: *Richard J. Bauckham, *Jude, 2 Peter* (WBC); Dallas, TX: Word, 1983.

Revelation
For the general reader: Gordon D. Fee, *Revelation* (New Covenant Commentary Series); Eugene, OR: Cascade Books, 2011; Robert H. Mounce, *The Book of Revelation* (NICNT); Grand Rapids, MI: Eerdmans, 1977; Grant R. Osborne, *Revelation* (Baker Exegetical Commentary on the NT); Grand Rapids, MI: Baker, 2002.
For the advanced student: G. K. Beale, *The Book of Revelation* (NIGTC); Grand Rapids, MI: Eerdmans, 1999.

Scripture Index

Genesis

1 53
1:28 170
1:31 254
2:17 277
6–7 47
15:18–21 109
18:11 49
20:6 242
24 96
31:35 49
37–50 97
37 . . . . . 99, 102, 103
37:2, 3–4 98
37:4, 5, 8 102
37:5–11 . . . . 98, 100
37:6–8 102
37:6–7 100
37:11 . . . . . 100, 102
37:12–17 99
37:25–28 103
37:26–27 100
37:36 . . . . . 99, 102
37:39–40 99
38 . . . . . 97, 100, 101
38:27–30 . . . 100, 102
39 100
39:1 102
39:2 . . . . . . 98, 103
39:3 98
39:7 100
39:8–9 100
39:21, 23 98

40:8 103
42:30–34 101
42–45 . . . . . . 99, 100
44:18–34 101
45:4–13 101
45:7 103
45:8 . . . . . 236, 237
46:8–27 97
46:12 102
49:1–28 97
49:9 265
49:10 100
50:15–21 99
50:18 . . . . 100, 102
50:20 . . . . . 98, 103
50:24, 25 103

Exodus

1–18 168
3–4 192
7–10 270
12:38 168
13:19 103
17:1–7 208
18:20 169
19–Num. 10:10 . . . 168
19–34 96
19:6 265
19:16–25 216
20–Deut. 33 171
20–Lev. 27 172
20 170
20:2 171

20:7 194
20:13 . . . . 182, 194
20:14 . . . . . . 97, 194
20:16 194
21:12, 27 182
29:10–12 184
31:3 237
33; 40 168

Leviticus

1–5 170
9:9, 10 177
9:13, 14 177
11:7 183
19:9–14 176
19:18 . . . . . 174, 175
19:19 184
20:1–13 208
20:14 204
26 172
26:3–13 185
26:14–39 191
26:14–38 190

Deuteronomy

4:15–28 191
4:25–31 . . . 192, 198
4:25–27 171
4:26 172
4:32–40 190
5:11, 17, 18,
    19, 20 194
6:5 . . . . . . 174, 175

12. 222
14:21 184
14:28–29 185
14:29 245
15:12–17 . . .179, 180
15:14, 15 180
16:11 245
17:18–19 172
18. 195
18:18 195
20:15 194
22:5, 9, 12 26
22:8 . . . . . . 26, 174
23:15–16 183
24:16 183
26:12 245
26:13 245
28–33. 172
28:1–14 190
28:15–32:42. . . . 191
28:20 171
28:53–57 229
30:19 172
31:9–13 172
32:35 229
34:9 237

Joshua
1:8 169
2:6 248
24:32 103

Judges
1:8 109
5:7 237
6 112
6:36–40 108
11:29–40 34

Ruth
1–4. 104
1:1 106
1:6 106
1:8–9, 13, 20–21 106
1:8 103
1:10, 16, 17 104
2:3–13 105

2:4 106
2:11–12 106
2:19–20 106
2:20 103
2:22 105–6
3:10–12 105
3:13 106
4:9–10 105
4:11–12, 14 106
4:17–21 105
4:17 105
4:18–21 105

1 Samuel
1–2. 99
8:16 40
11:9 204
14:2 237
20:14, 17, 41, 42. .109
22. 189

2 Samuel
5:6–7 109
7 189
7:14 210
11. 97
11:25 204
12. 189
12:1–14 193
13:3 239
13:14 49
14:20 237
20:16 237
24. 189
24:11–17 193

1 Kings
1 189
3:9 237
3:12 . . . . . 237, 239
4:29–34 239
11:1–13 254
11:4 239
17–2 Kgs. 13 . . . 197
18. 96
19:16 193
21:17–22 193

2 Kings
3:18–19 193
16:2–4, 5, 7–9 . . .199
22. 189

1 Chronicles
7:14–15 109
20:14–17 193

Ezra
1–2. 208

Job
1–2. 251
3:1–42:6. 251
3 250
6–7. 250
9–10. 250
12–14. 250
15:20 235
16–17. 250
19. 250
21. 250
23–24. 250
24:2–3 245
26–31. 250
32:19 239
38–41. 250
42:7–17 251
42:7–9 250
42:7–8 235

Psalms
1–41. 218
1 219
1:1, 2, 3, 4–6 . 54–55
2 . . . . 219, 221
2:7 210
3 . . . . 220, 223, 226
3:1 224
3:2 224
3:3–6 224
3:7 . . . . 225, 229
3:8 225
4:4 228
8 221
11. 222

12. . . . . 220, 229
14:1 234
16. 222
18. . . . . . . 220, 221
19. . . . 175, 214, 221
20. 221
21. 221
22. 220
23. . . . 213, 216, 222
23:5–6 228
24. 222
27. 222
29. 222
30; 31; 32. 220
33. 221
34. 220
35. 229
36, 37. 222
39. 220
39:5 252
40. 220
42–72. 218
44. 220
45. 221
46. 222
46:1 215
47; 48; 49. 222
50. 221
51:5 215
51:16 218
53:1 234
57. 220
58, 59. 229
59:7 216
62. 222
63. . . . . . . 218, 222
65. 220
66. . . . . . . 220, 221
67. 220
69:7–20 228
69. 229
70. 229
71. 220
72. . . . . . . 219, 221
73–89. 218
73. 222
74:147–150 218
75. 220

76. 222
78. 221
80. . . . . . . 218, 220
81. . . . . . . 218, 221
83. 229
84, 87. 222
88. . . . . . . 213, 220
88:3–9 228
89. 221
89:27 210
90–106. 219
90. 219
91. 222
92. 220
92:5 195
93. 222
94. 220
95–99. 222
98. 228
100. 221
101. 221
103. 221
104. 221
105. 221
106. 221
107–150. 219
107. 220
109. 229
110. 221
110:1 210
111. 221
111:10 236
112. 222
113. 221
114. 221
114:4 216
116. 220
117. 221
118. 220
119. . . . . . . 175, 217
120. 220
121. 222
122. 222
124. 220
125. 222
125:2 38
127. . . . . . . 219, 222
127:8 227

128. 222
130:1 230
131. 222
132. 221
133. . . . . . . 222, 228
135. 221
136. . . . . . 220, 221
137. . . . . . 220, 229
137:3–9 213
137:5, 7 229
137:7–9 229
138. . . . . . 220, 226
138:1–2, 3 227
138:4–5 227
138:6–7 227
139. 220
139:22 230
140. 229
142. 220
144. 221
145–47. 221
146–50. 219
147:1 221
148. 221
149. 221
150. 219

Proverbs
1:1–6 246
1:7 240
1:10–19 240
2–3. 246
2:5–6 239
2:16–19 240
2:22 240
2:27 240
3:5–12 240
3:7 239
4:14–19 240
5:3–20 240
6:1–5 240
6:7–11 240
6:12–15 240
6:20 246
6:23–35 240
6:27–29 241
7:4–27 240
7:4 239

8 . . . . 222, 246
9:10 236
9:13–18 . . . 240, 242
9:17 242
10:1 239
14:1 237
14:7 234
15:1 246
15:3 240
15:8–9 240
15:11 240
15:19 247
15:25 . . . . 244, 245
16:1–9 240
16:3 243
16:10 246
16:21 246
16:23–24 246
16:27–28 246
16:33 236
18:4 246
21:16 239
21:22 246
22:9 240
22:11 248
22:14 246
22:17–29 246
22:23 240
22:26–27 244
22:26 246
23:10–11 245
23:13–14 240
23:19–21 240
23:22–25 240
23:26–28 240
23:29–35 240
24:18, 21 240
25:24 248
29:12 244
30:15–31 239
31:10–31 . . . 239, 247
31:22 247
31:30 252

Ecclesiastes
1:1–11 252
1:2 252
2:16 237

3:1–8 239
3:2 234
3:12–14 253
12:8–14 252
12:8 252
12:9–11 252
12:13–14 . . . 252, 253

Song of Songs
1:1 254
1:2–4 156
1:8 256
2:8–9 256
2:16–3:5 256
3:1–5 256
3:6–11 . . . 254, 256
4:1–6 239
4:1–4 255
5:2–6 156
5:9 256
6:8–9 256
7:11–13 256
8:11–12 . . . 254, 256
8:13 256

Isaiah
1:10–17 206
2:2–4 151
3:13–16 201
3:13–14 201
3:14–16 201
3:17–26 201
5:1–7 255
5:10 . . . . 47, 48
5:21 237
6 192
6:9–10 175
7:14 210
11:1 265
11:4–5 151
11:6–9 151
20. 202
20:3 203
20:4 203
29:13–14 237
38:1–8 204
40:3 41

42. 195
44:22 205
45:1–7 202
49. 195
49:2 265
50. 195
53. 195
53:5 151
55:8 195
57:13 252

Jeremiah
1 92
14:14 192
18:18 237
23:21 192
26:7–24 193
27. 192
27:2, 3, 4 193
27:8–22 193
27:11 193
28. 192
28:15–16 193
31:1–9 202
31:15 210
31:31–34 . . . 151, 197
31:34 273
32:38–40 151
35:17–19 204

Ezekiel
1–24. 198
1–3. 192
1:24 265
4:1–4 203
23. 108
25–39. 207
27:8–9 237
33–48. 198
33:32 254
36:25–27 176
37:1–14 208
37:12–14 208
37:15–28 207
38. 207
39. 207
49:23 207

Daniel
7:9 265
7:13 265
10:6 265

Hosea
1:2 192
1:4 193
1:10 187
2:2–15 255
2:16–20 202
2:21–23 202
3:3–17 201
4:1–19 201
4:2 194
4:4–11 193
4:22 210
5:5–8 193
5:8–12 . . . . 198, 199
5:8, 9 199
7:8 261
7:11 260
7:14 205
8:14 191
9:3 191
11:1 210
13:2–4 206

Joel
2:28–30 151
3:1–3 208

Amos
1:3–2:16 204
2:6–7 271
2:6 206
5 200
5:1–3 200
5:4–17 200
5:5–6 200
5:7–13, 14 200
5:16–17 200
5:18–27 200
5:18–20 200
5:21–24 200
5:25–27 200
7:10–17 133

7:14–15 192
7:17 193
8:1–2 50
9:11–15 191
9:11–15 202
9:11 202
9:12, 13 202
9:14–15 202

Obadiah
21 205

Jonah
1:1 192

Micah
2:1–5 202

Habakkuk
2:4 187
2:6–8 202

Zephaniah
2:5–7 202
3:8–9 208

Zechariah
9:9 210
11:4–17 203
12–14 203
12:10 265
13:1 151

Malachi
1:3 230
2:1–9 193
3:1 41
4:6 211

Matthew
1:22–23 210
2:1–11 207
2:15 210
2:17–18 210
5–7 137
5:3–11 144
5:3–4 245

5:13 . . . . . 136, 260
5:17 170
5:18 169
5:21–48 174
5:21–37 174
5:22 . . . . . 229, 230
5:29–30 136
5:31–32 137
5:38–42 149
5:41 149
5:48 149
6:7–13 144
6:19–21 144
6:20 144
6:21 136
6:24 144
7:6–8 136
7:28 137
10 138
10:1–9 137
10:5–42 138
10:5–12 138
10:5–6 138
10:10 137
10:16–20 138
10:16 136
11:2–6 152
12:1–8 129
13 163
13:1–52 138
13:3–23 163
13:10–13 154
13:44–46 165
13:57 147
15:11 246
15:15–20 246
16:2–3 136
16:25 164
17:25 136
18:1–35 138
18:6–9 163
18:10–14 . . . 163, 166
18:12–14 162
18:18–19 194
18:23–35 167
18:23–34 48
18:24–28 47
19:1–30 145

19:3–11 248
19:16–22 150
19:23 29
19:30 145
20:1–16 . . .30, 145,
         162, 166
20:20:1–6. 167
20:1–15 145
20:16 145
20:17–34 145
20:20–28 150
21:18–22 147
21:33–44 157
21:45 155
22:40 174
23–25. 138
23:13–39 144
23:23 178
23:37–39 144
24:15–16 143
24:15 142

Mark
1:1–8:26. 139
1:1 138
1:2 41
1:14–3:6. 147
1:14–15 . . . 147, 152
1:21–28, 29–34 . 148
1:21 148
1:23 148
1:27–28 148
1:28 148
1:29 148
1:30 148
1:32–33 148
1:34 139
1:35–39 148
1:37 148
1:45 148
1:40–45 148
1:42 148
1:43 139
2:7 148
2:16 148
2:18 148
2:23–28 129
2:24 148

3:1–6 148
3:12 139
3:13–19 148
3:24 136
4 163
4:3–20 163
4:10–12 148,
         154, 156
4:11 . . . . 139, 156
4:34–41 148
5:43 139
6:4 147
6:45–8:26. 147
7:24 139
7:36 139
8:22–26 139
8:26 139
8:27–33 139
8:30 139
8:31–33 139
8:35 164
9:30–32 139
9:43–48 136
10:1–52 145
10:1–12 137
10:17–22 . . . 24, 150
10:19 194
10:24 29
10:31 145
10:32–45 139
10:35–45 150
11:12–14 147
11:20–25 147
12:1–11 157
12:13–17 137
12:40 245
13:14 . . . . 142, 143
13:15 34
14:3–9 150
16:18 34

Luke
1–2. 99
1:52–53 245
3:7–17 151
4:1 129
4:14 129
4:18 129

4:24 147
5:27–30 150
6:1–5 129
6:20–23 144
6:27–28 136
6:40 138
6:43 157
7:36–50 159
7:40–42 159
8:3 150
8:5–15 163
8:9–10 154
9:2–5 138
9:24 164
9:51–19:44. 144
10:3 138
10:7 137
10:16 138
10:25–37 155,
         160, 230
10:36–37 155
11:2–4 144
11:20 152
12:2–9 138
12:11–12 138
12:16–20 164
12:33–34 144
12:33 86
12:51–53 138
13:34–35 144
14:12–14 144
14:21 152
14:25–27 138
15. 165
15:1–2 . . . . 152, 161
15:3 155
15:11–32 160
16:1–8 164
16:16–17 173
17:20–21 152
17:33 138
17:37 260
18:9–14 167
18:9 155
18:18–23 150
18:20 194
18:22 86
18:24 29

19:1–10 150
19:11 155
20:9–18 157
21:12–17 138
21:20–21 143
22:20 173
22:24–27 150
24:44 195

John
1:45 195
2:6 47
4:44 147
5:39 96
7:23 174
7:46 141
8:7 54
9:1–3 250
12:15 210
12:31 250
13:34–35 173
20:30–31 146
20:31 147
21:25 . . . . . 111, 146

Acts
1–12 116
1–7 116
1:1–6:7 . . . . 116, 120
1:6 152
1:8 . . . . . . 116, 123
2:38–39 119
2:42–47 119
3 152
4:32–35 119
5:35–39 114
6:1–7 . . . . . 119, 120,
         121, 126–27
6:1 121
6:7 116
6:8–9:31 . . . 117, 120
6:8–8:1 121
6:8–15 120
6:8 123
6:9 120
8–10 116
8:1–25 119
8:1–4 121

8:1 121
8:5–25 121
8:5–7 121
8:9–13 122
8:14–17 122
8:20–23 122
8:24 122
8:38–39 128
9:1–19 114
9:31 116
9:32–12:24 117
10:28 169
10:38 . . . . . 123, 129
11–28 116
12:1–19 114
12:2 118
12:17 118
12:24 116
12:25–16:5 117
13–28 116
14:23 118
15 118
15:13 118
15:23–29 58
15:29 86
16:4 116
16:6–19:20 117
18:26 89
19:20 116
19:21–28:30 117
20:35 137
21:8 121
21:9 89
21:18 118
28:28 116

Romans
1:3 50
1:17 187
1:24–28 90
1:29–30 83
3:20 178
3:23 . . . . 57, 78
5:18 170
6:1–3 128
6:14–15 172
6:23 57
8:1–11 178

8:1 152
8:18–23 250
8:30 77
8:32–34 210
9:18–24 77
9:26 187
12 83
12:19 229
12:20 . . . . . . 46, 230
12:21 230
13:1–7 88
13:1–5 86
13:14 23
14 83
15:19 118
16:1–2 86
16:3 86
16:7 86

1 Corinthians
1–6 63
1–4 . . . . . . 64, 65, 78
1–3 66
1:10–4:21 . . . 64, 67
1:10–12 . . . . . 63, 65
1:12 66
1:16 77
1:18–3:4 . . . . 65, 67
1:18–2:5 . . . . 63, 237
1:18–25 . . . . . 66, 67
1:18–22 66
1:26–31 . . . . . 66, 67
1:26 50
1:27–28 66
1:30 66
2:1–5 . . . . 66, 68
2:10–16 66
2:6–16 68
3:1–4 68
3:3 66
3:4–9 66
3:5–23 66
3:5–17 . . . . . . 67, 69
3:5–9 68
3:6–9 68
3:9 . . . . . . 52, 68, 86
3:10–15 . . . . . 68, 80
3:10 68

3:16–17 . . .69, 79, 80
3:18–20 . . .65, 66, 69
3:21–22 66
3:21 66
3:22 152
4:1–21 67
4:1–5 . . . . . 63, 66
4:6 66
4:8–21 63
4:10 63
4:14–17 63
4:18–21 66
4:18 63
5 57
5:1–13 64
5:1–11 81
5:1 . . . . 45, 63
5:2 63
5:6 63
5:11 83
6:1–11 . . . . . 64, 79
6:1–8 63
6:2–3 91
6:6–11 79
6:7 79
6:9–11 63
6:9–10 . . . . . 83, 86
6:9 90
6:11 . . . . . . 61, 86
6:12–20 64
6:18–20 63
6:19 69
6:20 41
7–16 64
7:1–24 64
7:1–14 248
7:1 . . . . . 49, 63, 242
7:10–11 149
7:10 . . . . . . 91, 137
7:12 92
7:14 77
7:25–40 . 57, 64, 248
7:25 63
7:36 . .36–37, 50, 277
8–14 64
8:1–11:1 64
8–10 . . . . 64, 81

8:1–13 63
8:1 63
8:7–13 81
8:10 . . . . 63, 81
9:1–18 63
9:1–2 81
9:1 81
9:14 . . . . . . 82, 137
9:19–23 81
9:20 169
10:1–13 . . . . 77, 129
10:1–4 209
10:1 209
10:2–4 209
10:2 209
10:3–4 209
10:4 . . . . . . 96, 209
10:14–22 . 80, 81, 87
10:16–21 91
10:16–17 81
10:19–22 81
10:23–11:1 . . 81, 83
10:23–29 86
11:2–16 . . . .23, 58,
            64, 87
11:2–5 89
11:2–3 . . . . . 23, 76
11:5 . . . . 86, 89
11:6 87
11:7 87
11:10 . . . 71, 87, 277
11:13–14 87
11:14 76
11:15 76
11:16 87
11:17–34 64
11:17–22 82
11:26 152
12–14 . . . . . . 57, 64
12:1 63
12:2 63
12:13 63
13:1–2 64
13:3 42
13:8–10 53
13:8 64
13:10 78

14 78
14:1–5 76
14:26–33 76
14:34–35 . . . .23, 76,
            86, 88
14:39–40 76
15:1–58 64
15:8 81
15:12 64
15:29 . 34, 71, 72, 73
16:1–11 64
16:1 63
16:10–11 63
16:12–14 63
16:12 . . . . . . 63, 64
16:13–24 64
16:16 63
16:17 63

2 Corinthians
3:6 176
5:10 152
5:15 46
5:16 . . . . 32, 46, 50
6:14 80
6:16 69
10:16 81

Galatians
1:15 77
3:3 51
3:11 187
3:24 175
4:28 51
5 51
5:13–26 51
5:16 57
6:2 174
6:12 82

Ephesians
1:4–5 77
2:8–10 211
2:8 . . . . 57, 78
2:19–22 69
4:26–27 228
4:26 228
5 83

5:2 57
5:19 219
6:9 88
6:10–17 152

Philippians
1:12–26 70
1:13, 17 70
1:27–2:18 . . . 70, 78
1:27–30 70
1:27 70
1:28–30 70
2:1–4 71
2:1–2 71
2:5–11 71
2:12–13 . . . . 71, 113
2:14–18 71
2:14 21
2:25–30 70
2:26 70
3:1–4:1 70
3:10–14 152
3:20–21 152
4:2–3 . . . . . . 70, 86
4:10 70
4:14–19 70

Colossians
1:12 232
1:13–15 210
1:22 50
2:7 232
2:11–12 77
2:16–23 83
3 83
3:12 78
3:16 219
3:17 232

1 Thessalonians
1:3 . . . . 45, 52
1:6 52
4–5 64
5:22 28

2 Thessalonians
1:3–10 267

2:1 77
2:3–4 273
2:3 71
2:5–6 72

1 Timothy
2 89
2:9–15 88
2:9 89
2:11–12 88
2:12 86
2:15 277
5:3–15 77
5:11–15 89
5:17–18 82
5:17 77
5:23 76
6:17–19 . . . .

2 Timothy
2:3 75
3:2–4 83
3:6–9 89
3:14–16 76
4:13 75

Titus
1:5 . . . . 77, 118
3:5 77
3:7 61

Philemon
16 88

Hebrews
1:3 52
2:1–4 59
3:7–19 59
5:11–6:20 59
6:4–6 77
8–10 173
9:22 . . . . . . 173, 184
10:19–25 59
10:32–34 59
11:16 110
13:1–25 59
13:22–25 59

13:22 59

James
1:5 236
1:27 211
2:18 211
3:13–18 236

1 Peter
1:1 118
2:13–14 86
2:20 251
3:19 71
5:7 225

2 Peter
1:13 75
2:3 107
2:20–22 77
3:1–7 60

1 John
2:7, 12–14, 19, 26 59
2:18 273
2:20–23 273

3 John
2   24, 34, 59

Revelation
1–3 268
1:1–11 268
1:3 261
1:4–7 262
1:5–6 . . . . . . 59, 265
1:9 . . . 258, 261, 266
1:10–11 261
1:12–20 . . . 264, 269
1:13 264
1:17–20 267
1:18 264
1:19 260
1:20 165
2–3 261
2:1–3:22 269
2:3 266
2:13 267

2:14, 20 86
3:10 266
4–5 269
5 265
5:5–6 264
6–7 269
6 264
6:9–17 268
6:9–11 264, 266, 267
6:12–17 . . . 258, 264
6:12–14 265
7:14 . . . . . 266, 268
8–11 . . . . . 269, 270
8–9 . . . . . . 265, 266
9:7–11 265
9:10 261
11:1–10 258
11:15–19 273

11:15 270
12 264
12:1 261
12:7–12 271
12:9 265
12:10 270
12:11 . . . . 266, 267
12–22 270
12:17 266
13–20 266
13–18 86
13–14 . . . . 270, 273
13 266
13:1 261
13:7 266
14:9–13 266
14:11–12 267
15–16 . . . . 269, 270

16:5–6 266
17–22 . . . . . 269, 270
17–18 265
17 264
17:9 265
17:18 265
18:20 266
18:24 266
19:1–22:21 273
19:2 266
19:10 261
20:4 261
21:7–8 267
22:10 261
22:18–19 261
22:21 . . . .

Names Index

Adler, Mortimer J., 30
Aland, Kurt, 144
Anderson, Bernhard, 222, 228
Augustine, 12, 19
Barker, Bill, 15
Bauckham, Richard, 259
Bishop, Steven, 223
Bonar, Horatius, 139
Bratcher, Robert G., 56
Deissmann, Adolf, 58
Ferguson, Everett, 136
Jeremias, Joachim, 120
Jordan, Clarence, 45
Justin Martyr, 135
Lamsa, George, 55
Long, V. Phillips, 15
Longman, Tremper, III, 205, 223, 228, 251
Luther, Martin, 215, 271

Michaels, J. R., 19
Mickelson, A. Berkeley, 16
Mickelson, Alvera, 16
Montgomery, Helen, 55
Nicole, R. R., 19
Peterson, Eugene, 46
Phillips, J. B., 46
Provan, Iain, 252
Scholer David M., 85
Spittler, R. P., 19
Sproul, R. C., 16
Stein, Robert, 136, 149, 150
Taylor, Ken, 46
Van Doren, Charles, 30
Waltke, Bruce W., 15, 39, 97, 100, 102
Weymouth, F., 55
Williams, Charles B., 55
Young, Robert, 45